Here is what people worldwide are saying about Jan Ruhe and *MLM Nuts & Bolts*

"When you read Jan Ruhe's rags to riches story, she will inform, involve and inspire you. But *MLM Nuts & Bolts* is so much more than the story of a Champion. It's a powerful, practical, step-by-step guide that shows you exactly what to have, be and do, so you can be a Champion, too!"

John Milton Fogg
Author of *The Greatest Networker in the World*

"Jan Ruhe is one of the preeminent MLM leaders in the U.S.-if not the world. Creativity, determination and boundless energy are but a few of the reasons for her success—year, after year, after year!"

James E. Preston
Chairman of the Board
Avon Products, Inc.

"Jan Ruhe is a woman who is the model of a successful person in the MLM business industry as well as her attitude. When I first saw her on the stage, I felt that she is the person who will fire up the flavor of MLM in Thailand and help Thailand to recover from the worse economic crisis in 30 years to make it Booming up again, before we go into the year 2000."

John Lertthanasarn
President, C.B.P. World. LTd.
Bangkok, Thailand

"After attending your Seminar in the States, I carried a suitcase full of *MLM Nuts & Bolts* books back to South Africa because I just knew that my Managers each HAD to have one! I was right! It motivated them, inspired their Teams and boosted their cheques! *MLM Nuts & Bolts* is their MLM handbook and their MLM Bible too! Thank you, Jan!"

Sue du Preez
Director of "Exclusive Touch" Fashion Accessories, South Africa

"Ambition, Jan Ruhe has it. And she'll empower you to get it. I like all of her resources and I encourage you to get them."

Randy Gage
Gage Research and Development

"Jan's book has 21+ years of how to, which we have proved to work in practice. If you are serious about a MLM lifestyle, this mega book must be bought and read over and over again. It will take you to the top of your company's compensation plan. We highly recommend this book to you and your team."

Gavin Scott & Bonnie Arapes
Top Kleeneeze Distributors
United Kingdom

"Have you ever had the experience of moving from a state of standing still to becoming instantly motivated? The level of energy and focus is incredible! How would you like to have that whenever you desire? You can. Read *MLM Nuts and Bolts*, and learn from a Master who has been there and done it all."

Larry Michael
President, Shinetop Productions

MLM Nuts & Bolts is full of proven tips which help you achieve the next level in your business. Jan has been a friend of mine for years and this book is the genuine story of her success and her experiences."

Randy Ward
Author of *Winning The Greatest Game Of All*

"It's been said, "Success leaves clues." When it comes to the success women can enjoy through MLM, Jan Ruhe is one of our industry's premier role models."

John Kalench
Founder/President
Millionaires in Motion, Inc.

"Jan Ruhe teaches you how to lift everyone you touch with unstoppable spirit and genuine compassion. If you want to bound out of bed each morning with vitality and purpose, and know once and for all that who you are makes a shining difference--then take action now and read this great "How To" book, by my inspiring friend, Jan Ruhe!"

Brian Biro
Author of *Beyond Success: The 15 Secrets of a Winning Life*

"What great information!... What an inspiration!..." These are comments you'll hear over and over again from your downlines when they read Jan Ruhe's *MLM Nuts & Bolts*. Make sure everyone in your group has a copy today. Is what Jan Ruhe writes true? It is. I know. Jan is my upline, mentor and friend. And what she says works for me!"

Elise Ragland
Emerald Sales Director, Discovery Toys

"Most of the people in Networking are women. It's great to read a book written by one of these women. Especially one like Jan Ruhe, who is at the very top of the profession. She knows what she's doing and shares her help freely."

Venus Andrecht
Author of *MLM Magic* and *Net Working Girls*

"*MLM Nuts & Bolts* is filled with Champion tips from my friend Jan Ruhe, who lives and works the lifestyle of a Champion."

Dave Edwards
Linebacker #52, super Bowl Champion-Dallas Cowboys

"This is stimulating book by one of the most creative people I know. Jan has had a lot of peaks and valleys in her life. Through sheer perseverance, she has overcome them and is a real Champion. You will be a Champion too, when you read and take action on the information in this great book!"

Ken Pontious
T.E.A.M. Paragon
Enrich International

"By the example she has set for others, Jan Ruhe has empowered people to make a big difference in their lives. Her presentations are lively, dynamic and inspiring. The audiences love her!"

Rita Davenport
President, Arbonne

"I got really excited after reading this book, because I know the impact *MLM Nuts & Bolts* is going to have on those of you who read it and take the actions.

Robert Butwin
Author of *Street Smart Networking*

"I am constantly searching for new materials for the purpose of providing attitude adjustments for others. Jan Ruhe's *MLM Nuts and Bolts* is high on my list of "Empowerment Manuals." I'll bet you can't read it just once!"

Mark B. Yarnell
Author of *Power MLM* and *Your First Year in Network Marketing*

"Jan Ruhe's book cuts to the chase and gives you the exact formula for achieving financial success, without sacrificing your happiness and well-being. Because she is not only someone I respect professionally, but a friend as well, I know first hand she has lived the philosophy and methods presented in this extraordinary book. Read it and reap the rewards!"

Danielle Kennedy
Author of *Seven Figure Selling*

"You cannot come away from a conversation with Jan Ruhe without feeling better about yourself. Jan's story, teachings, insights and philosophies will make you more than a better networker, they will make you a better person."

Peter L. Hirsch
Author of *Living with Passion*

"*MLM Nuts & Bolts* is a must have book for serious business builders. Everyone in MLM and Direct Sales can get many many ideas out of this "How To" handbook. I highly recommend it. I know Jan's incredible story. It's genuine. Jan is my friend. I know the information in this book will help you to succeed. Count on it."

Shirley Hutton
Retired as #1 in Mary Kay
Author of *Pay Yourself What You Are Worth*

"Prepare to be a master at MLM! Whether you are an ambitious person in MLM or brand new hoping for a better world and a better lifestyle for yourself and those you love, or just excited about the possibilities for personal improvement, this book will give you a jolt! This book is a "How To" manual full of nuts and bolts and concrete suggestions for all who are in MLM. You can trust Jan and her experience to help you help yourself get all you can in life. Jan and I are friends and I can tell you she is a Master at MLM."

Dayle Maloney
Mr. MLM

"Jan Ruhe is one of the most dynamic and successful practitioners in the MLM business I've ever known. She practices what she teaches... she walks her talk... and is enjoying her dream. You can enjoy the fulfillment of your dreams, too, if you'll do what Jan teaches. Read her words, follow her directions.. to the letter... and watch your world expand!"

Ed Foreman
Author & Speaker
Former United States Congressman, Texas & New Mexico
Success Business Entrepreneur & Self-Made Multimillionaire

"Ambition–that volatile combination of vision, passion and supreme confidence that fuels our roaring fires of accomplishment. It is an honor and an inspiration to be Jan Ruhe's friend. Jan, keep pouring it on the world!"

Richard Brooke
Chairman and CEO, Oxyfresh Worldwide, author of *Mach II With Your Hair on Fire*

"Jan is the most motivated, upbeat MLM role model I know."

Tom Schreiter
Author of the *Big Al* series

"If you are up to "taking on" MLM, Jan Ruhe is who you would want as a prospect, distributor, upline, mentor or friend. She is electricity in motion! Her enthusiasm and heart are matched only be her genuineness and capacity to inspire, by tellin' it like it is, was and can be for you!"

Russ DeVan
President, Success By Design

MLM Nuts $ Bolts

By Jan Ruhe

MLM Nuts & Bolts
Jan Ruhe

Printed in the United States of America.
First Edition: March 1997.
Second Edition: October 1998.
Third Edition: April 2002.
Fourth Edition: June 2003.
ISBN: 1-890344-04-4

Cover design by Amy L. Hill Graphic Design.
Typesetting by Dan Poarch.

An Upline® Press book.

Published by:
Proteus Press
300 Puppy Smith
Ste. 205-290
Aspen, CO 81611
970-927-9380, phone
970-927-0112, fax
http://www.janruhe.com

10 9 8 7 6 5 4

To my precious three children:
Sarah, Clayton, and Ashley White.
How blessed I am that I am the one you call 'Mom.'
You were the reason I worked for the lifestyle.
There is no healthier partnership between a mother
and her children than what we have.
Always remember, you are Masters.

Acknowledgments

To Billy, my husband, my Sales Directors, the PowerTeam, to my friends around the world and family. I am so thankful for each of you. I am the most blessed woman in the world.

In Special Loving Memory:
My grandmother, Edith Penniman Knowles
1899-1985
My father, Joe Kelley
1915-1997

Table Of Contents

The Early Years: BMLM; First Marriage; First Two Babies; How I Was First Introduced To MLM; The Need For Extra Money; How I Got Involved The Second Time; First Loan; Third Baby Is Born; Here's What To Do If An MLM Event Ever Takes Priority Over Your Child's Birthday Party; Here's *How To* Handle Chaos If It Happens In Your Life; *How To* Get Out Of An Abusive Relationship; *How To* Survive If The Word Divorce Comes Up; Do You Worry If You'll *Ever* Make Any Money In MLM?; Divorced And In Debt?; Custody Of All Three Children Was Awarded To Me; You Can Make Money In MLM Even If You Have Very Little To Start With; Advice For Those Who Fear Letting Go Of Their Children; Advice To Those Who Are Ready To Make A Change; Fate Took Another Turn: Here's What Happened That Started Me On The Path To Becoming A Millionaire; *How To* Let Challenges Propel You To The Top; *How To* Be Happy During Challenging Times; How I Met A Princeton Man; Second Marriage; *How To* Handle Challenges When You're Happy; The Reasons I Didn't Give Up In MLM; With Work Patience, Information, Education, Preparation, Inspiration, Motivation, Determination And Perspiration. . .Dreams Do Come True

What Is MLM?; Why MLM Is For You; Facts You Should Know About MLM; *How To* Learn About The MLM Business And The Industry; Here Are The Benefits Of MLM For You; Here Are 12 Success Principles You Should Know; Here's *How To* Make It Happen; *How To* Make Money In MLM; Here Are The Main Reasons People Fail In MLM; *How To* Be Prepared If Your Friends And Family Aren't Interested; *How To* Handle Rejection; *How To* Handle Disappointment If No One Initially Supports Your Decision To Join MLM; Questions You Should Ask Yourself Before You Start To Build A Huge Organization

How To Get Clear On Your Goals; Here Were My First Goals; *How To* Set Higher Goals; *How To* Be The Merchant Of Your Dreams; *How To* Ignite Your Passion; Write A Powerful Vision Statement; *How To* Set Goals That Will Bring You Riches; Do You Know About Single Daily Actions (SDAs)?; *How To* Set Success Goals; *How To* Handle Disappointment If You Don't Meet Your Goals; *How To* Set Goals With Your First Level Leaders As Well As Your Lower Level Leaders; *How To* Set Reasonable Goals That Get Results; *How To* Develop A Game Plan; Here Is *How To* Set The Goal Of Getting To The Next Achievement Level In Your Compensation Plan; *How To* Set Long-Term Goals; *How To* Go From Wanting To Be A Millionaire To Being A Millionaire; Here Is A Five-Year Goal Master Plan

Discover Your Values; Be An MLM Pro On The Telephone; Ask Powerful Questions *And* Listen To The Answers; Make An "Always" List; Perform At Your Best. . .Get Fabulous Results; Buy Only A Few Items For Your MLM Business; Invest In What You Need To Help You Succeed Fast; Get Rid Of Stuff That Gets In The Way Of Your Success; Make Choices That Will Propel You To Success; Take Action—Activity Breeds Productivity; Get Organized For Success; Creating Wealth; Come From Contribution; Be Prepared For Change; Have Fun!; Sell Your Products; Be Positive, Not Critical; Be Determined To Succeed; Work With

Your Entire Successline; Work On Your Leadership Skills; Forgive Everyone Who Has Hurt You; "Be"; Be A Great Listener; Take Care Of Yourself; Be On Time; Be Enthusiastic; Pay Close Attention To Successful People; Be Self-Motivated; Concentrate; Believe In Yourself; Think Great Thoughts; Get Busy; Set Short-Term And Long-Term Goals; Pay Close Attention To The Word "Don't"; Have A Great Day, Every Day

Come And Can't Wait To Come Again; What If No One Comes To Your Meeting?; Here Are The
Benefits Of Attending The National Convention Or Leadership Seminars; *How To* Respond If People Say
No To Attending Meetings, Especially The National Or Leadership Seminar; *How To* Hold A Big Event

Wealth is not be things we own
A stately house upon a hill.
Paintings, rugs, tapestries
Servants taught to do one's will.
In luxury a man may dwell
As lonely as a prison cell.

Wealth is not a plentious purse
The bonds that one has stored away,
A boastful balance in a bank
Nor jeweled bobbles that fools display
Things that really gratify
And things that money cannot buy.

Wealth is health— a cheerful heart
An ear that hears the robin's song.
A mind content— some treasured friends
And fragrant memories lingering long.
Living is an inward art— all lasting
Wealth is in the heart.

Longfellow

Introduction

Calling All Network Marketers Ready To Shift Into High Gear For The Twenty-First Century....

MLM Nuts $ Bolts

This book provides you with *nuts and bolts, wrenches, screwdrivers, hammers.* . .every tool you need to Master Your MLM Success

"If it's doable for me," Jan says, "it's doable for you.
I'm going to show you how *you* can succeed!
I don't have the only way to do MLM . . .
but my way works—and will work for you, too!"

Who Should Read This Book?

- You—if you're prepared to be open-minded, willing to drop your preconceived ideas and ready to learn new concepts, study and then *take action!*
- You—who understand the power and potential of MLM.
- You—if you're looking for proven principles and tried and true techniques proven to work in your business.
- You—who want to double, triple or quadruple the bonus check you're currently earning. (And you will, if you practice the strategies shared in this book.)
- You—who demand proven, powerful, real world "how-to" information on building a huge Network Marketing organization.
- You—who want to *fast forward* your MLM business to the top!
- You—if you want more dynamite hands-on, how-to ideas to build your MLM business bigger, better and faster than you've ever seen before!
- You—who love having fun!

This book is full of practical nuts and bolts taken from over 17 years of business-building experience. Pay attention please. There's no beating around the bush. Jan shares the facts and just the facts. She'll tell you how it is. She'll tell you how it can be. She'll tell you what's possible and what's necessary for you to do, step by step.

And it's up to you to take action. That's your responsibility.

Read this book over and over again. The "how-tos" here are true and truly from Jan's own experience. Fact is, few people want to hear the whole truth and nothing but the truth. But those who fail to face the facts, and the obvious experience of the past, won't be successful in the future.

There are many "posers" out there who will give you advice about MLM—but ask them this one question: "Have *you* ever succeeded in MLM?" Listen to those who have been there and done it successfully, or who are following step by step those Masters who have.

If you are hired in a business office, normally there's a guide to show you "how to" do that job. There's an instruction manual created by someone who did those same steps over and over. That's what this book is: a training manual created just for you with step-by-step instructions on exactly "how to" succeed in MLM.

Being successful in Network Marketing means changing yourself from the inside. Education, allows you to develop your inner self, which in turn reflects what you desire to accomplish. Your thoughts determine what you receive in your life and work.

The degree of success you achieve
is directly related to how well you can
train others to do what you have done.
It's called being "duplicatable."

As you go through each chapter in this book, remember,
these are Jan's ideas and experiences. They're a place for you to start.

This Powerful "*How-To*" Book Will Show You *How To*:

- Be a master prospector.
- Be a master recruiter.
- Be more effective on the telephone.
- Develop actions which, if you take, will change your life for the better and will help you help yourself to transform into the Master you are.
- Develop your leadership abilities.
- Develop your own success habits.
- Do your MLM better to get quicker results.
- Empower your successline.
- Feel empowered.
- Find seminars that give you major breakthroughs.
- Gain more confidence.
- Get along with personalities different from your own.
- Get a philosophy.
- Get coaching from someone who has walked the walk.
- Get confidence in your own abilities.
- Get ideas and worthwhile strategies.
- Get started in MLM.
- Give recognition.
- Have actual ideas that work.
- Have music that motivates.
- Have people stay in your program.
- Have powerful thoughts.
- Have your MLM business explode.

- Improve your relationships.
- Know how to sell benefits.
- Learn powerful ideas on how to recruit.
- Learn techniques that will help you close sales.
- Make dynamite choices.
- Pro-actively deal with chaos in your life.
- Read great books that will empower you.
- Recruit people who sell.
- Share Jan's 17+ years of experience.
- Survive and thrive if you are a single parent.
- Use magic words that get results.
- Work with your upline.

Ready?

Based on Jan's experiences, you might as well begin right here and now knowing that you already have what it takes to be a Master. Napoleon Hill said:

"When you are ready for a thing, it will make its appearance."

This book shares with you the idea that success is not luck and that leaders are not born. Jan shares her own personal experiences, so you can see what she endured to get where she is today. Allow her the honor of being your teacher and let her be a guide in your life and work. It's been said that:

"When The Student Is Ready The Teacher Appears."

Here is a suggestion: Give a few of the ideas in this book a try. If even one idea works for you, *great!* Use it. It's yours.

If an idea doesn't work for you, let it go and move on. Take the best and leave the rest.

You may not agree with what's written here. Jan isn't writing this book to *please* anyone. She is not selling anything. She's just giving you the facts she's learned from 17+ years of experience on the phones, in the coffee shops, on stages, in the living rooms and corporate offices of MLM. In fact, if you find yourself disagreeing with something in Jan's book, pay special attention! That could be the very thing that changes your life for the better forever!

Being at the very top of the industry, in the upper 1/10th of 1 percent of what all American women earn, gives Jan the right to be heard. Clearly, she's done a lot of some-things right.

One of the fastest ways to success is to follow in the footsteps of someone who has done it and made it to the very top. Not almost to the top... not on the way to the top. . .not someone who knows people at the top. . .but someone who has made it to the top! Don't follow the followers. Follow the leader!

Do you know that less than 5 percent of the people in our world slow down and listen long enough to find out how the rich got rich?

Napoleon Hill once said: "At some time in your life you are going to have to deal with procrastination." No matter what you're doing now, I am asking that you let Jan help you by furnishing you with the leadership skills and the tools of the trade to make sure you succeed.

Some of you won't get the message. The message is that your success is up to you and for you to begin today! You may be determined to go back to those old habits of reinventing the wheel. Don't waste any more weeks of your future. Trust this, if you do not begin today, put this book away where you can find it again. For sooner or later—and when you're ready—try MLM Jan's way.

Make each day of the rest of your life a masterpiece. Forget the mistakes of the past. Forgive yourself and press on to the greater achievements of today and all the tomorrows of your future. Make the choice right now to get started on your expressway to success. Let this book be the wind beneath your wings.

The message in this book is hot.
If Jan Ruhe can be a Millionaire in MLM,
SO CAN YOU!

This book will be one you will refer to over and over and over and over, as you rise to different levels in your business. You are going to get a ton of great ideas in this one, single. . .

"How-To"

book that promises to take you to the next level in your MLM business—and the next and the next. What a great book to give your new distributors, sales reps, new leaders and every associate and consultant in your successline. So get ready. It's all here. Jan's walked the walk, so she gets to talk the talk.

"Believe nothing, no matter where you read it,
or who said it,
no matter if I have said it,
unless it agrees with your own reason
and your own common sense."
- *Buddha*

This book will help you. Big time. Dream BIG, your dreams will come true.
Becoming a MLM pro can be the stuff that dreams are made of.
Step into the high life, plan to see the world, you can have it all!

Here's to your bright, successful future. Life is not what happens to you. It's what is happening right now—this minute. Life is what you make of it.

This book will inspire you to throw the door of the present open wide, step on through and take control of your life. Quit waiting for someone else to make it happen.

The Successful Implementation Of One Good Idea Is Worth More Than One Thousand Ideas Not Acted Upon.

Love from the mountaintop,
- Jan Ruhe

A Bright Future Awaits
You In MLM !

Meet The Author

Jan Ruhe joined Discovery Toys in 1980, and has risen to the top of the company as a Diamond Sales Director. She has trained tens of thousands of people, and has personally sponsored over 500 representatives in to the company. She has written three books on Network Marketing including *MLM Nuts & Bolts* and *Fire Up!*, and has been featured in *Working at Home* magazine and numerous Industry publications. Jan is an *Upline*® Contributing Editor, has inspired thousands of people at her Upline® Masters Seminar appearances, and is in high demand as a speaker and trainer worldwide. She lives with her husband Bill in Aspen, Colorado.

> "I am convinced that in MLM, you must give yourself time,
> you must take risks and
> you must be willing to grow and change.
> I believe we are more alike than different.
> You must have the determination to succeed…
> *more than anyone else you know!*"

Now you can join the thousands who have heard Jan speak and train about MLM. She is a world-class Network Marketing/Sales/Training Master. Her powerful information and belief will give you the knowledge and confidence you've been searching for to build a large successful network and live the lifestyle of your dreams.

Jan will show you how to utilize the most important resource in MLM: You!

When you are ready to listen to someone who has succeeded in MLM, Jan is the person to listen to. Many people who have not succeeded in MLM give advice like they have walked the walk…not Jan. She's put her time in and is now reaping the rich rewards. Jan is a real-life living and breathing example of what works. If she can make it in MLM, you can, too.

Let Jan be your personal MLM trainer. Her information isn't *the latest, greatest, best and newest*, or any other hype 'n hustle. It's just her experience *and* how you can do it too. And by the way, Jan is absolutely sincere in her belief that YOU can have it all!

Jan is congruent with her message. She *IS* the message she brings. She says, you don't have to start great, to be great. She motivates, teaches, inspires and enlightens everyone. Her income and fulfillment have come directly from empowering others. Jan is committed to your success.

If the idea of building a huge Network Marketing Organization, making a fabulous income while you help others make powerful, positive changes in their lives appeals to you, act now! Read this book today!

Jim Rohn said of Jan…

"She IS the American success story"

Upline® Magazine introduces Jan as one of the…

"Greatest Networkers In The World"

In MLM people are looking for nuts and bolts: *how to* recruit more people; *how to* raise sales; *how to* make money; *how to* build huge organizations; what books to read; *how to* balance success and family.

This book has all that and more, because Jan has done it. Here are her actual duplicatable methods, techniques, skills you can learn, and strategies Jan used to go from divorce, being in debt over six figures, staying focused on her passion, being a single parent, remarriage, to building her dream home and becoming a millionaire.

Jan makes a difference. She can tell people exactly what to say, what to do and how to do MLM. She is a Master. A pro's pro. This book should be in the hands of every single person in Network Marketing who has decided now is the time to succeed. After all, which is a better teacher, theory or experience?

The Fire of Desire
Here Were Jan's Desires...

- To provide a phenomenal lifestyle for her children.
- To be a role model: working out of her home and being hugely successful.
- To have the enduring respect and admiration of her children.
- To be financially independent.
- To slay the fear of not having the lifestyle she deserved when she got older.

In The Late Nineties, What Are The Buzzwords In MLM?
Duplicatable, Transition, Transformation, Shift, Click, Cocoon, Go To The Next Level, And More.

When I started in MLM, it was with great expectation, hope and passion. I had no knowledge of any of the buzzwords. They didn't matter to me in the grand scheme of things. I discovered a product that fit for me. I could stay home with my babies, and my babies could enjoy my product. I was excited about MLM from the first day I joined. Seventeen years later I'm still excited! I never whined or moaned through the years that I couldn't do it. I jumped right in.

Why?

Because I envisioned the lifestyle of my desire.

Many years ago, I bought a poster of the Aspen mountains beautifully blanketed in snow. I hung it over my desk in Dallas. I gazed at it every day for years. I placed my car keys on an Aspen key chain for six years.

I live in Aspen in a custom mansion built from only the money I earned.

Put your desire to work for you today!

What I Was Willing To Work For To Have In My Life

- A breathtaking view.
- A fabulous hot tub.
- A fancy guest bathroom.
- A home decorated with the latest home furnishings.
- A home where I owned the street so no one could drive by unintentionally.
- A home gym.
- A library.
- All the leisure time I want—when I want it.
- An ambiance finer than that of any five-star hotel in the world.
- An investment counselor.
- A peaceful environment.
- A Pentium computer.
- A safe home.
- A sexy master bedroom.
- At least two of my children to graduate from Aspen High School.
- A warm, cozy and big mountain home with a fireplace.
- Cars for each of my children.
- College funds paid in full.
- Educated children.
- Fabulous designer luggage.
- Financial independence, never to need anyone to help me out again.
- New dishes for every occasion.
- New linens (for every occasion).
- No boss—never!
- No debt—ever!

- No yard to take care of, no poison going into the earth to kill the weeds.
- Peace—abiding internal peace.
- Ralph Lauren comforters and linens on all the beds.
- R-E-S-P-E-C-T.
- Sorority funds.
- Successful friends.
- Time to meditate.
- To contribute to others.
- To be a respected, successful speaker and author.
- To be able to visit my children when they are in college and afford for them to come home any time they choose, not just on holidays.
- To make a positive difference in the lives of others.
- To work when, where, and how I want to work.
- Unlimited travel funds.
- Up-to-date appliances. (Have you seen the new digital washing machines and dryers?)

**The benefit of sticking with it today and every day?
Having It All!
Every last thing on my "What-I'm-Willing-To-Work-For-To-Have-In-My-Life" list is mine!**

Go After Your Dreams With Total Passion

Most of all I wanted a stunning lifestyle for myself and my family. After my divorce, from 1985 to 1989, I didn't look up once in five years to catch my breath.

If I had it to do over again, I'd have taken a vacation, even one day off. I can't change that, but I can caution you: **Take Care of Yourself** today. Take a day off for yourself once in a while. Twice in a while!

In the early years, I had $10,000 in debt on my credit card and felt like I would never pay it off. Through the years I have had many, many months where my credit card debt has been much higher than that! And I pay it off at the end of every month effortlessly.

Here's What Your Dream List Could Have On It...

- **Financial Freedom**, achieved within three to five years. A life of free choice, contribution and creativity.

- **Self-Empowerment** is the foundation of success. You have the self-esteem, self-motivation, belief, communication power, relationships, values and life purpose of a true Master.

- **Leadership** is the highest paying business profession. Helping others help themselves achieve their goals. Apply yourself to your profession with the highest integrity, humility, listening, service, courage, honor, empowerment and vision.

- **Vision** is your habit. Continually nurture your vision. Continue to have a powerful relationship with your own motivation.

- **MLM** is the most effective means by which you will achieve financial freedom. It is recognized as the most powerful method of marketing and distribution in the world.

- **Your Company** is recognized as the leader in Network Marketing opportunities. Its products are of the highest quality and everyone who buys them will benefit greatly.

How To Create Your Own I'm-Willing-To-Work-To-Get-It-In-My-Life List

Just begin. Right here. Right now. Create your Master Dream List.

If money was not an issue, what would your life look like? Feel like...? Be like...? Begin today. Dream BIG. Work hard on your dreams. Check them off as you bring each one into reality.

MLM Was My Only Hope.
I Had To Make It Work.
There Was No Other Way!

After All I Have Accomplished and Accumulated,
Here Is What I Really Treasure In My Life:

My health. The respect and unconditional love of my children, husband and parents. Friends all over the world. My grandmother's china and her ring she wore every day. My wedding ring. My photograph albums and framed photos of the children. A tea set Sarah brought me from China. A beautiful, safe home.

There is not enough money to pay me for the above list.
Name your price, even if it is the millions, the above list is not for sale.
I worked for it. I own it. I love it.

What Do You Treasure In Your Life?
I'll bet money can't buy it.

Letting Go of My Children

It's really been difficult for me to emotionally let go of Sarah and Clayton. However, Sarah comes home from Colorado University, Boulder, at least twice a month. I'm so glad she can come home whenever she chooses. Clayton lived at home while he attended his first year of college. He now attends a major university.

It was a celebration when Sarah and Clayton each graduated from high school. But a part of my life as she had known it, was over. On to the next step. Their independence. I still feel like I have so much to teach them as young adults.

Although I was overjoyed at what I had provided for her, the day I watched Sarah sail away on the *S.S. Universe* for her adventure trip around the world, I was bent over on the dock, with my hands on my knees, crying.

The day Clayton had to sign up for the draft was a difficult day for me.

The first time Ashley drove away by herself in her car was difficult for me.

How can anyone leave their children and go to work full time? Man or woman? I just cannot comprehend it. My goal has been to raise independent children. Does that mean letting go of them has been easy? They are the ones who brought me happiness. They have been my life.

There is not enough money or big enough benefits an employer
could have paid me to have missed these last 20 years of
being a mother.

Where would my children and I be today if I hadn't taken the risk?
Where will you be in 20 years if you don't take action today?

What will you do when you've reached your lifetime goals?
Make new goals!

Don't Miss Recruiting Someone Like Me!

How I Learned I Earned My First One Million Dollars

In August 1991, it was announced in Minneapolis, Minnesota, at a National Convention, that I had earned my first *ONE MILLION DOLLARS*.

When they asked me what was the most important thing about my 11 years with my company that could be shared with the 2,000 people in the audience, my answer was:

"The luxury of raising my children while staying at home, while enjoying incredible personal growth."

Incredibly, as of 1998, I am now working on earning my *fourth* million!

In the summer of 1995, while living on the top of the mountain in my home in the Aspen valley, my banker, attorney, CPA and investment banker had a meeting. They all called me into a meeting and announced that as of June 1995 I had a net worth of **ONE MILLION DOLLARS!**

This business has brought me grand teachers. And, oh yes, critics beyond belief. But most of all, this business has brought me unconditional love and support from a precious handful of people. Amazingly, I have worked with people with enormous egos. All kinds of wacky ideas have been tried. Some very tough choices were made. The end result: a Millionaire. Financial independence.

Some Facts About Jan Ruhe's Life

* She only wanted to be married, have a man financially support her and be a mother.
* She went to work every day, fought the traffic, just to work and fight the traffic home again. She hated it.
* She married in 1972 for the first time.
* Daughter Sarah was born in 1976.
* She joined MLM the first time—and quit.
* Son Clayton was born in 1978.
* She joined MLM for the second time in 1980—and has stayed with the same company for 18 years.
* Daughter Ashley was born in 1980.
* Her divorce was final Halloween day, 1985 (Boo!).
* She remarried in 1990.
* Sarah left for college in 1994 and graduated from the University of Colorado in Boulder in December of 1997.

- She moved to the Aspen valley in 1994.
- She became a millionaire in 1995.
- Clayton graduated from Aspen High School in 1996.

"Hello, My Name Is Clayton White...

I am here tonight in my first speech class in college to introduce Jan Ruhe. She is an author of several multi-level marketing books.

Ten years ago, Jan was over $100,000 in debt. Also 10 years ago, Jan visited Aspen, Colorado. The beauty of that town inspired her and my step-dad to move her business and her three children from her home of Dallas for 24 years, to the Aspen valley where we live today.

Jan was divorced a decade ago and through a bitter court-jury battle, won custody of her children. She had three children, became a single parent and had $130,000 in debt in attorney's fees. What a tower to climb. She started with MLM 18 years ago, to be able to work at home so she could raise her children. She took her financial situation and her company to extremes that no one could imagine. She's gone through one hundred times more challenges in her life than any average human being.

Jan Ruhe is my mother and the inspiration in my life.

I have a story I want to share with you.

During my senior year in high school I got hurt playing football. I was able to return for the last game of the season playing against the number one team in Colorado. My coach didn't want to play me. He finally put me in the game—and I stunk. I couldn't run like I used to, so he took me out of the game. Here I was, coming off the best performance in Colorado history the previous year. I had broken three Colorado high school football records my junior year, in 1994. But there I was, now sitting on the bench. I couldn't believe it. I motioned my mother down to the bottom of the stands and told her that I wanted to leave the game at halftime and walk away. She thought it over and said:

'No, Clayton, you must finish what you have been working for the last eight years tonight. Get back in there and run like you know you can.'

I went in the locker room at halftime and talked to my coach. He put me back in the game in the second half. In the fourth and final period I had one hundred yards working. On the last play of the game I went forty yards to score the only touchdown of the game. I got down on one knee and thanked the Lord for my last eight years.

I could not have accomplished this feat or any other without the guidance and inspiration from my mother.

She's the best mom and person anyone can ask to know.

Here's my mother…Jan Ruhe."

By Clayton White, 18 years old

This is a copy of a speech Clayton wrote for his speech class his first year in college in 1996. A copy of this speech is with Jan always.

Sarah White, Jan Ruhe's Daughter, Traveled Around The World On "Semester At Sea" on the S.S. *Universe*

Sarah attended classes aboard ship with 500 other American students while sailing around the world for a semester. I accompanied Sarah to Nassau, Bahamas to see her off on her world voyage; the hardest, most painful day of my life. Watching the ship leave the harbor with my baby, letting go of my Sarah.

Sarah, Ashley And Jan Go On A Mother-Daughter Safari In Africa

One of the 11 ports-of-call the ship visited was Mombasa, Kenya. When the students arrived in Mombasa, many of them rode the train all night to Nairobi to meet private guides to take them on a safari. I took my younger daughter, Ashley White, then 15, to Nairobi to meet Sarah and the other students at the train station and join them on the safari.

When the students arrived, the guides took us to private airplanes. We flew out to the bush, landing on a strip on the ground, climbed in safari jeeps and began our photography safari in the Masai Mara of Kenya, Africa. Astounding!

Sarah had just turned 20 years old aboard the ship, while crossing the equator from South America to Africa. Her best friend on the voyage was Virginia Amato. They had become such good friends. Virginia hosted Sarah's birthday party. Virginia was on the same safari with us, in our safari van. Virginia passed away on this trip, their next stop in India. Some day Sarah will write that story.

MLM provided me the financial freedom to take my daughters on this African safari. After this safari Ashley and I continued on in Kenya on two other safaris.

Here is a personal letter written by Sarah White and handed to me when we met

Sarah in Nairobi in 1996:

Mama! It's the day before we get to Kenya and I was just sitting out on the deck thinking about how I am so excited for our safari adventure! Who would have thought a year ago that we would be in Africa together? I am so proud of you, how far you've come, how you never lost sight of your values, dreams or priorities. You are such a strong woman and I am so lucky to have you as my mom!

I guess this is the time you told me about, you know, *"some day you will thank me"*! I don't know how you were always right. You tried to tell me what to do, looking out for me, but let me make my own decisions and learn from them.

You are the only teacher I value and respect and have really learned from. You helped me shape my values, set high expectations for myself and those I surround myself with. With this trip, you have given me my wings, my independence and have furthered helping me become the person I want to become. I've learned more about myself than about anything else. I have discovered the values I uphold and have always held to be true, that most people laughed at or thought were strange, but that I know are right and the basis for living this precious life that is mine: rationality, independence, integrity, honesty, justice, productiveness and pride.

I look to you as the only other person I've encountered in this world who also upholds all of these. You never let anyone destroy these visions, despite whatever shattering events or people tried to block your way. You've showed me how to cherish my life as my own, to live it to the fullest, and for that, I love, thank and respect you as my mom, my mentor and best friend.

I think you already knew this, I just couldn't wait to thank you again for this wonderful opportunity. I am so glad you are here.

I love you,
Sarah

Chapter One

Begin Today Writing Your Own Personal Success Story Here's Mine...

If you don't wish to read Jan's success story,
simply skip over this chapter and go on to the next.

*"It's a funny thing about life,
if you refuse to accept anything
but the very best, you very often get it."*

—Somerset Maugham

Many people have asked, *"What did you do after going through a divorce, a bitter custody trial, being totally over your head in debt: How did you become a millionaire? Will you share your story with me?"*

There is only one right answer, *"Yes, I will share my story with you."* I can't keep my story inside me. I am so sad for people in bad relationships, bad marriages, afraid to get out. There is no way for me not to be melodramatic about this. Here is the story, my message that it took me years to have the courage to write.

It all started when I was in college at Texas Tech University, in 1970. One day I got a little booklet in the mail called *The Daily Word*, which Unity Church distributed. It had daily sayings that were empowering for me. The booklet came from my grandmother. It was the first time in my life I had ever read anything so purely positive. And it would be years before I ever read anything positive again. Years.

Six years later, at 4:30 a.m. in Baylor Hospital in Dallas, Texas, on March 7, 1976 my life changed forever when my daughter, Sarah Janell White, was born. At the time I first saw Sarah my decision to become somebody was made. Sarah's and my life would be a masterpiece. After all, here in my arms was all the reason I'd ever need to succeed.

From the day Sarah was born, I've realized there are angels watching over me. There is no doubt in my mind that there are angels. As you read through this book, look for their signs. The angels directed me all the way.

Almost 22 years later, here I am in the Aspen Valley. I'm a millionaire. But once, I had a sickness. The disease of being broke and sick of asking my husband for money. I was filled with fear about having no money for the future. What did I really want out of life? A lifestyle. A great lifestyle! Others had great lifestyles. Why not me?

Success would be mine. I would not be denied.

Unfortunately, I had the expectation that my husband would provide that lifestyle. It became clear that my husband was not going to be able to produce what I wanted. He didn't want to. I wanted to. So I went out and made the lifestyle I wanted. And so can you.

It will be no accident that you rise to the TOP position.
It will not be the result of chance or luck.

Finding a product to believe in and then becoming the student of sales, sales training and marketing was one key for me. A real key. Passion, determination, goal-setting, dreaming, commitment and many more attributes are so very important. When you decide to study successful people, you will take your life to the next level.

The product I represented was children's toys. The marketing strategy was MLM.

The Early Years: BMLM

Those were the days when computers filled up entire rooms. There were drip-dry clothes, no credit cards, laser beams, ballpoint pens, pantyhose, car air conditioners, central air-conditioning (only window air conditioners). It was before the U.S. space program began. And very few people had even considered venturing into inner space.

Closets were for clothes, not coming out of. Bunnies were little rabbits. Rabbits were not Volkswagens®. Designer jeans were worn by designers. Having a *meaningful relationship* meant getting along with most of your cousins.

There were no fast food chains and no drive-through food places. There were no gay rights, dual careers or computer marriages. Day care centers, group therapy and nursing homes were unheard of. No tape decks, electric typewriters, artificial hearts, word processors or yogurt.

Guys never thought of wearing earrings. A "chip" was a piece of wood—on or off your shoulder. Hardware meant hardware and software was not even a word.

In the 1950's **Made in Japan** meant junk. The term *"making out"* referred to how you did on your exam. Pizzas, McDonald's®, Burger King®, Whataburger® and instant coffee were unheard of.

There were *Five and Dime* stores, where you actually bought items for five and 10 cents. We had phone lines that were called party lines. You had to wait your turn if someone else was on the phone line.

Aids were helpers in the principal's office. *Grass* grew on lawns. No one knew what a trash compactor was. We filled up our pens with ink from bottles. We wouldn't think of pumping our own gasoline into our car.

My favorite color ink was peacock blue, and my pen always leaked in my purse. Teachers cared about handwriting. We didn't have microwaves, push-button phones, cordless phones, CD's, tape cassettes, car phones, beepers, phone-answering machines, pagers, fax machines, Fed Ex®, Mailboxes, Etc.®, e-mail, voice-tel, Jiffy-Lube®, Wal-Marts®, K-Marts® or Bizmarts®, hand-held calculators, laptop computers, modems, burglar alarms, car alarms or car phones.

My First Marriage

About three years into my marriage, my husband became involved in an organized fundamentalist religion. It was a religion of control. My husband went to Bible study after Bible study. He began to change and I didn't know how to handle this drastic shift in his personality. He changed into someone I did not like or respect. I didn't feel safe.

For the next nine years I lived in a terrible situation. He is like a stranger to me now.

My First Two Babies

When Sarah was born in March 1976, she was a beautiful, healthy and perfect baby. I loved Sarah more than anything or anyone else. I decided that she would have a happy, *incredible* life. For the first time ever, I felt the emotion of love and adoration. I still feel that way about her today.

My husband and I were growing apart. He studied his religion with a passion. My grandmother, Nana, would come to visit Sarah and me every day. We had more fun with Sarah. Sarah was like her own baby. Sarah and I would go to see her frequently. She had her own Real Estate company. Her office was near my home. I would sit and listen to her. I always listened to her very carefully.

In March 1978, my son, Clayton, was born two years and two days after the day of Sarah's birth. He was my pride and joy. I held him most of the time. The three of us were inseparable.

When Clayton and Sarah were babies, I would take them to a shopping mall to keep them cool during the summer or warm during the winter. We couldn't afford the air-conditioning or heating bills at home. I made most of their clothes. I owned only one dress myself. We spent most of our time playing, reading and enjoying being together.

How I Was First Introduced To MLM

When Sarah was a baby, in 1976, a neighbor invited me to a skin care home party. I was so excited about the concept, I booked a demo in my home, too. After the demo the sales rep said, *"You seem to be a very gracious hostess."* It had been years since anyone had said something nice to me, other than my grandmother and mother. That simple statement of recognition changed my life's direction. I joined the company and attended my first MLM training.

The training was terrible! Everyone at the training was so much older than I and acted as if they knew what they were doing. I didn't know where to begin. I bought a lot of products and off I went to tell the world about how great they were.

Only a few close friends ever bought the product from me (including my grand-mother). After six long months, I gave up and quit.

The Need For Extra Money

With the little money I saved, I was able to send Sarah to a prestigious private school called Lamplighter. Sarah had been on the waiting list to attend this school since her birth. It was a very expensive school and I was determined my children would get to attend. I realized that my scrimping on household bills was not enough. I would have to supplement my husband's income. I began again looking for opportunities to sell some sort of product from my home.

How I Got Involved In MLM The Second Time

During Sarah's first year in preschool, in November 1979, a friend of mine invited me to a home toy party in Dallas. It sounded intriguing and fun, so I went. Sarah was almost four, Clayton was almost two, and I was pregnant with soon-to-be Ashley.

The sales rep explained she could not find enough people interested in selling toys. The company was only two years old and she was planning on quitting. However, I was *very* interested. When I asked her for more information, she gave me her green business card. *WOW!* Was I impressed, a woman with a business card!

By March of 1980, while pregnant with my third baby, Ashley, I made the decision to try MLM again, this time with that toy company. Man oh man; three children, toys, birthday parties, holidays, I could sell toys. Not even a question in my mind.

At the time, I was unhappily married. Even though I was committed to my vows, I wanted badly to have an equal relationship. As it turned out, that relationship could never be equal.

I saved that green business card. When I called the company sales rep, she had quit the company ages ago. She referred me to another sales rep. I called and joined on the spot! My grandmother paid the $300 total investment for my kit. She told me she was making a *stake in my future*. She encouraged me to stick with this company and to make it great.

Here Are Some Powerful Ideas For You:

- Be ready for chaos if it comes, and thrive on it…it's just a passing fate.
- Be prepared for change, it will happen.
- Recognize when destiny takes a turn.
- Start MLM as early as you can in life…the payoff is worth it.
- You can be unhappy in your life and still build a successful MLM business.

There were times when I was overwhelmed. I wanted to quit my business really only once—out of total frustration. The phone was ringing constantly. I couldn't think. So many people calling wanted to join my organization.

I Felt Guilty:

- A lot of the time.
- If I wasn't spending time with my children.
- When I wasn't working on my business.

I Felt Resentment:

- I had an unhappy marriage and we had very little money. We were house poor. We had a nice, clean home, but no money to decorate it. No money to travel or have a life.
- I was cooking, cleaning, being a mother, wife, daughter, sister, neighbor and friend and owned a thriving business. No time to myself.
- No time to spend with friends.
- I got positive and negative feedback on an hourly basis of what I could and should be doing differently. What expectations people had of me. What I should be planning. Everybody telling me what to do.
- There was too much paperwork, too many opinions, too many chiefs, too many different personalities.

Here Are Some Powerful Ideas For You:

- Change your attitude. Don't feel guilty. Ever.
- Don't set business hours.

- Go to a personal growth and development seminar.

- Get an up-to-date haircut.

- Invest in a new wardrobe, or at least one new, nice up-to-date outfit.

- Get a sitter for two hours a day.

- Give up guilt.

- Know that quality time is better than quantity time.

- Never say you are putting anything on the back burner. Where did that silly saying come from anyway?

- Spend quiet time by yourself.

- Tell others when you are available for conversation.

- Quit letting other people control your time.

- Realize you should not feel guilty. Instead, feel excited about what you are going to be able to provide for your family.

- Take a break, even only a short break, every day.

- Take time out for you.

- Take vacations.

- Vow to never, ever quit.

My First Loan

Have you spent money on getting your business started, money that you don't have? Did you pay all your bills and you don't have enough money to buy business cards, make long distance calls, go to conventions or anything else?

Well, guess what? I didn't have any money either, so here's what I did.

Into the local bank I went. After explaining to the loan officer all the excitement about my new business, I took out my first loan. A loan? For $500. Me? I realized I didn't want to quit my MLM business. I was not willing to regret giving up what I sought so hard to build. So I moved big time in the direction of making a better lifestyle for myself and my children.

Here Are Some Powerful Ideas For You:

- At the first sign of feeling overwhelmed, call time-out. Mentally and physically come to a complete stop.
- Attach more fear to not moving forward and taking some risks than to just doing it.
- Begin again.
- Believe in yourself.
- Break off the rearview mirror of your past.
- Decide to dream big. Your dreams are going to see you through.
- Educate yourself.
- Move forward.
- Prioritize.
- Remember, there is no limit to the number of times you can try.
- Say to yourself, *"So what, I can handle this debt."*
- Take control.
- Take a risk.

My Third Baby Is Born

In August 1980, my daughter, Ashley, was born. My precious little baby girl.

My MLM business was going strong. I had about 16 people in my group. The idea of staying home, selling a product I believed in and making money part-time while raising my three children really appealed to me. Now I had those three little children and I was making extra income, so I could stay home with them. This really made sense to me. There was a port-a-crib in my office so Ashley could be right next to me. An important transition about this time was made. **I went from being involved to being committed.**

Here Are Some Powerful Ideas For You:

- Buy in bulk, so that you don't spend so much life time at the grocery store.
- Get an easy haircut.
- Get a housekeeper to do the laundry.
- Get up early.
- Have a park day, take a picnic and the children to two or three parks. Tell them there will be another park day next week if they respect your time on the phone.
- Make the transition from being involved to being committed.

- Plan your weekly menu on the weekend.

- Read time management books.

- Set a buzzer. Tell the children, if they leave you alone, when the buzzer goes off you'll have a surprise for them.

- Take time every day with your children.

- When you are tired, take a break.

- You can be successful in MLM with children at home.

Here's What To Do If A MLM Event Ever Takes Priority Over Your Child's Birthday Party

We had National Conventions each March, which always coincided with Sarah's and Clayton's birthdays. For six years I missed their special days. However, I always had a fabulous party to celebrate their birthdays *before* I left home.

If you have to miss your children's special days, they'll survive. It's okay. Just because your traditions may say that you can't do that and be a good parent, I'm here to tell you that it's time to break with those limiting traditions. Birthdays don't have to be celebrated on the exact day. You'll make it through. I promise.

As long as your children are happy, it doesn't matter what day their birthday is on. I've heard of parents asking their child's approval to change the date of the birthday party. Oh, please! Who is the parent? Who is the child?

Here Are Some Powerful Ideas For You:

- Celebrate the event, not the day.

- Give up guilt.

- Involve your child in the planning of the party.

- Tell your child that their party will be on a day prior to your trip.

Here's *How To* Handle Chaos If It Happens In Your Life

For those of you who have children, focus your love and energy on your children *and* your growing business. Embrace the joy of "and." Release the bitterness of "either/or." I never, never envisioned what was about to happen in my life. Chaos.

I realized I hated being controlled and emotionally abused. Here's what I discovered: In the future I would only contribute to people and allow people to get close to me who would not try to control me. Not even a little. If people try to position themselves as being above me in any way, I will not permit them into my inner circle. No way! Conversely, I don't want to be above anyone else who is close to me. I only want equal relationships. Other than that, don't bother.

Here Are Some Powerful Ideas For You:

- Become a serious student of MLM.

- Begin a study of sales, human relations and MLM Masters.

- Make the decision of what you will and will not tolerate in a relationship.

What Will You Do If You Find Yourself In An Unhappy Marriage?

My husband's religion now dictated rule after rule that I could not live by nor would I raise the children believing. Now I had to make some serious choices. Actually, in the end they were not too difficult. I did what I thought was right and best at the time. That choice was easy.

Here Are Some Powerful Ideas For You:

- Begin a meditation time.

- Do not complain about your situation, take action.

- Do not let anyone take away your self-worth.

- Get help.

- Hang out with only those people who will love you and support you.

- Know that you are worthy.

- Read self-help books.

How To Get Out Of An Abusive Relationship

It took years for me to get up the self-confidence to take control of my situation, to put a stop to the emotional and verbal abuse the children and I had been living with.

Here Are Some Powerful Ideas For You:

- Alert your spouse that his or her beliefs are interfering with your life, and the lifestyle you want for your children and for yourself.

- Communicate to your spouse he or she can have his or her own belief system—you'll have yours.

- Communicate when their beliefs are suffocating and stifling.

- Decide that you will be equal but not submit.

- Do not demand anyone to submit to you in all things.

- Do not demand total control and obedience to your will.

- Do not get angry, cry or pout.

- Keep recruiting, training, going to meetings.

- Make it clear that you are not going to put up with his or her beliefs anymore.

- Permit no one to control you.

How To Survive If The Word Divorce Comes Up

Right after my grandmother passed away, I made the decision to file for divorce. It was March 1985. At this point, I didn't know just how much I wanted to be financially independent. All I wanted was to get out of my marriage. I had made a decision. It was the right decision.

I filed for divorce. My first divorce attorney normally prepared wills and got first time offenders out of jail. He was not a custody attorney. His fee was $5,000. I didn't think there really would be a court battle. Man, oh man, was I wrong!

My husband's attorney had the reputation that he could obtain custody of the children for the father. My husband was very serious and was determined to get custody of the children. He had lost control of me and was going to fight to control the lives of our three children.

Here Are Some Powerful Ideas For You:

- Ask your spouse questions—maybe you can reconcile your differences.
- Continue personally growing and developing.
- Don't make a decision to divorce in the heat of an argument.
- Decide what you can and cannot forgive.
- Don't seek counsel of well-meaning friends.
- Do not stay married only for the children's sake. That's not what's best for them.
- Do what is best for the children.
- Listen to your own heart, not your parents, friends or anyone else.
- Make benchmarks, see how things are going in a week, a month.
- Put your spouse first, try and see through your spouse's eyes what is happening.
- Seek counsel or professional help.
- Seek to understand.
- Seek to be understood.
- Try to compromise.

A Custody Trial. Can You Survive?

Imagine this: I filed for divorce, my husband counter-filed, asking for a trial by jury seeking total custody of our three children. Can you imagine that, a trial by jury?

I fired my first attorney and hired a more aggressive and tough attorney. My husband finally moved out. It was such a relief. I kept working on my MLM business and it continued to prosper.

Here Are Some Powerful Ideas For You:

- Dedicate yourself to your children and to your business. Often, I worked well into the early hours of the morning. My children were nine, seven and five at the time of the trial.
- Don't be in a hurry to date or have a serious relationship with anyone.
- Enjoy being by yourself with your children.
- Enjoy the stress being gone, the conflict being gone.
- Go on building your MLM business. Don't shut down.
- Learn, change and get on with your life.
- Make your home very, very happy.
- Take time for yourself with your children to build a new life.
- Tell very few friends of your strife at home and the heartache you are experiencing.

Do You Worry If You'll Ever Make Any Money In MLM?

My MLM business kept going, but the growth of my business seemed so slow. I doubted I'd ever make a lot of money. All of a sudden, I got a check for $5,000 for one month. I was floored!

You will make money. Take action today. The only way to make money in MLM is to move those products. If you are moving the products and getting others to do the same, you have to make money.

Here Are Some Powerful Ideas For You:

- Do not ask your spouse for permission to succeed.
- Don't fight or be jealous of those who are successful.
- Don't talk about failing.
- Give yourself permission to succeed.
- Go to more seminars.
- Immediately leave a meeting when and if it turns negative.
- Read more books.
- Listen to more tapes.
- Listen to the Masters.
- Move more products.
- Move the product yourself *or* get others to move the product with you.
- Study the ones who are making your business work.

- Work on yourself.

Divorced And In Debt?
The Secret Is: *Take Control* And *Get Ambitious*

I had never been in debt and we never used a lot of credit. So to have any debt at all makes me extremely nervous. How about you? Hey, money is just paper, and you can survive major debt. I did.

I decided to play hardball, go all out to make sure I won custody. NO MATTER WHAT. I would win this custody battle and would get the top attorney in Texas. I decided to hire a tough lawyer with a reputation for winning custody battles. After researching the Dallas market for the representation that fit my specifications, I hired a well-known attorney. His retainer, win or lose, for my case was $25,000. I borrowed the money. That was the first $25,000. Several more $25,000 bills followed. Big Time Debt. Big! It didn't matter, money just didn't matter. Maintaining custody of my three children was all that mattered.

I spent many hours preparing for the trial. It was frequently postponed. My nerves were shot. The attorney's bills were piling up. My hair was turning from brown to shocking white. Although filing for divorce was a tough decision, I knew it was the right one. But oh man!

The reality is, challenges are just a part of life. Life is a never-ending stream of challenges. None are fatal. They're just life.

The longer I live, the more I believe you have to enjoy every moment. There are many challenges that await us all. We just have to be prepared to deal with them. Being in debt is just a challenge. It is not life-threatening. I understand that some of you are feeling very burdened by debt. Please know YOU WILL SURVIVE.

I was really scared about paying off my bills. I had no money. My only hope was my MLM business.

Put YOUR back up against the wall and see who wins.

All I was sure of was that I was sick of the money worship. I wanted the money to get out of debt and to have a fabulous lifestyle.

I was going to succeed!

Here Are Some Powerful Ideas For You:

- During the hot summer months, put fans in your bedrooms and turn off the air-conditioning. Pray for rain, so that you don't have to water your yard.

- Every month, pay something on your bills.
- Go to the library and begin to read and outline self-improvement books.
- Keep personally growing, invest in your mind.
- Keep recruiting and writing newsletters.
- Keep working your MLM business.
- Take time for yourself.
- Know that there is a law of averages. It guarantees that if you just keep trying, sooner or later things will work out.
- Make phone calls at off-peak time.
- You can live on less than you think.
- Take your newsletters to give to your successline at meetings to save postage.
- Think prosperity.

Custody Of All Three Children Was Awarded To Me!

The jury trial lasted one week and totaled more than $100,000 in attorney's fees.

*The experience of listening to the judge read the verdict
that I won total custody of my children was one of the
happiest and the most intense moments of my life.*

At last, it was final. The chaos was over, or so I thought. This trial had taken its toll on me. I had experienced emotional abuse, divorce and a custody battle. Don't criticize or abuse until you have walked a mile in my shoes. No longer will I permit abusive people into my life. Never again!

The divorce became final in February of 1987. I was given the responsibility of all the repairs and upkeep on the home, all lawn care, half the debt prior to separation, the bulk of my attorney's fees and 100 percent of my credit card debt.

The fabulous part was, I had total and complete custody of the children *forever*. Joint custody would not have worked for our situation. The future years have shown me that my decision was the right choice. Dead right. No, strike that: Live right!

You Can Make Money In MLM Even If You Have Very Little To Start With

After the divorce, I became very self-sufficient, doing everything I could do to keep the children happy and to be careful how I spent our money. Although my override checks were larger than most everyone's in the company, 90 percent of the money was going to attorney's fees and debt reduction.

Ask yourself, *"Can you afford to not attend your national convention or to invest in books or tapes to help you speed up the information that you need to succeed?"*

Ask your family to give you nothing but self-help books and tapes for birthdays and holiday gifts.

Here Are Some Powerful Ideas For You:

- Box up all your old clothes and cheap accessories and take them to the Salvation Army. Charge a new wardrobe.

- Get a credit card.

- Go to the library and check out all the self-improvement books.

- Invest in yourself and take action on the new information you learn.

- Keep recruiting and training others to recruit.

- Keep making enough money to survive. I looked through pants and shirt pockets for quarters that might be hiding.

- Know that you will survive. You will survive.

- Listen and watch the Masters. Duplicate their methods.

- Never, ever say: *"I don't have the money,"* or *"I can't afford to."*

- Pay off your credit cards at the end of every month.

- Put a pen to what you will be spending if you go to work eight to five.

- Recruit more people.

- Replace old, worn-out belongings with new ones.

- Share with no one how miserable your financial situation is.

- Sell all the cheap old paintings on your walls.

- Sell all the old furniture.

- Sell all old pieces of everyday china and every wedding gift you received and don't use.

- Sell or give away every knick-knack.

- Throw away the clutter.

Advice For Those Who Fear Letting Go Of Your Children

The weekends that the children left to spend time with their dad were devastating for me. I missed them terribly and worried about them constantly. Chaos that I thought was over was raging in my life and in my children's lives. I was relieved when the children came home, only to have to face those emotions again for the next visitation.

It was a very sad time in my life, an emotionally stressful experience I simply had to endure. I had poured so much of my life into these three children. I had the empty nest syndrome 15 years early. When they all left, our once busy home was dead quiet.

The children called me from 10 to 20 times a day from their dad's, wanting to come home. Those precious little voices.

There were many lonely days and nights. I survived. For those of you who are going through this, or who fear going through this, you can survive, too. You will!

Here Are Some Powerful Ideas For You:

- Always have pretty candles burning when the children come home.

- Build a life for yourself. Your children are going to grow up and leave the nest.

- Build memories.

- Get some rest when your children are gone.

- Have lots of love to pour into them when they return home.

- Make sure the house is spotless when they come home.

- Re-assure them of your love and that you are okay.

- Take an interest in what they did while they were gone.

- The best gift you can give your children is independence. Begin today to help your children do for themselves.

- Tell your children to have a good time while they are gone.

- You will be a better parent if you take a break from your children.

- Your children need you more the older they are.

- Your children will survive without you there.

Advice To Those Who Are Ready To Make A Change

The children were surviving without me fretting and moaning at home. My MLM business was growing all over the country. Marvelous people came into my organization. Exciting group growth! Wonderful people—a recruiting explosion had begun!

I needed money to stay in my home, pay the attorneys and raise my children. I kept recruiting, training and studying. My successline began to explode. Money started to flow in from my MLM business.

I refused to:

- Get a nine-to-five job.

- Take my children to a day care center.

- Have a boss tell me what to do and when to take vacation days.

- *Ask to take time off.*

I had already experienced that office life. I found it disgusting. You never see the outside, except for a short lunch break. There was a better way to earn a living. I knew I'd found it. If you're serious about a fabulous future, then MLM is The Only Way!

It was time to change. Everything changes. Take responsibility and begin to change yourself.

Here Are Some Powerful Ideas:

- After a divorce, there's an adjustment time to grow into the new life.

- Begin to calm down.

- Enjoy your time alone.

- Get busy outlining self-help books and learning from others who are earning money in all sorts of successful businesses.

- Get your depression under control.

- Realize: If you can't change the situation, then change the situation.

- All you really have to change is yourself. No matter what.

Fate Took Another Turn
Here's What Happened That Started Me
On The Path To Becoming A Millionaire

On an ordinary afternoon in Dallas in 1988 I went out to my mailbox to find a Jiffy Bag with my address on it. It was marked *Personal and Confidential to Jan White* (my name at the time).

I opened it to find a cassette tape inside. There were no markings on it at all. I popped the cassette into a tape player in the house and a strange man began to talk to me. Here is a portion of what I heard:

"Hello, Jan, this is George. I inquired about you in Denver at a booth in a Denver Mall. I asked who was the top person in your company and got your name and address from a sales rep in the booth. I hope you don't mind this rather weird way of approaching you, but I would like to give you some valuable information. You see, I was very successful with a MLM company many years ago, and I have some information that I bet will prove very valuable to you in the near future. Here is my phone number in Denver. If you would like to call me, I will make myself available to you. No charge. No strings attached. I've heard a lot about you and would like to be part of your life."

Well, blow me away! I was intrigued and simply amazed. So I called George. We talked half the night. He was 30 years older than I, a recluse, and very knowledgeable about MLM.

Every day for months afterwards I received a Jiffy Bag with a personal cassette tape and letters from him on how to do MLM and Sales in a First Class manner. We became telephone friends immediately. He was so different. He had no agenda except to help me become the best I could be in this business.

As time went by, he gave me tremendously valuable advice. Many ideas in this book came from ideas that originated with George. As we became better friends one time on a telephone conversation, he said to me, *"Jan, you need to marry a man who graduated from Princeton University."* I said *"Princeton University, George, I am from Texas, I have no way to meet a Princeton man."* He left it at that.

He was one of very few people that I truly **listened** to. Many people tried to control me or tell me what "I ought" to do or who "I ought" to listen to. George was not controlling. He took a sincere interest in me. Ultimately, I flew to Denver to have dinner with him and to meet the face behind the voice. He was a special person to me during those years.

Here Are Some Powerful Ideas For You:

- Be self-motivated.

- Become a new person.

- Begin to take risks and be willing to make mistakes.

- Begin to see the people who you think are your friends, but who really are not, through new eyes.

- Begin to take and keep copious notes on everything.

- Buy a Mont Blanc® pen and begin buying only *the best* of everything.

- Choose to go for greatness *always*.

- Be a pioneer.

- Do not blame others for your failures (a very important lesson).

- Face the fact, this is your life. Quit keeping peace with others.

- Get determined.

- Go get what you want in life.

- Go through a metamorphosis. Transform yourself.

- Stop letting others get in your way.

- Have only one credit card and make it an airline mileage card and put every single dollar you spend on that card accumulating airline miles. (This tip is worth thousands of dollars!)

- Know that change will not take place overnight.

- Leave those who don't want what you want out of life behind or out of your life.

- Let success rub off on you.

- Life is a do-it-to-yourself program.

- Listen, research, probe and evaluate *always*.

- No matter what, resolve to become the best you can be.

- Quit taking responsibility for those who fail.

- Realize you have to detach yourself from some people.

- When relationships become a struggle, resolve to work it out or move out, life is not meant to be a struggle.

- Save 10 percent of your check every month and put it into a bank account called (Your name) **Wealth Account.** No matter how much it is, forget it's there and do not spend it—*no matter what.* After about three years you'll be surprised. I paid my last debt payment with that nest egg and then built another Wealth Account in December 1989.

- Take responsibility for yourself, your team and your family.

- Think success.

- Unhook yourself from those who do not have like goals.

- Write down all your goals. Writing this book was on my goal list.

- You are the one to make the final decisions about your business and your life.

- You don't need unmotivated, negative people in your life. Give them away.

How To Let Challenges Propel You To The Top

We all have challenges, no doubt, but it's important to learn to keep from blowing them out of proportion. Most people put money or financial challenges at the top of their lists. I can tell you, financial challenge was close to the top of my list, but not at the top. My children's well-being and happiness were at the very tip top of my list.

By this time in my life, I knew all about chaos. I was thriving on it. I knew that I could survive it. Bring it on. I would win. Chaos would not control me. It would propel me upward!

During the years, the adjustment of having to leave home to visit her father was a terrible struggle for Sarah. She refused to go to visit her father in 1990, when she was almost 14. She wanted to see her dad but not under the strictness of the court order visitation. She had a social life that sometimes conflicted with these visitations. Her father demanded that she visit him according to the court's rulings.

This, of course, made major challenges for me. In Texas, if you go against the court order, you can be held in contempt of court and go to jail. I did not want to go to jail. The child must be made to go to the visitation. But Sarah refused to go!

I was not quite out of debt when this challenge began. I was responsible for the upkeep of the house and was considering having some remodeling work done to update our home. The court had given me total custody of the children, but only as "tenants in common"with my ex-husband on the ownership of my house. I got bids for the remodeling job, went to the bank and was approved for a home improvement loan, only I needed my ex-husband's approval.

Of course, he would not approve. I was left totally responsible for repaying the debt. He said that in his opinion the repairs weren't needed. Are you surprised? I wasn't.

Here Are Some Powerful Ideas For You:
- Believe in lots of hugging.
- Limitations and expectations aren't real. Only you can make them so.
- Choose to listen to children's feelings.
- Expect your children to be the best they can be. Set high expectations.
- Help children make the right choices.
- Make your home a safe place to make choices and to learn.
- Remember, children are human beings and have the right to communicate.

How To Be Happy During Challenging Times
All through the years, my children have been involved in activities beyond school. I kissed them good night every night. Rocked them and read them books every day. I called them every day when I was traveling all over the world. They never knew about the nights I worked all night. The price I paid to keep moving forward was incredible. Was it worth it? Yes. Now, yes. As lonely and hard as it was, I was happy.

Here Are Some Powerful Ideas For You:
- Dream big.
- Get enough rest, water and sunshine.
- Go to movies.
- Invest in seminars.
- Feed your mind.
- Say goodbye to those who hold you back, those who discourage you.
- Smile.
- Take care of yourself—FIRST!

How I Met A Princeton Man
It became clear that again, I had to seek out an attorney and settle the challenges my ex-husband presented in the only way he could understand.

My next attorney came highly recommended. He was a tough attorney, and interestingly enough, *a Princeton graduate*, a retired Navy Commander, a Vietnam Veteran, a Navy pilot and a gracious gentleman. It was several months before I met him. I heard about him from several different sources.

I met Bill Ruhe at a charity party I attended in Dallas. We said hello. I briefly explained my situation. He gave me his business card and asked me to schedule an appointment with him the following day.

On my first visit with Bill, I shared with him my wonderful MLM business. I also shared with him the terrible debt I had been climbing out of. I retained him to help me with Sarah's situation and a remodeling challenge.

Bill and I met frequently and we quickly became friends. I called him from all over the world. He called me the minute I walked into my home. Every day. However, he was an attorney, and he billed me for every communication. Now I was in debt to him for a total of $7,000.

Ultimately, he helped Sarah modify her visitations and the remodeling on the house was done. Months later, he called and requested that I see him for a very important meeting. I was sure he wanted the total payment due. I was shocked.

He told me he was not available to be my attorney anymore. Now, let me tell you, I was sick. I needed him to be my attorney. We had been in the courtroom together, he knew my situation, he loved the children and he was my dear friend. Now I would have to start over again to find another attorney. I would have to build another relationship. I truly was so sad. I was so, so sad.

My Second Marriage

In the next few moments, my mind was completely blown!

The reason, Bill told me, that he could not represent me was an ethical question. He told me *he was in love with me and the children* and asked me, *would I marry him?* That moment will live forever.

We had never talked about love, marriage or even held hands! Was I surprised? I realized that those months of pouring out my story to him, I had felt safe with him. For the first time I had been open and honest in expressing my feelings with a man. We had become very close friends and remain so today. We married several months later in Las Vegas.

How To Handle Challenges When You're Happy

In 1990, a former VP of my company wooed away one of my top people to help start up a new MLM company. At the time she assured me she would not be contacting her successline to leave with her. I thought she was leveling with me. She wasn't.

Ultimately, five of my top people left within two months. Sad but true, the company they left for went out of business only two months later. They lost all the equity of their building years. However, I was the recipient of a fabulous group of new leaders.

They lost it all.

Not everybody is going to like you or care about your opinions. Most losers see only with tunnel vision and hear what they want to hear. For the longest time I wanted to believe that those leaders were champions. They weren't. So what? Don't worry, be happy. Hakuna Matata.

Here Are Some Powerful Ideas For You:

- Realize challenges are just an interesting part of your success story.
- Don't be intimidated.
- Give leadership to everyone in your organization.
- Help those who want your leadership. Give it to them.
- Never let anyone else have power over your successline.
- There are people in your successline, I promise you,
  who want your leadership.
- Your successline is your successline.

The Reasons I Didn't Give Up In MLM

- I am not a quitter.
- I decided that I would strive to be on top—the bottom is too crowded.
- I decided to face my fears.
- I had a purpose: to raise my children and to get out of debt.
- I knew it could be done.
- I made a commitment to succeed.
- I wanted the lifestyle. I was determined to get it.

With Work, Patience, Information, Education, Preparation, Inspiration, Motivation, Determination And Perspiration... Dreams Do Come True

The great news is, dreams do come true. They do it all the time! I am living, walking, talking testimony that dreams do come true. I don't know anyone who can say that they have achieved their life goals. As of the writing of this book Bill and I are working on our future goals.

As of 1996 my dreams and goals have all come true:

- No debt.
- I am married to Bill Ruhe. We have been married eight years.
- We live in our 14-room dream mansion in Aspen, Colorado.

- Sarah has graduated from college. Clayton is in college, I am paying his college bills effortlessly. Their dad takes no financial or emotional responsibility to help them through college.

- Ashley is in high school. She's on the varsity soccer team and is the #1 top varsity cheerleader.

- All three are excellent, well-behaved, energetic, interesting, athletic, talented, happy children. In spite of being raised by a cosmopolitan, independent, single, determined businesswoman, they have turned out to be darn good kids!

- They are the wind beneath my wings. They are, after all, the major reason I *had a purpose.* My children have given me a purpose to live, to work hard and to achieve greatness.

- I am so thankful to my successline and to those who were my mentors, teachers, friends and critics, and for my health. I did it and so can you!

- My parents have moved nearby, here in the mountains in Colorado. Sadly, my father passed away in 1997.

- Many organizations and companies ask me to speak for them.

- People change their attitudes and make life-changing goals after attending my seminars.

- I listen, talk, give help to everyone who calls me—as long as they take action and get results. It's addicting to hear the excitement of people's success from all across the nation. In one day, people call me from a dozen different states. My team is awesome. We have the momentum we worked hard to get. We get results. The leadership in my organization has studied and learned all about this business called MLM. I am so proud of the leadership of my organization.

- I still work from my home.

- I don't have a secretary.

- My business brings in over ten million dollars annually to our company.

- I am considered a Master in the MLM industry.

- I am hired as a success coach at $250 an hour.

- My story is now told in lots of other books as well.

You are going to make remarkable progress in a short time. As you read this book, you will find ideas and encouragement rarely found anywhere else. Here's to your success story. I can barely wait to read about you!

Chapter Two

How To
Get Started In MLM

Are you tired of looking for answers about just how to get started in MLM? Well, your frustration is over, because this chapter is a been there, driven that road map on how to get started.

In this chapter, I have cut through all the stuff that others won't or can't tell you and let's you get down to business now.

How would you like some general information from someone with experience who will give you straight information that just doesn't seem to be easy to obtain, that will help you build an organization and get paid for decades?

Great! Here it comes.

What Is MLM?

MLM stands for Multi-Level Marketing, Another title is Network Marketing. MLM is a system of marketing and delivering products or services directly to the end user. Goods or services are moved through a "network" of independent contractors. It's a system that cuts out the middle men. And it's hot. Multi-Level Marketing has made thousands of men and women independently wealthy in America alone.

You can have a lot of fun in MLM
and it's financially rewarding.
Hurry up and get involved,
get committed and take action.

Today, do it right now!

Why MLM Is For You

- The success stories are many, and this book is one of them.

- MLM is available for everyone.

- If you have two to 10 hours a week, you can accrue income of several hundred to several thousand dollars a month.

- Most MLM companies offer a very low cost to you of starting your business, so if you find one is not for you, you haven't spent very much money up front.

- One thing is for sure, with companies downsizing, job security isn't what it was for most of our parents. It's frightening!

- Most people can't retire on what they're earning—even if they could keep that money coming in.

- Who really likes exchanging their lifetime hours from nine to five for not enough money at the end of the month? I tried. It was impossible for me.

- There has never been a time any better than right now—this minute—to build a gigantic MLM business.

- If you need a little or a lot of money to live like you want, give MLM a try.

- You can make a lot of money in MLM.

Facts You Should Know About MLM
Is it easy? No!
Is it doable? Yes!

- Building a very good income in MLM takes some time. Plan for three to five years.

- Learn while you earn—if you learn a lot fast, you'll earn a lot fast.

- In MLM, you have the ability to become a legend in your own time.

- In MLM, you can't get to a certain level and quit working. When you get to another level, you just do business differently.

- Most MLM plans are set up for optimum productivity, not minimum performance.

- Find a product you love that is marketed through MLM and join today. **Hurry!**

- Sad but true, most people quit because they expect MLM to come easy. They would rather simply sit in front of their TV.

MLM...

...pays for performance, production and service, not for potential.

...companies are not illegal pyramid schemes.

...has decreed that you may have anything that you desire, if you go the narrow way, which allows no distractions and no stopping.

...is not easy. It is not a get rich quick scheme. Rewarding, very. Easy, no way.

...takes time, a little money, effort, desire, commitment and action.

Here Is An Amazing Study Of MLM. Where Do You Fit Into The Game?

Look at all the people who are in the game.

There are those who make the game. There are the players, the game makers. There are the pieces. The pieces are moved by the players and the game makers. The damaged or broken pieces believe that they can't play anymore. Of course they're still playing a game—the game of being broken pieces. And there are the spectators. They just watch everyone who is playing.

Now, take these different roles and apply them to your MLM business.

If you are a game maker, you will build your own business. You will not wait for your upline or your recruiter to show and tell you what to do. Those with excellent training are successful much faster. Is now the time for you to jump into the game?

My advice? Become a game maker!

How To Learn About The MLM Business And The Industry

- Attend all local meetings about your business.

- Become a student of your business.

- Commit to attending your next National Convention or Leadership Seminar.

- Go with your upline to his/her presentations.

- It's your responsibility to review all the information your company has available.

- The upline's job is to support you if you have any questions. That person may not always know the answers, but there is someone who does. Keep searching until get your questions answered.

- Read books, listen to tapes, attend seminars.

- Read your upline's newsletter.

- Subscribe to *Upline*® magazine.

- Join Jan Ruhe's Book-of-the-Month Club at www.fireup.com.

Here Are The Benefits Of MLM For You (Take a close look at this list, What appeals most to you?)

- All business-related activities are tax deductible.
- Attend every sports event, play, performance, award ceremony possible in your children's schedules.
- Be one of the parents who isn't complaining that they are looking for a job.
- Be there for your children when they need you.
- Develop your leadership skills.
- Earn extra income.
- Enjoy ongoing personal growth and development.
- Everyone who joins MLM has the same opportunity, man or woman, college or none, support from others or not.
- Get a savings plan for retirement.
- Get a top-flight education, unlike the one you got in school.
- Get great products at a discount.
- Have a part-time career.
- Have many successful people in MLM who are willing to show you the light on the trail.
- Have no need for day care.
- Have low overhead.
- Have the most flexible work hours.
- Make many new friends.
- Pay for your child's college education with ease.
- Spend more quality time with your children.
- Take and pick up your child/children from school.
- Travel, travel, travel.
- Wear the clothes you choose.

Work:

- Only the hours you choose.
- Out of your home.
- With champions—people who are positive, who have desire, drive, eagerness and ambition.
- With whom you choose.

Here Are 12 Success Principles You Should Know

1. Use your company's products.

You have to be your own best customer to know how fantastic your products really are. If you're not convinced, return your kit and try something else. And remember, you *are* buying wholesale.

Here's your key to product knowledge: Each week purchase four new products. By the end of three months you will be an expert product user, not wasting time being a product expert.

2. Cultivate an attitude of acceptance.

Look for the benefits of your sales plan and the good features about the products. As you purchase each product, week by week, throw away all the competitive products you previously used. Make that commitment to your business.

Never dwell on some feature of the plan or some company policy you would like to see changed. The company is not about to change such a successful operation to suit anyone's personalized ideas. If you wish to recommend a change, put it in writing and it will get consideration, but don't waste energy "fighting the system."

Accept your sponsor and your leader. He/she is the only one you have, and no one is in a better position to help you.

3. Ninety percent copy.

This is a common sense principle. In the beginning, develop your business along the lines that have proven effective for others. Your success will be assured if you will direct 90 percent of your time and energy this way. Use the other 10 percent of your abilities to explore new ideas and to match your business to your own personality and unique circumstances.

4. Set goals to get goals.

Just as a ship would not be moved from its berth without a destination, you should not begin your MLM adventure without setting goals. You'll find many suggested goals you can use as guidelines in this book.

One of the reasons why the Five-Year Plan (see Chapter 3) has helped so many people is that it's a goal that really works. It's one of the most perfect examples of a compelling goal you'll ever see. The Five-Year Plan has a very definite starting point, a definite time span, inspiring reward at the end and progress checkpoints along the way.

If you focus on your goals daily, write them down and write them down again and again, say them aloud and tell them to your friends. They will begin to come true.

As if by magic? Magic works for me.

If you do not have a more specific goal in mind, adopt the Five-Year Plan as your goal.

5. Attend and conduct meetings.

Meetings are the backbone of your business. Attend as many as you need to learn the sales plan, and then begin conducting meetings of your own. Continue to attend other meetings periodically to refresh your ideas, to broaden your knowledge and to observe different presentation techniques. Always remember that your meetings are where you will learn the most. The greatest teacher in the world is your own experience.

A meeting as a pre-scheduled occasion—in your home is fine—where you give a "stand-up" presentation. If no one comes, give the meeting anyway. Give it to your spouse, give it to a tape recorder. A friend of mine once gave his presentation to six pillows!

6. Teach the sales plan.

Every meeting should be a "discovery session" for probing the many unique features and benefits of your company's sales plan. While the plan may be simple in concept, it will become fascinating and complex if you will just think of yourself as a student of business, or mathematics, or even human psychology.

Your business opportunity can fill the needs of anyone. It appeals to young and old, rich and poor, and every other category of person you can imagine. Although many people will not take the time to study and understand what you have to offer, you can continue to present it with confidence and pride. You only have to touch the hot buttons of a handful of people to have a fabulous business. Never give up and you'll succeed.

7. Emphasize your most exciting products.

These products lend themselves best to your plan, *because* they are exciting…*because* a small customer often buys a large order…*because* the resale potential is high…*because* they have a fast consumption rate…and *because* your distributor's own families can consume or use a large volume all by themselves.

8. Be positive.

Positive thinking is the one technique that allows you to use the greatest amount of your potential.

None of us uses but a fraction of our total ability. Optimistic, confident, goal-oriented thinking, programs our subconscious mind in a positive manner that encourages possibilities. This brings out ideas and actions we might otherwise overlook.

Negative thoughts are traitors to your cause, and you must eliminate all negativism from your personality. If you have a complaint or an excuse, don't voice it! If a negative thought creeps into your head, immediately replace it with a positive thought. "I can't sell" must become "I will continue talking to people until the laws of probability grant me a customer."

Remember: "What you think—you do, what you think—you look, what you think—you are." Think about this success plan and you will do it. Think about your happy future and you will look happy. Think like a leader and you will soon be one.

9. Do your business every day.

Busy people are the best Network Marketing distributors.

One advantage of the Network Marketing business is that you can take advantage of fleeting moments to "talk business" to a friend or fellow employee. You can "think business" and organize your thoughts while you drive your car. You can use your products many times every day and each time think about how tremendous the products are and how everyone ought to be using them. If you will keep your business in the front of your mind every day, you will be amazed at the progress.

For the strict spare-timer it is possible to concentrate most of your work in one day per week—one busy day—but you still must take advantage of every working opportunity during the other six days. If you walk past a potential distributor without at least making some small attempt to "talk business," you may be passing up a future master who will, eventually, join someone else's group.

10. Set a fine personal example.

You don't make money "off the work of others" in our business. You must provide leadership for the distributors you recruit. Don't ask or expect others to do anything you won't do yourself. If there are challenges in your organization, you must look to yourself for the solutions. Set a better example—and your challenges will disappear.

11. N. D. A. O. P. C. C.

"Never do anything other people can't copy." Your success will be in direct and exact proportion to how simply you can get the job done. Many people need to follow in your footsteps. If you set a complicated example, you will lose much of your following along the way. Keep it simple.

This doesn't mean you should avoid hard work! Just don't stray off on a complex tangent that other distributors won't be interested in following. Remember, in the long run you make very little from your personal sales. In fact, a master leader makes very little from his own leadership bonus. The big money in MLM comes to those leaders who blaze a simple trail and help many, many others to follow along.

12. Never give up.

The Five-Year Plan (see Chapter 3) is based on your finding only one ambitious person per year. Now, suppose that person is destined to come along in your tenth month? Do you give up if you haven't found someone after only six months?

There are a number of people in Network Marketing who make over seven figures annually. Where would they be if they had given up after only a few months? I know for a fact some of them did very poorly in the beginning. "Never give up and you'll get paid!"

I do not believe a person can follow these principles consistently without far exceeding the Five-Year Plan, even on a spare-time basis. How's your endurance? A person who won't be stopped can't be stopped. Persistence with this fantastic plan will lead you to a $50,000 per year income in only five years. What will you have if you let your opportunity slip away? Some people in Network Marketing make a 5-6 figure income per month! I do!

When your own business stops growing, know right away that you must be overlooking one of these "12 Success Principles."

Do You Make Any Of These Mistakes?

Do you:

- Spend tons of money on advertising?

- Spend tons of money on leads?

- Decide to invest in the MLM business, get really busy, sign up just a few people, sit around to see what will happen?

- Figure you will become financially independent after only 0-6 months? It doesn't happen that way, does it?

Here's *How To* Make It Happen

Duplicate methods that get results. Train others on how to get results. Promote leaders direct to you. Give yourself time to do it all. You will become financially independent.

How To Make Money in MLM

- Commit to always and ever changing and improving yourself. Those who won't commit to change, transformation and personal growth are missing a fabulous life.

- Check out your company's history.

- Go into management/leadership/partnership from the very beginning.

- Have someone who is knowledgeable about the comp plan explain it to you. Learn exactly what you have to sell and how many people you have to recruit to start to make those larger percentages. There is a lot of money to be made in MLM. Far too much of it is left on the table every month by people who don't know the comp plan.

- If it's a good opportunity today, it will be good tomorrow. Be able to take immediate, consistent action on your opportunity today.
- If there is no product being moved, watch out—no money!
- Make sure you sign up with someone who is working the business.
- If anyone tells you that you can make a lot of money in a very short time, run the other way.
- You can make money, big money in MLM. How? Study the Masters. Do what they do.
- Say *"Yes"* to the opportunity, it might have major value for you.
- The people who make the money are the ones who are more constant, more enthusiastic, more ambitious and do not quit.
- There are some success stories of fast cash in MLM, but not many. Fast doesn't last.
- Those who are positive and enthusiastic will find they won't be able to resist the urge to get started, keep going and earn the money they know they can.

There are many people in MLM who earn $100,000 or more a year. Some earn that much in a month—and more. Where would they be if they had given up after only a few months? Where will you be in the future if you don't make MLM work for you?

A Word Of Encouragement And A Word Of Caution

There is no doubt in my mind that you can become a success in MLM. Be careful, very careful, whom you let coach you. Let only those who are succeeding in MLM be your coaches. Talk is cheap. Results are expensive. Beware and be aware of those who give you advice who have never done MLM, or won't tell you in what MLM company they succeeded.

Step One: Invest In A Product Kit

- You can recommend the products to someone since you have tried them.
- You get all of the support materials you will need to begin your business.
- You save money, compared to purchasing all of the items separately.
- When you use most of your products, you'll experience the benefits for yourself.
- When you invest in your own product kit, you can explain the benefits of your product kit to others.

- It helps to have some knowledge of the products, and from the beginning, you must have the paperwork to fill in to enroll others, such as the Kit Request forms or Distributor Sign-up forms, or company Agreements.
- You can earn while you learn in MLM. Begin with the knowledge of just a few of your products.

Step Two: Get Product Knowledge

- Buy every product you can use from yourself.
- Buy only your own products to use in your home and to give as gifts.
- Collect stories about how others are benefiting from your products.
- Earn while you learn; you don't have to have knowledge of all of your products to begin.
- Get your product knowledge from those getting results, so you can genuinely recommend the products to others based on proven experience.
- Get to a product training within your first two weeks. If you don't have knowledge of the products, how can you recommend them?
- If you don't have a need for a particular product, find a friend or relative who could try the product and give you feedback. This will allow you to share their personal story about that product as well.
- Learn all the benefits of your products, backwards, forwards and in your sleep. Read about them, use them, go to product training seminars.
- Throw away or give away all the products in your home that are competitive with yours.
- You don't have to like or use all of the products. And there is high value in trying all of the products, so you can choose your favorites. That way, you will know why the benefits are so good and why they provide such a strong base for your business.

Learn to:

- Explain the unique benefits of your products to others.
- Explain how the products are used.
- Explain the benefits for you personally of your favorite products.
- Share your personal product experiences and provide ideas for other product uses.
- Emphasize the necessity of using every product, so you can identify

your favorites.

- Explain the benefits so well that you can convey them even if you don't have samples with you.

- Expand your knowledge (information with belief) so you can speak powerfully about the products.

Step Three: Recommend Your Products To Others

- Identify: The First Three People You Are Going To Contact To Either Present Your Product Or Talk With About Becoming A Recruit.

- Be confident enough to begin recruiting from your first presentation.

- Develop retail customers.

- Follow up on all your customers. Ask for referrals or to book future demos. Determine if and when they are ready to become a recruit.

- Maintain scrupulous records.

- Once you have used some or all of your products and have seen their benefits and value, you can begin to recommend them to others.

- Just recommending products is a great way to start your MLM business.

- Some people recommend handing out tapes, booklets, pre-approach packets. Not me. I didn't even think of doing that. I didn't have any money to start with, so that was not an option for me. I don't have experience with that kind of recruiting. But, hey, try it if you like. It seems to work for many others.

- Start recommending your products to other families and friends. This is a critical step for your business building. Be prepared to go outside of your family and friends before too long.

- Who are the first three people you are going to pinpoint to help you share your products?

- You will gain confidence when you can first speak powerfully about the products.

Step Four: Create A List Of Names Of At Least 100 People You Know

Through the years I have heard many people tell others to make a list of 100 names. It's a great way to begin. But why not get some guidance about that list that will truly help you get started? Here's that guidance:

Making a list of who you know is very helpful. Just start. Once you make the list, put a star by those people you know will support you from the beginning. Many people in MLM will tell you not to start with them. **Well, I sure would and here's why...**

If you are sold on your product, you will want to contact those people who you know will benefit from the product and who will at least let you give them a presentation. Don't bother yet with the people you haven't seen in years. Those people might be prospects later. Also, I always worried that someone else would get to my great prospects before me. What if you walk into a meeting and there is your friend, signed up with someone else because you were afraid to approach him? You will be sick!

- Keep in mind, you don't have to contact anyone you don't want to contact.
- Make a list of who you are going to call on.
- Use a spiral notebook or keep track on a computer program. Keep track from the beginning.

Here Is Some Powerful Information On *How To* Create A Names List:

Ask yourself, *"Who can I introduce my products to, so that I can begin to see my products moving through my business?*

Begin with your family and close personal friends: moms, dads, sisters, brothers, aunts, uncles, cousins (first, second, third), neighbors, church members, business associates, business clients, businesspersons for whom you are a customer, butcher, baker, candlestick maker, club members, high school friends, college friends, persons you know on sight, people who know you.

Do you have 100 names yet? If not, then go to the yellow pages and identify persons you know associated with business for which your product would have an immediate interest and appeal. Who are the doctors, dentists, nurses?

Still not at 100 names? Go to all your lists.
- Class lists, wedding list, any list of people you know.
- Friends and family.
- Go to your DayTimer and address book and write down all of the names listed.
- Go through lists you already have.
- Go through every category of every list you have and write down anyone you think of who is a friend, acquaintance, associate, anyone who would recognize your name if you called.
- Your holiday card list.

Here Are The Main Reasons People Fail In MLM

1. Negative attitude.
2. Because they expect to.

3.   Low self-respect and self-esteem.

4.   Lack of family togetherness.

5.   Wishful thinking.

6.   Failure to conduct good meetings.

7.   Failure to recruit.

Help others with these challenges and don't accept any excuses—especially your own!

How To Be Prepared If Your Friends And Family Aren't Interested

OK, you're told to start with your family and friends. So you do. And they clearly are not interested. Oh no! Should you quit MLM?

Make a note of this answer: **No!**

My family and my friends were totally not impressed that I joined an MLM company. I got no support from them at first. Boy, do I know what it feels like to not have your family and friends interested! Everyone says to start with your friends and family. That's exactly what I did. How I wish that someone had prepared me for the lack of support I received.

I couldn't wait to get involved with my company. With only about 15 minutes of training from my sponsor, I was ready to go! When I asked my friends and family to help me get started, I was surprised that there wasn't much interest. Like none! I finally asked people I barely knew—the neighbors, acquaintances and preschool moms in Sarah's class—to come to my home and see these wonderful products. I kept on asking.

A few people booked home parties with me. My first goal was to book six home parties. I would not be denied. I kept asking until I got six. At my first six home parties, I just let my sincere enthusiasm spill out (actually, "gush" out is more accurate).

My First Home Party: How I Got Started, March 1980.

There were 20 people there. I was really nervous. I was pregnant with my third baby and unsure of myself. It was pouring down rain. I knew the benefits of just a few products. I was excited though. I knew I had found a gold mine. I sold $75 in product and couldn't sleep all night. A few people actually bought from me!! No one joined. But…I booked another party.

Here's What Has Happened Since That First Party

From that first party, I booked more parties, and from those, people began to line up with me to have home parties. Sometimes the lines were so long they went down and around entire hallways!

Through the years I have had over 500 home parties and several hundred presentations, have gotten individual orders for over $5,000 many times over, and have sold over $125,000 in product by myself.

My successline has grown to over 7,000. I hold the record in my company for promoting the most individual leaders and have won at least one of every award my company has presented in the past 17 years.

Ten years after joining MLM, I got a phone call from a woman in Miami, Florida. She called to say she had been at that first demonstration, that rainy night and had thought about it over and over through the years. She said she was ready to join me *and* she would only join with me. She did!

So, after all, 10 years later, I did get one recruit from my first home party. Patience…

How To Handle Rejection

The is one of the hardest parts of the business for most Network Marketers. It wasn't for me. I knew that MLM was a numbers game and I would keep asking everyone until I got recruits. I crossed the "R" word (rejection) out of my personal wealth dictionary. So should you.

It's true, this business does involve lots of rejection. People who you know and don't know will tell you, *"You'll never make it," "No, I'm not interested in joining you."* If you take rejection personally, it can hurt. Do you hesitate to present your opportunity to certain people? Have you ever quit because you just couldn't handle the rejection?

Here's *how to* handle rejection. Ask questions like:
Are you familiar with (your company)? It's a home-based business opportunity. Have you ever considered having a part-time business out of your home?

Here are the common responses:
1. I've been looking for something to get involved with.
2. Maybe, but I'm really not interested right now.
3. No, I'm not interested at all.

1's are keepers.

2's you ask to be ambassadors.

3's you want to say, "I'll wait for you. If you ever decide to join an MLM business, remember I want you in my successline."

See that? There is no rejection. This is the technique that will build you a strong organization. It reduces fear and, right from the beginning, you know who to talk to.

How To Handle Disappointment If No One Initially Supports Your Decision To Join MLM

- Ask friends and family questions about why they won't support you in your business.

- Ask your family and friends to be your ambassadors, to help spread the word about your new business.

- Get new friends.

- If your family or friends make fun of you, just laugh with them. You'll show them.

- Know that many times when you start something new, that change can create fear in your inner circle of family and friends.

- Know that many times your family and friends secretly hope you do not succeed. That way, they can be there for you, helping, protecting, needed, when you fail.

- Re-assure your family you are going to make time for them.

- When you become successful, just know that they will begin to pay attention. Show them.

Quit talking about it. Do it. The sooner you begin making some money the sooner all of these people will support you. Sad but true.

Here's What Happened When My Son Clayton Joined MLM

In July of 1996, my son Clayton came into my office and asked me to recommend a MLM company for him to join. He was 18. I had met a Master in the nutrition industry who I felt my son would listen to and learn from. I felt that a nutrition company would be great for him, so that he would learn more about great nutrition and how to take better care of himself. It's perfect for him to do part time while attending college. I love the company's products. Clayton joined, attended the first Leadership Seminar of his career and came home full of hopes and dreams. Fired Up! I clearly remember 17 years ago how much I wanted my family to believe in me. *I rushed to be his first and best customer!*

How To Support Your Friends And Family Who Are In MLM

If you have a family member or friend involved in MLM, call and ask for a brochure or catalog right now. Begin supporting that person in their quest for success. I've never understood people who would rather support a grocery store than their own family or friend. Just amazing. It's so sad. Do you really love your friend or family member who is in MLM? Guess what? You're not giving them that message when you don't support their new business.

Step Five: Set Up Your Own Home Office
My First Office

In our fourth bedroom, I set up my office. My grandmother gave me an old desk from her real estate business. It was missing one leg, so I propped it up with the a couple of copies of old yellow pages. She also gave me an ancient, heavy, army green filing cabinet that was in my grandfather's office in the coal yards in Dallas. I put up a bulletin board over the desk and had a phone line installed. The drawers of the desk stuck and the filing cabinet drawers were so heavy and hard to push that finally I got rid of them.

I started my business in this playroom. Sarah and Clayton played right by me while I did my business.

My Current Office

Now, 17 years later, I have a fabulous office on the second floor of my three-level home with gorgeous views of the Aspen Valley and surrounding snow-capped mountains. The furniture is all different types of fine wood. Just spectacular. I have candles all around, a stereo, the most up-to-date Toshiba® phone system with intercoms connecting to the 14 other telephones in my home, a Pentium® computer, fax machine and a TV in my office. Incredible! Who would have dreamed it when I first invested in MLM? Not me.

How To Set Up Your Office

Every large MLM business started in a basement (like $7-plus billion Amway® did), garage, card table, corner of a room, on the floor or in an extra bedroom. Some even started in a closet, on a dining room table or in half of half of a room.

No matter where you start, you must have a space to get organized, a phone, a writing area and a small display, if not shelves, for products. You'll feel more like you are in business. Your friends and neighbors will be impressed with your commitment.

- Size doesn't matter. It doesn't have to be an expensive office.
- Get a place to store your products.
- Get a spiral notebook, calendar and a pen.
- Get your own phone and get on the phone.
- Let your family know, when you are in "your office," you are not to be disturbed.
- Make your office a place where you really like to be.

Step Six: Getting Started In Your Business

- Ask for help.
- Attend personal growth and development seminars.
- Be unique.
- Become a saver (as well as maker) of money.

- Become an investor of money.

- Call prospects and ask if they have eight to 10 hours a week and a desire to make some extra money representing your company.

- Discipline yourself to do it. No excuses. You just have to make the decision to do it.

- Duplicate the people in your business who are getting results.

- Find a way to do the business better.

- Get busy.

- Get enthusiastic.

- Go to product training.

- Hand out a business card to everyone you meet. Try to give away 10 every day.

I made no fewer than 20 phone calls a day, sometimes 30. How? I just made a plan to do it. The children were home, normally playing where I could watch them. You can do it.

- Never make any excuses.

- Realize that you don't need to depend on your upline. As the upline's business branches out, your upline has less and less time to support you. Also, you'll find, as your business grows, you will need your upline's leadership less. Your goal is to become the upline.

- Search for information on being the best you can be in MLM.

- Set achievable goals so you can get your goals.

- Study leadership.

- Never, ever give up.

- Once you get the names down on your list, begin calling and letting the world know what you're doing. As you begin to prospect, you will get more names than you can possibly ever follow up on in a lifetime!

- Tell everyone about your business. Without realizing it, you will become a Master Prospector. Every time you get someone's name and phone number, write it in your spiral notebook. Nothing fancy.

- Use your product.

- Use your product some more.

Make...

- A commitment to become a student of human relations.
- A commitment to go to work on yourself.
- A decision to succeed.

Questions You Should Ask Yourself Before You Start To Build A Huge Organization

Are you willing to discipline yourself?

Are you willing to hold yourself accountable?

Do you have passion?

How are your people skills?

How are your leadership skills?

What do you have to do to change yourself?

What knowledge do you need?

What level are you willing to take yourself to?

Always Remember,
The #1 Key Person In Your Organization Is...
YOU!

Chapter Three

How To Set MLM Goals That Will Bring You Riches

"Stop, take a moment, listen to your inner self. Dream big, focus on your dream,
ignite your passion, let no one discourage you, get a determined attitude.
Begin today to work toward a better, brighter tomorrow.
Goals are necessary. Call goals your dreams.
Goals are dreams with deadlines."

Decide what it is you are working toward. Go for it.
If it's doable for someone else, it's doable for you.
Conceive it. Believe it. Achieve it.
Never shrink your dreams to match your income.
Grow your income to meet your dreams.

This chapter is for all of you who are pursuing the dream of owning your own life through MLM. It seems that Network Marketing just works better for some people than for others. Do you ever wonder why? Here are some powerful suggestions that will make you extremely successful—if you take action.

Today Only Comes Around Once.
You Can't Rewind Or Fast Forward It.

Today is a brand new day. God has given me this day to use as I will. I can waste it or use it for good. What I do today is important, because I'm exchanging a day of my life for it. When tomorrow comes, today's place will be gone forever, leaving behind something that I have traded for it. I want it to be gain, not loss; good, not evil; success, not failure; in order that I shall not regret the price I paid for it.

How To Get Clear On Your Goals

- Crystallize your thoughts and beliefs.

- Don't focus on income alone.

- Indefinite goals produce indefinite results.

- Keep focused on your lifetime goals.

- Make your goals uncommon, never be content with average.

- No goal is too big.

- People who work toward their goals and stay focused are normally rewarded.

- Plan for prosperity. Predict it. Start organizing for it.

- Put your goals in writing.

- People who take care never go anywhere. Take charge, instead; set your goals and take action.

- Plan ahead, to get ahead.

- Plan your work, then work your plan.

- Take action on your goals.

- Take interest in others' goals.

- The future belongs to the people who prepare and plan for it.

No matter what else you do right, if you associate with the wrong people, it's virtually impossible to achieve your goals. Be first the master of yourself, and only then a master of others. Remember, you always have a choice.

Your Success Is Up To You.

It's time to take action on your goals.

Based on evidence, a good way to start getting what you really want, is to develop the habit of imagining you already have it.

Nothing can make up for firsthand experience in MLM.

Here Were My First Goals

When I joined Network Marketing, I dreamed of being able to afford private schools for my children. Then I dreamed of being able to afford dance lessons for Sarah, recital costumes, baseball and soccer uniforms for Clayton, paying off our credit card debt. When these goals were met I began dreaming again of a new car, a better wardrobe, money in the bank, airline tickets to exotic places.

The power of the dream.

In a musical that I love, *South Pacific*, there's a song called, "You've Got to Have a Dream." In the song it says, *"You've got to have a dream, if you don't have a dream, how you going to have a dream come true?"*

My main goal was to get out of debt and to stay home with my children. Later, my goal was to become financially independent. The **only way** I could reach that goal was **to help others succeed in MLM.** Another one of my goals is that as rough as life was at times, I would **never** give up…

No Matter What!

Advice To Those Of You Who Are Mastering MLM— Get An Attitude! Here's Mine: Either Lead Me. Follow Me. Or Get Out Of My Way!

In the early years of my business, I worked at least 12 hours a week. Being totally passionate about my MLM business got me through all the obstacles—real and imagined. Having those first, early goals helped me focus on achieving all my bigger goals.

The Truth About Reaching Goals In MLM Is— You must:

- Be faithful to your dreams.
- Get really clear on what you really want out of your business.
- Hang out with successful people.
- Listen to motivational tapes every day.
- Identify your dreams.
- Let no one nor any challenge stand in the way of accomplishing your dreams.
- Don't just sell products.
- Do not let anything or anyone permit you to become sidetracked.
- Practice your approaches and your presentations, and learn from others who are successful.
- Set priorities.
- If your goal is reasonable, if you believe you can achieve your goal and are willing to work toward your goal every day, it must come to pass. IT MUST!
- It is not always easy to reach your goals.

- Most people get discouraged in MLM the first three months. Are you most people?

- The great news is you will achieve your goals, if you work your business and give it time.

- You will reach the goals you decide to go all out to achieve.

- Your goals must be pursued every day. This can be part time, but never just sometimes.

- Your goals must be challenging but attainable.

How To Set Higher Goals

- Answer this question for yourself: *Why not me and why not now?*

- Be willing to pay for information.

- Become a sincere student of those who **Have Done It.**

- Do not let anyone or anything distract you.

- Know that big goals come with higher price tags.

- Make a clear decision that you are going to do it.

- Make a plan, plan to work, and work, work, work your plan.

Advice To Those Who Have A Goal To Become Financially Independent Here's Where To Begin: Set A Goal To Save

Start saving even when you don't think you can afford to save. As you began to make more money, save more money. Choose to stay in a modest home and drive a Toyota—even though you can choose to live in a large home and drive a Mercedes or a Jag—and save the rest. Make choices and have big dreams for the lifestyle you want for your family and yourself. Pay yourself first. Put 10 percent of your check in the bank first—just for you—then pay your bills. Ultimately, you can have it all.

How To Be The Merchant Of Your Dreams

To be at the top of a thousand-person sales organization and travel all over the world giving speeches, motivating people, sharing and enjoying spending time with them—know that you can.

- To get out of debt—know you can.

- To have a group of positive people who want what you want—know you can.

- To have a small group around you who are your customers—know you can.

- To make a lot of money—know you can.

- Dream Big! You can.

- Know that your dreams will come true. They do. They will. It just depends on you. It depends on how much time you devote to recruiting, building your business and improving yourself.
- If you get a passionate attitude about what you're doing, you will get remarkable results.

There is a day when you get into MLM.
There is a day when MLM gets into you.
Until then, you are either a Master in the making or
You're just average.

How To Ignite Your Passion

- Believe in the **inevitability** of your dream, and it will happen.
- Big dreams don't come cheap—they come very dear.
- Fantasize, don't be paralyzed by negative thoughts.
- Have a vision bigger than you are.
- Go for achieving all your goals. Be totally unstoppable.
- Say this, "I want to have more to live for tomorrow than today."
- If you don't have a dream, you have nothing to lose. Go into that place and time where as a child you went to dream. Look around... .
- Limitations are illusions.
- Motivation comes only through vision.
- Stand in your own private Disneyland® and dream.
- The size of your dream determines the power of your action.
- You have a great gift: Your mind cannot tell the difference between reality and your imagination.
- What is your vision? Embody your vision.
- Work on getting a little better each day.
- You have to take personal responsibility, no one else will do it for you.

Write A Powerful Vision Statement

- It will support you in creating your successful future.

- Powerfully support your leaders in understanding the need for having a vision themselves, and in writing one that will truly support them.

- Your ability to create and use a powerful vision—and your ability to have your leaders do the same—will directly affect the success that you have in your MLM business and your life.

Identify Your Reasons For Pursing A MLM Career
Have Those Who Want To Be Leaders Identify Their Reasons For Pursing An Income In MLM Representing Your Company

How To Set Goals That Will Bring You Riches

- Be clear why you are in your own MLM Business. Be specific and include as many points as possible.

- Become very clear about what your life will look like when you have accomplished your goals. Keeping that vision ever present in your mind will support every action you take day to day.

- Continue to revise your goals as your business grows.

- Decide what you want.

- Decide if you are going to make your business a part of your daily life.

- Decide the number of hours per day and per week that you are willing to commit to building your business this year.

- Decide how many prospecting conversations—quality conversations for possibilities—you are willing to commit to having per day or per week.

- Decide where you would like to be in one year: what position you will achieve and what your monthly income will be.

- Answer this: Do all of the aspects of your goals match or fit?

- Find out from the beginning what others' hopes and dreams are.

- Find out what other people in your successline dream about and help them reach *those* goals.

- Get crystal clear on what your dreams are.

- Get powerfully passionate about what you are doing.

- Make your own goals. My goals cannot become your goals.

- Goal-setting creates a structure that will help to direct your actions and conversations toward goal-getting.

- Goals help you to determine what actions you reasonably think will be necessary to accomplish your bigger vision.

- Goals keep you focused on a specific path. You choose your own time frame.

- If you don't know where you're going, then you don't know what steps to take or in what direction to go. MLM is not a Sunday drive!

- In Network Marketing, you have to commit to the long-term benefits that this residual program has to offer, never forgetting for a minute it is not a get-rich-quick scheme.

- If you could not fail, what would you want your life to look like?

- Make a master dream list.

- Make a five-year plan and then work it.

- Make up your mind to succeed. Succeeding is up to you.

- Talk about your goals

- Look at much more than just material possessions.

- Write down the reasons for your goals in bullet points first. Reasons are what having the goal will get you or give you.

- Once you have a really clear picture of what your life will look like when you have accomplished your goals, you will be so excited that you won't be able to contain yourself.

- Read your goals at least once a day. Twice is better. As many times as you can is best.

All this is what will provide you with the self-motivation necessary for you to take all the steps you'll need to take.

And More Powerful ideas On *How To* Set Goals That Will Bring You Riches

- Once you decide on your goals, know that you will refine them, change them, reach them and begin again with new goals.

- Recognize others' achievements.

- Set goals, then set more goals.

- Set goals that are measured in money.

- Say your goals out loud and write them down.

- Start with 10-year goals. Where will you be in 10 years? In five years? In one year?

- When you set a goal, you have taken the most important step toward achieving personal success.

- Show other people ways they can be successful.

- Sometimes just going to a meeting and hearing others' goals will help you crystallize your own goals.

- Sometimes one line in a book or one lyric in a movie or song will help you decide on a goal.

- Tell people all about your company.

- The only way to not achieve your goals is to quit trying.

- The power of the dream is the most powerful power.

- Use goals as guidelines to help evaluate your actions.

- Write down your goal, write it out as a vision in first person present tense, as if it has already happened.

- We are in a free enterprise system and you are free to go for your goals and manage your business in any way you choose.

- Ask, "What actions do I have to take to achieve my dreams?

- When you're passionate and you believe in what you are doing, you stay committed for as long as it takes to get the job done.

- When you are passionate about what you are doing, you will begin to observe that champions take action differently than average people.

- Working part time, not spare time, will bring you a part-time income, if that is your goal.

- Work toward your dreams and the universe will accommodate you.

- Your game plan will require a partnership between you and your upline leader.

Do You Know About Single Daily Actions (SDA)?

Do you have a set schedule for your daily activity?
Every day my goal was to call no fewer than 20 people and reach each one of them. Answering machines didn't count.

Do you have a daily goal of how many people you are going to call to get new recruits? How many appointments will you make every day? How many people are you going to recruit every week? How many times a day will you present your opportunity?

Only if you work on your MLM business every day will you grow a huge Network Marketing organization.

- Commit to do specific actions on definite days.

- Decide which Single Daily Activity (SDA) you will commit to each day. It can be different each day. The point is: Make them up. Lay them out. Do your SDAs. You are in total control of whether or not you do those SDAs.

- Make a very specific schedule so you know where your hours are going and going to come from.

- Realize that just doing your SDAs over and over, week in and week out, will generate tremendous income for you. Tremendous!

- SDAs are those small, simple actions that you commit to taking each day: making five customer calls, five follow-up calls, five leadership calls. Sending out three catalogs. What they are is up to you.

- Always make one of your SDAs focus on the number of prospects you will contact each day.

- You must coordinate this action with the income you set as your goal. If you intend to make $10,000 per month by the end of the year with a five-hour per week effort, there's a discrepancy in terms of your expectation and reality. Those figures just don't fit.

- Your SDA efforts must be reasonable ones that truly support your expectations.

How To Set Success Goals
Think: What if money were no longer a concern—whether that means an extra five, ten or fifty thousand dollars—what would your life look like in the following areas:

- What qualities would you be known for: generosity, contribution, leadership, fun.

- What would you do?

- What would your days look like?

- What could you be doing every day for the rest of your life?

- What feelings will you have?

- What values of yours will be honored by being involved with your company?

- What will you drive?

- What possessions will you have?

- What qualities will you possess?
- Where will you live?
- Who will you contribute to and in what ways?

Here are the two main reasons to ask these questions:
- It keeps you focused, when doing your MLM business becomes inconvenient.
- It will support your new sales reps and leaders in creating their visions.

How To Handle Disappointment If You Don't Meet Your Goals

- If you don't accomplish a goal, evaluate your actions: What was missing and what do you need to put in place the next week or month to support your new goal?
- If you have the opinion that you MUST meet every goal, you set yourself up for failure.
- In MLM, if you set team goals, you can't promise to accomplish your team goals, since you are not the only person involved.
- You are not in control of what other people do or do not do. You are responsible for recruiting and training others to work the business. **And, you are responsible for you.**

How To Set Goals With Your First Level Leaders, As Well As Your Lower Level Leaders

- Determine goals for your successlines.
- Have three specific goal areas to decide on before the next call with your upline/successline, or before the next meeting or phone conference.
- Develop a very powerful relationship with goals and then be able to support your leaders in doing the same thing.
- As a leader, empowering your leaders with their goals, say, *"Every month we will be setting goals together, and then at the end of the month we can evaluate your progress and look together to see what was missing and what can be put in place to get better results next month."*

How To Set Reasonable Goals That Get Results

- 20 quality prospecting conversations = 1 recruit
- Sponsoring 4 distributors = finding 1 potential leader
- 80 quality conversations = finding 1 leader

- 4 quality conversations per day, 5 days a week, 4 weeks per month = 1 leader per month

- Contacting 8 prospects per day will increase your ratio, resulting in 2 leaders a month.

- It's always better to talk to more people than you have to. There is geometric value in momentum. When you have lots of prospects, it just turns into a numbers game. The more people you sort through, the better your presentation becomes. There is no desperation (and none in your voice) when you always have more people to talk to.

> ### "Whether you achieve your goals or not is ultimately determined by your activity."

How To Develop A Game Plan

Ask yourself and your successline questions such as:

How many:

- prospects will you contact per month?

- recruits can you reasonably expect from those prospects?

- retail customers will you have who purchase products from you directly?

- wholesale customers will you have, who only want to use products?

How much:

- inventory a month will you invest in for your own use?

What:

- is the number of customers to be generated per month from those prospects?

- month do you intend to advance to the next level based on your group volume?

Asking these questions will dramatically increase your monthly income. With all of these numbers and information, you can create a monthly income goal based on the position you hold right now and the total volume that you can expect each month.

Here Is *How To* Set The Goal Of Getting To The Next Achievement Level In Your Compensation Plan

Take a look at your company's compensation plan. Find out exactly where the profit-generating position kicks in and get there as soon as possible. In some companies the scenario is this: When you have a group volume, which includes you and everyone else in your business of $X,000 over a two-month period, then you will advance to a leader. Once you are there, you will earn far more in commissions on the same volume. This is definitely where you want to be!

How To Set Long-Term Goals
First, you must determine:

- How many people you will need to talk with to find leaders.

- That you will not support those distributors under you who are not open to your leadership or who are not taking leadership steps themselves.

- The income per month that you would like to be earning in 12 months.

- The number of leaders you intend to develop over the next year.

- That you will learn, understand and master the career/compensation plan.

- The total volume that you will need in your organization to earn that income.

You can estimate that 3 to 8 percent of your total volume will be your income. If you want to be earning $2,500 a month, you need to have a total group volume of $50,000 per month. This will vary from company to company.

There Are Only Two Success Steps For Goal Setting in MLM.

Step One: Set A Goal

If your goal is financial independence, no one will stop you. No one can. No One. Money—what many people say is the root of all evil and surely not to be talked about in polite company—will get you the lifestyle you want. Let me assure you, money can bring you a fabulous lifestyle. It did for me. There is nothing wrong with being successful. Humans are meant to succeed. And isn't America the best land of opportunity of all? I have been rich and I have been poor, and rich is better!

Step Two: Take Action

- Become your own best customer, give only your products for gifts.

- Commit to your dreams. Your dreams are going to see you through.

- Focus on contributing to others' success—not just to a friendship club.

- Work your business with a passion and you will be able to give your family an unbelievable lifestyle.

- Keep recruiting and training others how to recruit.

- Know there is raw power in your dreams.

- Know that MLM isn't easy. It takes time. Have patience.

- Never complain when you have to miss special events with your children.

- Offer to teach product knowledge to others as soon as you can, because what you teach, you internalize. It just gets easier and easier.

- Only work with those people who are positive and want to build a business.

- Quit saying *"I know."* Unless you are at the very top of your company, you don't know.

- Start accumulating inventory to sell and supply new recruits. Never fill up your closet or garage with inventory just to meet your qualification quotas.
- Use your products only. Throw out **ALL** other competing products.
- Work your business every day.

How To Go From Wanting To Be A Millionaire To Being A Millionaire

- Ask millionaires for their input. Ask them to critique you and be open to their advice.
- Become a MLM expert. Recruit and train others to recruit.
- Duplicate your upline who is getting results.
- One of your goals must be to study millionaires, take them to lunch, to dinner, interview them.
- You must think like a millionaire.

Know that there is a price tag for success:

- More is expected of you.
- You must be able to withstand the critics.
- You will have to miss some of your family's activities, not all of them, but some of them.

Here Is A MLM Success Program
A new recruit's first goal should be to attain the first rank in the company as soon as possible.

Commitment And Planning
Here are the two keys to your success:

- Your personal commitment.
- Your planning to obtain that success.

One very obvious fact stands out in MLM. Those who make a **personal commitment** to work their MLM business are **always** successful. It's never failed. It will not fail you either. Those who are reluctant to make the commitment never get started. It's usually not because the need is not present; it's not because there is no time; it's not because there is no help available.

Here are the only two reasons that keep a new recruit from getting started:

1. Failure to make the commitment.
2. Failure to plan.

Attention New Sales Reps!
Here Are The 10 Commitments To Make Today!

Your success consists of many factors. Commit to these 10 goals and your success will be guaranteed.

1. Be your own best customer.
2. Write down your personal goals.
3. Set a personal leadership example.
4. Concentrate on the opportunity.
5. Be positive and do not allow negative influences to affect your thinking.
6. Teach others to teach others.
7. Follow the training of the person who is getting or has gotten the best results.
8. Have a weekly evaluation with your upline leader.
9. Spend a minimum of 40-60 hours a month building yourself a future.
10. Commit to work your company's opportunity for at least one year.

Here Are 10 Commitments For Upline Leaders

1. Answer all of your new recruits' questions, or direct them to the knowledge.
2. Conduct and teach how to conduct opportunity presentations.
3. Counsel your new recruits.
4. Help new recruits meet and go through any challenges.
5. Help your new recruits in all areas of the business, as long as they are working.
6. Help your new recruits sponsor their first four recruits.
7. Motivate and inspire your successline at all times.
8. Set a proper leadership example.
9. Supply product and plan knowledge.
10. Teach one-on-one presentations.

Work only with workers. If your recruit stops working so do you!

Here Is An Exact Formula, A 13 Week Plan You Can Follow

Week One:

Understand and appreciate the opportunity you have. Less than five percent of people in the U.S. have ever been offered the MLM opportunity. Really, you've got to understand what an amazing gift you have to offer. It's incredible!

Complete training with your upline on your starter kit. Understand how the contents of this kit and the literature it contains will help you build your business.

Place your "Starter Order." Every recruit is different. A businessperson with plenty of money seeking fast growth may start with a $2,000 order. A housewife or college student might start with a few highly consumable or non-consumable products with a $100 or $200 order. If you don't use your own products you don't deserve to be successful. Leaders don't waste time on those who will not work their products into their budget. Become your own best customer.

Start your list of 100 names. Get started with your spiral notebook. (See Chapter 2)

Set your meeting nights. If there is a local meeting in your area, attend it. If you start your own meetings, remember, it is your meeting—set it when you want and stick to it. Monday through Thursday evenings are best. Never be discouraged by the turnout. Large businesses are built on small meetings. (See Chapter 9)

Sponsor one person this week. Try to recruit someone in your first 48 hours. Have your upline help you sponsor this person. This doesn't mean your upline will give you a new recruit. Get a good prospect and have your upline go with you to help you. Remember, you are being trained. Use whatever aids your leader is using—sponsoring books, catalogs, products or scratch pad. (See Chapter 8)

Meet with your upline. Bring at least one person with you. (See Chapter 7)

Study your company's sales manual. Anyone who wants to be a leader in a short period of time has to have the common sense to seek out answers. Ninety percent of the answers you want are found in your company publications. But remember, no fortune has been earned in school. Fortunes are earned by applying what you have learned.

Develop a sponsoring attitude. Webster says a sponsor is one who takes responsibility for others. Here are some sponsoring realities:

- Ask yourself, *"What do I have to gain?"* with this person.
- Don't give up on slow starters or big talkers, but don't wait on them either.
- Everyone you sponsor isn't going to be a "superstar."
- MLM is a growth business; because of this, you need to develop and practice *patience*.

Study the Compensation Plan. In the long run there is nothing more motivational than a thorough understanding of your company's marketing plan.

Week Two:

Sponsor your second recruit. Your goal during the entire 13-week period of this program is 12 recruits. Sponsoring is the lifeblood of the business. You must leverage yourself to build a big business.

Hold a meeting in your home. Present it yourself or your upline will present it for you. Have prospects committed and confirmed to attend to insure having at least five in attendance.

Plan your first product workshop. Product workshops are great for involving everyone and building belief in the products. Workshops are vital to building your consumer base. Your friends will realize the products are superior, that you are committed, and that your business is fun.

Prepare a Presentation Book and learn to present your company sincerely and enthusiastically. Here is what to put in it: A company brochure, copies of your upline's checks, photos of you with your upline, photos of you at your National Convention. Your photo with Masters in the industry.

Have a rubber stamp made. Example: Mary Doe, Sales Representative For *Getting the Lifestyle You Deserve, Inc.* 1234 First Class Drive, Aspen, CO 81234 (303)332-1234

Open a business checking account. Put all of your business income in this one account. Pay all of your business expenses from this account. Don't get your money mixed up. When you commit to becoming a Leader with your company, your earnings should be channeled into your business instead of supplementing your income.

Invest in a quality tape recorder or CD player. A great percentage of your training will come from listening to tapes. You will want to play the *Fire Up!* music.

Begin your tape and book library. You can probably only digest and learn from one to two tapes per week. Begin ordering tapes and books recommended by your upline today. Turn your car into a classroom.

Week Three:

Sponsor your third recruit. One new recruit a week is a minimum effort necessary to reach your big goal. It is not uncommon for a real leader to double or even triple this pace. Such an individual will grow four to nine times as rapidly. Just do it!

Hold your second meeting in your home. Some of the people from your first meeting should be there, but always have someone new coming. Remember, success doesn't come from big meetings but many consistent small meetings.

Have your first product workshop in your home. Your new recruits, friends, relatives and neighbors will realize your company is not "just another thing" once they try your products. Invite your upline. When you and your upline show off the benefits of the products, the people who come will see that you have a real and exciting opportunity.

Be ready to present and explain your attitude toward the business, and how to get started in the business.

Meet with your Upline. Bring someone with you, be attentive and learn.

Replace all competitive products in your home at a rapid pace.
Put every product that your company can replace into a large box. Use your company's products and only use the old product when it is superior to your company's product. Take a picture of the competitor's products and make up a cost comparison sheet. Wouldn't you rather buy from yourself? Some can become leaders while others are still using up brand X.

Learn to demonstrate your main product's benefits.

Show and explain the products in your kit. Share your fabulous products with 12 friends.

Set aside an area in your home for your office. (See Chapter 2)

Keep your Prospecting Notebook up to date.

Add five more names this week.

Week Four:

Sponsor your fourth recruit. Hurry!

Help your recruits learn to recruit. In order to really grow in MLM, you must work on your depth. There is only so much you can accomplish all by yourself, but by teaching others to teach others to teach others, there is no end to your potential.

Visualize your goals. Write your goals on paper. Have a **I-am-willing-to-work-for** list complete with pictures. Make sure your goal is clearly defined and has a date on it. Goals not written are simply wishes. And wishing just won't do it!

Hold your third meeting in your home. You conduct the meeting. Everyone started in MLM at the bottom. By the time you have conducted 600 meetings (over a four-year span), you will be on top.

Give your second product workshop. This can be in your home or the home of one of your key recruits. Invite your people over just to share the benefits of all of the products.

Work as a team (if you are married). You can make it alone if you have to, but it is more fruitful, fun and productive to have common goals and ambitions with your spouse. Develop an understanding of what areas of responsibility each one of you wants to handle. Ninety percent of the time, one spouse starts more quickly and does more than the other, but always try to be helpful, cooperative and above all *supportive*. The results will be a better business and a better personal life as well.

Take *Urgent* Action.
- Be an action person.
- Do not procrastinate.
- Do not self-impose any roadblocks.
- You are on the road to Success.

Back up your commitment with inventory. It is smart business to "buy up" to the next bonus bracket (providing you have a Commitment and Plan and you're working the business and the business is working). Figure the increased percentage you'll earn from being at different bonus levels. Be a good businessperson. It is not necessary to have a garage full of product. Only buy extra inventory if you can afford it. It's always a good idea to have inventory for your new recruits, if you are determined and sold on your opportunity.

Take your top producer out to dinner. They deserve it and so do you. Everyone likes to be recognized and appreciated. You will develop good rapport and better understanding with social time together.

Week Five:

Sponsor your fifth recruit. You should understand your company's benefits enough now to know that you're offering the greatest business in the world. Think of their interests—you are doing them a favor. Don't hold back. Go for greatness!

Hold your fourth meeting in your home. The numbers are growing and you're becoming the leader of your group.

Decide, with your upline, which of your direct recruits should start having meetings in their homes. The only way you ever gain success and security in MLM is by helping others be successful. You should have a monthly team meeting together but weekly meetings are where you begin to become a leader—and where you'll be creating your new leaders.

Help others build their business and you will not have to be concerned with the growth of your own. Build your people and they'll build your business.

Review your Prospecting Notebook. Prospecting is the lifeblood of any business and so important to your success!

Start your own newsletter. Give your recruits the information and recognition they need to succeed. A newsletter lets you do and say something once, yet thousands of people can get your message.

Study the marketing plan and be prepared to present it to your upline. If you are going to be enthusiastic and tell a prospect you have the greatest MLM opportunity in the world, but then you stumble over the figures, your prospect will have about as much confidence in you as you would in a doctor who didn't know which side your appendix was on. Learn while you earn.

Give your third product workshop. The primary purposes of your product workshops are: to share the benefits with your customers, communicate that you stand for quality, book more workshops and create new customers.

Meet with your upline and some of her other successlines. Volunteer to help in exchange for gaining valuable experience. Your attitude at meetings can inspire everyone. Be enthusiastic, cheerful, positive and friendly. People like to congregate with like-minded and same-hearted friends.

Week Six:

Sponsor one new distributor.

Hold your weekly meeting in your home. Allow your recruits to help you. It's important to teach them leadership. Train from my *Duplicatable Training System.*

Conduct a meeting for your strongest first level leader in his/her home. The goal is to always have four future leaders working at moving up in the comp plan.

Maintain contact with your "retail customers." They know people you do not know. Also, their interest may be piqued to become a recruit because of your growing success and your superior products.

Continue to build your tape library. Listen to the tapes while getting ready in the morning, driving to and from work, or as you do odd jobs around the house. Get your team to do the same thing. Have them buy their own tapes, so they will use them fully and not lose yours. If you play music at meetings make sure it is motivational music, such as "Fire Up!"

Analyze and study your goals and your progress. Always analyze your strengths and weaknesses. Be proud of what you are building, but not content or complacent. Your results will usually follow your work effort by two to three months.

Service your distributors. Product flow and meetings are the two areas where you can most quickly build faith and loyalty. Always be on time. Start and end your meetings when you said you would. If you don't have a particular product on hand, get it. Do the job of the person above you and soon you will have his title, too.

Build your inventory. With more inventory you will be able to better service and supply your recruits if a product gets discontinued. You will have it in stock. Inventory helps add conviction to your commitment. Your friends and neighbors sense your stability. You work harder and you really feel like you're in a thriving business when you have an investment in your products.

Give your fourth product workshop. They're more fun when you do a lot of them, simply because you're better at it now. Think of all the new friends you'll meet and how good you'll feel after the meeting.

Continue to improve... in every area and be the pipeline to pass all that knowledge on to your group. That is what leadership is all about—helping others to succeed and be strong.

Week Seven:

Sponsor another new recruit. Think that this recruit may be your top producer or the one who may sponsor your top producer.

Conduct your weekly meeting. Involve your "gung-ho" successlines. Devote two-thirds of the time to the marketing plan. You're not there to entertain anyone. Don't "baby-sit" those who are not interested in growing. Never discuss a negative thought at a group meeting.

Conduct the second meeting for your new first level leader. Do it in his/ her home. Start to identify and work with the leaders under him/her. Get to know them personally. Take a sincere and active interest.

Have another product workshop. You are setting a good example—and your successline will follow your example. You should be a qualified professional regarding your product by this time. Your goal should be to have at least 10 of your successline qualified as product professionals by the end of your 13 weeks.

Copy your residual check. Keep a record of every check you get. This allows you to visually show your progress. It is a great pleasure to look back on years of steady growth. Your checks can be your strongest recruiting tool. Make sure you put a copy of them in your Prospecting or Recruiting Book. Never have them direct deposited.

Identify and begin working with your second first level leader. You cannot afford to have just one or two strong first level groups. Your goal is to have four.

Study enough about the nature of your products to satisfy your

own curiosity and conviction. Your testimony of the benefits of your products will be built on the results you and others around you receive. Do not become technical—mechanics don't sell cars.

Work hard. Even if it's initially frightening and distasteful to you. Sales, contacts, meetings, phone calls, letters, newsletters, ordering, planning…these are the varied jobs of a Network Marketer. The more you put into this business the more you will get out of it.

Adapt to your particular strengths and weaknesses. It's imperative that you recognize your weaknesses—after all, they're only strengths you have yet to develop—and improve on those areas, but is much more important to recognize your strengths and adapt your plan to take advantage of what you do well.

Continue to improve. Everything is continually changing, consequently you need to continue to improve. People should not evaluate you just by where you are today, but where you are going and take into account all the progress you are making. This is a challenge—and an exciting one!

Week Eight:

Sponsor another new recruit. You've heard people say, "There's safety in numbers." Never more true than in your MLM business. With recruiting, more is better. If each of your successline people are following this plan for success and are equally as successful as you, you could relax on your sponsoring. However, your goal was and is to sponsor one new person each week. If you continue to sponsor a minimum of one a week you will be hugely successful! You will be at the top of your company in record time.

Conduct your weekly meeting. A store that closes early just because business is slow, is destined to fail. Copy things that work for others. Continue to hold meetings. Learn from your mistakes. Not every meeting will be equally successful, but they will all contribute to your growing business.

Conduct the first meeting with your second first level leader. These are the meetings that build big businesses. You can look back and realize this type of support in the group, by the leader, is why your business is growing.

Enjoy the business. Challenge yourself, but do not pressure yourself. Your business will grow much faster when others can see and feel all the fun you're having. You will work harder when you're having fun, because that's when hard work comes easy!.

Develop, understand and maintain the attitude and desire to build an organization to lead. You do not need to buy your way to the top—even if you could. If you want more from your business, produce more. MLM programs are designed for leaders, not salespeople.

Attend your upline's meeting. It's important that "your" successlines meet with someone who has been in the business longer than you have. Be an example for others at this meeting. Be enthusiastic, positive and attentive. Treat your leader with the respect you want from your people.

Evaluate your lifestyle. We all have character traits that can stand improvement. MLM is a way of life. Do you look the part? Are you turning people on or off? Ask your upline for an honest appraisal of those areas you could improve on.

Buy a "daily-memo" book. Get a system. Before you go to bed, write down what needs to be done tomorrow. Set your priorities daily. You can write down names of prospects you meet or think of. This will be invaluable to your organization. Before you go to bed, make a list of 10 things to do and make them special SDAs (Single Daily Actions) for the following day. This can be a spiral notebook or a computer program.

Continue to promote your product workshop program. Do this by conducting a workshop for one of your new people. You need to teach this distributor how to conduct their own workshops and how to schedule more workshops. By now you are making your products so exciting—people can't wait to have what you have.

Buy the services of others to help you. Don't let mowing the lawn, painting the house, fixing up your office or keeping your books stand in the way of having time to build your business.

Week Nine:

Sponsor a new recruit. Here's an exciting fact: You have not yet sponsored your best distributor! If you were prospecting for gold, uranium or oil, no one could tell when, where, or exactly how you would "strike it rich." But one fact is certain: Only the quitters lose!

Conduct your weekly meeting. Let some of your key people take part in the meeting. Make sure they are prepared. Have fun, but remember this *IS* a business meeting. Always keep in mind the results you want to accomplish at the meeting.
Conduct your second meeting for your second first level leader.

Have patience, but be firm about following a pattern that works. Teach others to teach others to teach others.

Get up one hour earlier. I've found that the one hour I take before all the interruptions of the day is equal to three hours later in the day. It also shows determination; plus most of us work better during those early morning hours. Your attitude is so much better when you get off to a good start. One hour per day is equal to 15 days per year. If you can get three times as much accomplished, you have picked up 1100 hours of super-productive time in just one year. Discipline pays. We all have the same amount of time. Don't squander it on hurry, worry and fear.

Reward yourself and your spouse. Promise yourself an immediate reward for achieving every goal you've set. Example: After you've recruited eight people you will have a romantic weekend away. If those eight people are using and recommending products as you are, your weekend will be a paid vacation.

Set up your bookkeeping system. The less time spent on busywork the better, but every good businessperson knows "where he is at." Make sure your figures tell the true story right from the start.

Progress on your product workshops. You should be busy training your successlines by having them come to all your workshops, or having trainings in your home for your new recruits and their new recruits. Remember, your purpose is to train them to do their own businesses. Make certain they have my *Duplicatable Training System.*

Subscribe to Upline®. America's #1 MLM magazine and resource catalog will give you a monthly boost and is an outstanding source of good common sense material.

Add more names to your Prospecting Book. Keep it constantly updated. Ask for referrals from all your customers and wholesale customers.

Go for the next level in your comp plan. Go after the new title and responsibility that will make you stronger. Always reach up for the next rung in the ladder of success. Otherwise, you will never get to the top. Hurry, you can't stroll to a goal.

Week Ten:

Sponsor a new recruit. Reflect on what you are doing—building a network of distribution that eventually will be nationwide, perhaps even worldwide. What you can do as an individual is limited. What you can do with an organization is unlimited.

Conduct your weekly meeting. Your meetings are beginning to take on your personality, because you are the leader. I've found the weekly meetings grow into more training and motivation and less recruiting as you develop, but new spark is always added by the new distributors. Always have your new recruits there. Always.

Conduct the third meeting with your second first level leader. This individual should be developing depth and strength now. She needs to be weaned then tested—give her a chance to do her own thing next week. Don't be like the doting mother who will not let go and keeps her children tied to her apron strings.

Make a list of your first four future leaders. Your goal by now should be elevating your people and yourself to the next level. And you can, because you've built the proper base. Four "going groups" is all that most people can work with effectively. Constantly replace the one that is breaking off or falling down.

Implement the rule of FOUR in your organization. Your goal is to build an organization in depth. Four leaders who beget four leaders who, and on and on. You will be the sales manager of a nationwide network of your company's distributors.

Take a good look at what you are doing *in depth*. There is always a better way. Keep improving. People are observing you and will be influenced by your actions and your growth. You go deep for MLM security.

Give a product and opportunity training. You should have a number of people in your group who are at varying steps of qualifying as product professionals. By allowing them to take over more of the work of planning and training, your team will look to them—and you're their leader. That's your goal. Be a leader of leaders.

Reaffirm your commitment to yourself, your company *and* your success. No other company offers higher rewards for the commitment you've given. Review your Goals, Planning and Commitment.

Run a health checkup on your business. How many people have you sponsored? How many meetings have you given? How many distributors are in your group? How much inventory do you have? How much self-improvement have you made in this 10-week period?

Develop a source of revenue. If you have not been in the business long enough to have earned the capital necessary for your inventory, or fortunate enough to have it saved up, you will need to borrow it. Many borrow from parents, many from financial institutions. Product inventory is simply another form of savings account—only these savings can be sold at a profit!

Week Eleven:

The most valuable gift you can give another is to set a good example. Do it now!

Sponsor a new high-quality first level recruit. By this time you realize you cannot prejudge people. Do not, however, just "sign up" anyone to fill your quota. Think of the type person you want and go after him. Always have handy a packet of literature and Prospecting Book to help the person decide to join you *NOW*.

Conduct your weekly meeting. I recommend trading meetings with other leaders to get a new approach and new ideas. Try to get someone as good or better than yourself. Remember, your goal is to build an organization. Keep your meetings geared to that goal.

Build an inventory to handle all your needs. When you follow this program, you will need to steadily increase your inventory. Build your inventory as it helps you qualify for the next level. Many factors need to be considered: Your personal financial situation, your group output, delivery time from date of order, what you are selling, etc. Back orders cost you plenty, so try to avoid them by building a good inventory and learning proper ordering procedures.

Conduct your first meeting for your third first level leader. Always have someone you are grooming for the next level. You are developing a pattern that will make you tremendously successful. You're developing your style. Make sure it's sincere and enthusiastic. Use this meeting to develop your first level into a leader and help build her organization.

Set long-range goals. A goal not written is merely a wish—write it down. Have pictures of what you want. Have a "power-picture" of what you want to become.

Keep your word. When you tell someone you are going to do something—do it! Don't make up excuses. I have seen many people fail just because they do not **follow up**.

Teach yourself not to make statements that conflict with your goals or interfere with your mental attitude. When you feel inclined to complain, hold it back. When you begin to doubt that you will reach a goal, don't mention it. To keep the best possible attitude, Stop Talking Failure!

Become a good communicator. Effective communication is a critical factor in every business, but none more so than MLM. Develop your own method for communicating with your organization—timely phone calls, newsletters, personal interviews, passing along information and being yourself and treating the other person as a capable individual and leader.

Make things happen. There are three kinds of people in MLM: People who make things happen. People who watch things happen. People who wonder "What happened?" Which one are you? Have a sense of urgency about your business. Challenge yourself to have specific things done by certain date.

Firmly entrench in your thinking that the only factor that will decide whether you are successful or not is *you*!

You can do it. So DO IT NOW!

Week Twelve:

Sponsor your eleventh recruit. You are probably way ahead of the one per week pace, which is all the better for you. The focus here is on consistency. The best way I know to become wealthy is to have an organization of people through which you multiply your efforts.

Conduct your regular weekly meeting. Many successful leaders in MLM established their business with a weekly meeting. These meetings will become a cornerstone and a pillar of your organization.

Give away one sample of your product every day this week. Explain to the person you give a sample product to that you are just qualifying for manager, leader, NSD, NUP, etc. in the *Greatest Business in the World*, and you're giving away this product rather than cigars. Do a lot of word-of-mouth advertising every day one week a month. It's a lot of fun.

Treat your spare-time business like a $50,000 per year business. Which it will be shortly *IF* you keep current a written list of your next four leaders. If you always have four new lines qualifying, you will be busy, happy and prosperous.

Have a copy of this plan on hand. Give it to people you have explained the program to, or prospects who live a distance away and others you meet and don't have a chance to visit with.

Set your meeting calendar and always have it planned one month

in advance. It is amazing how this will help you stay organized and busy, how your successline will value your time more and your meetings will be larger and more effective.

Utilizing the "Golden Hours"—7 to 11 p.m. Make your contacts when people are available. A helpful reminder is to put a display of your product on top of your TV. How did you invest or spend these hours before you started building your own business? To increase your G.V. (Group Volume) turn off your TV.

Have a leadership meeting with your top people. Every meeting should be positive. In this one, however, you will cover challenges. In MLM, you have fewer challenges than other corporations, but remember, you're human. You are the leader. Keep this meeting constructive. This association of leaders can turn into a powerful "master-mind" group.

Understand the concept of spare time. Spare time is all the time you regularly *waste*. The time that you are driving—you can listen to tapes. When you are having lunch you can have an interview. The time spent on elevators, in lines, on airplanes can be spent making contacts.

Week Thirteen:

Sponsor a new recruit. In doing so, you have 12 in a 12-week period! Less than one percent of all sales reps accomplish this feat. By working in depth, these 12 should grow to 60 distributors in your organization. Continue to sponsor on a replacement basis. Successful distributors and total group volume is your goal. And by the way, this is exactly what I did to become a millionaire.

Conduct your weekly meeting. Recognition is a big part of the fulfillment people want in MLM. You should now be recognized as having promoted to your next level at your meeting with the people you have helped and vice versa. You have proven this program works, you have a track to run on. Now there will be no end to your accomplishments.

Conduct your second meeting for your third first level leader.
Reinvest your bonuses and profits back into your business until you have at least $500 to $1,000 in inventory and everything is paid for. (You were able to survive without your MLM income three months ago, you still can today.) Think of your investment as the best interest-earning savings account in the world. You should be able to liquidate your inventory in two months easily.

Establish a firm understanding with your distributors of how you market your products:

- A good distributor should consume a minimum of $50 per month within his own home or buy $25-$50 of product per month.
- Focus on conversational selling.
- There are a multitude of opportunities to "slip" a product presentation into virtually every conversation you have. Use any method you may excel with. If you or one of your sales reps have confidence in door-to-door or party plan selling, and you want to pursue that method, that's great for you, but don't try to switch potential leaders to fit into this mold! Remember, it's got to be duplicatable.

What Are You Going To Do When, Someday, It's Too Late To Set Goals That Are Achievable?

- By completing this 13-Week Program, you have set a beautiful example for yourself and others.
- Learn and teach the value of being consistently consistent.
- Make an organizational chart that keeps track of your production.
- Make an organizational chart to keep track of your team's production.
- Know where your team volume is coming from at all times. Never let your team dictate what your volume will be.

Here Is A Five-Year Goal Master Plan

There are three key steps to building a highly successful spare-time MLM business in only five years. This one is too good to overlook. It should be the goal of every MLM distributor to be financially independent and have the option of retirement in just five years. You can do it. The question is: Do you want to?

Step One: Become a Leader Yourself

Here are the recommended goals to achieve in one year or less.

❑ Develop 30 customers who regularly buy your products. You have no quota or deadline for achieving this, and we're really not talking about a very large number of customers. This sales experience will help you be a better leader. You will also enjoy making a good retail profit and your personal sales volume will be up to $500 or more monthly.

❑ Sponsor 12 first level recruits as soon as possible. Experience has shown that one out of four who are properly sponsored will work seriously in the business. Work in depth applying the "Rule of Four." Continue sponsoring/recruiting after your first 12. As long as you keep your "edge," your leaders will be encouraged to keep theirs sharp, too.

❑   Conduct one regularly scheduled meeting per week at your home. This is excellent training for yourself, a good time for sponsoring, training and motivating others in your group and an excellent opportunity for your distributors to bring their prospects. Never cancel your meeting if no one attends...this will kill your business.

❑   Once you reach your first leadership rank in your company, begin stocking products, keeping records of your distributors' volume and their bonuses as well. Learn these simple aspects of the business on a small scale before you have a huge team.

❑   Continue to improve your meetings.

❑   Follow the proven success principles given in this book and teach these principles to your group.

Step Two: Help Your People Become Leaders

Identify and help your ambitious people advance to the next level.

❑   Ambitious people are easy to identify. If your other distributors lack self-confidence, you should encourage them to try, but don't push. Remember, you will be best at teaching the business the way you do it.

❑   Work closest with the people who are willing to cooperate with your methods. If you don't have enough ambitious people, concentrate on recruiting up, rather than on squeezing business out of reluctant distributors.

❑   Do everything within your power to help your ambitious people do the work listed above, but don't ever do their work for them. Tell them how. Show them how.

❑   Be patient.

❑   Give meetings at their homes and at the homes of ambitious people under your directions. Suggest ideas for them to try. Occasionally, leave them on their own for a few months, so they can know the meaning of responsibility. Always be ready to pick them up when they are down. Help them to work for their long-range potential, so that month-to-month challenges won't dull their enthusiasm.

❑   Give your other distributors the service they deserve. Stock sufficient products to supply the normal needs of your group. Order regularly.

❑   Provide training through group meetings and written material such as newsletters.

❑ Don't waste time trying to force someone beyond the rank of "distributor" if that is all they want to be.

Step Three: Go Down, Down, Down
Make certain your organization grows in depth.

❑ Educate your first level managers regarding how and why their group can expand. A first level manager who has no managers is still in the apprentice stage. Apply "The Rule of Four" once again. Look down in your successline leader's group for ambitious people and give them your first level attention.

❑ After a reasonable time, if you see no response from a potential leader you are trying to work with, use your time to develop additional first level groups. If you have explained the plan properly and provided initial encouragement, you have done all that is required.

❑ As your organization grows larger, insist that the senior distributors carry their own load. Work closely with those who cooperate. Give your other distributors the service they deserve. Communicate with them regarding new ideas, special meetings and so forth. Make arrangements to speak to their groups occasionally. Don't spend time trying to force someone beyond the rank of "Manager" (Executive, whatever) if that is all they want.

Step Four: Set Goals

Step Five: Track Your Progress

Step Six: Use The *Duplicatable Training System* By Jan Ruhe

Year A _____

January
Where I traveled: _____
Total Team Recruits: _____
Personal Team Recruits:_____
Total Team Sales: _____
Personal Sales: _____
Amount of Check: _____

February
Where I traveled: _____
Total Team Recruits: _____
Personal Team Recruits:_____
Total Team Sales: _____
Personal Sales: _____
Amount of Check: _____

March
Where I traveled: _____
Total Team Recruits: _____
Personal Team Recruits:_____
Total Team Sales: _____
Personal Sales: _____
Amount of Check:_____

April
Where I traveled: _____
Total Team Recruits: _____
Personal Team Recruits:_____
Total Team Sales: _____
Personal Sales: _____
Amount of Check:_____

May
Where I traveled: _____
Total Team Recruits: _____
Personal Team Recruits:_____
Total Team Sales: _____
Personal Sales: _____
Amount of Check:_____

June
Where I traveled: _____
Total Team Recruits: _____
Personal Team Recruits:_____
Total Team Sales: _____
Personal Sales: _____
Amount of Check:_____

July
Where I traveled: _____
Total Team Recruits: _____
Personal Team Recruits:_____
Total Team Sales: _____
Personal Sales: _____
Amount of Check:_____

Year B _____

January
Where I traveled:_____
Total Team Recruits: _____
Personal Team Recruits:_____
Total Team Sales:_____
Personal Sales: _____
Amount of Check: _____

February
Where I traveled:_____
Total Team Recruits: _____
Personal Team Recruits:_____
Total Team Sales:_____
Personal Sales: _____
Amount of Check: _____

March
Where I traveled:_____
Total Team Recruits: _____
Personal Team Recruits:_____
Total Team Sales:_____
Personal Sales: _____
Amount of Check: _____

April
Where I traveled:_____
Total Team Recruits: _____
Personal Team Recruits:_____
Total Team Sales:_____
Personal Sales: _____
Amount of Check: _____

May
Where I traveled:_____
Total Team Recruits: _____
Personal Team Recruits:_____
Total Team Sales:_____
Personal Sales: _____
Amount of Check: _____

June
Where I traveled:_____
Total Team Recruits: _____
Personal Team Recruits:_____
Total Team Sales:_____
Personal Sales: _____
Amount of Check: _____

July
Where I traveled:_____
Total Team Recruits: _____
Personal Team Recruits:_____
Total Team Sales:_____
Personal Sales: _____
Amount of Check: _____

Year C _____

January
Where I traveled:_____
Total Team Recruits: _____
Personal Team Recruits:_____
Total Team Sales:_____
Personal Sales: _____
Amount of Check: _____

February
Where I traveled:_____
Total Team Recruits: _____
Personal Team Recruits:_____
Total Team Sales:_____
Personal Sales: _____
Amount of Check: _____

March
Where I traveled:_____
Total Team Recruits: _____
Personal Team Recruits:_____
Total Team Sales:_____
Personal Sales: _____
Amount of Check: _____

April
Where I traveled:_____
Total Team Recruits: _____
Personal Team Recruits:_____
Total Team Sales:_____
Personal Sales: _____
Amount of Check: _____

May
Where I traveled:_____
Total Team Recruits: _____
Personal Team Recruits:_____
Total Team Sales:_____
Personal Sales: _____
Amount of Check: _____

June
Where I traveled:_____
Total Team Recruits: _____
Personal Team Recruits:_____
Total Team Sales:_____
Personal Sales: _____
Amount of Check: _____

July
Where I traveled:_____
Total Team Recruits: _____
Personal Team Recruits:_____
Total Team Sales:_____
Personal Sales: _____
Amount of Check: _____

Year A _____ (cont.)   Year B _____ (cont.)   Year C _____ (cont.)

August
Where I traveled: _____
Total Team Recruits: _____
Personal Team Recruits: _____
Total Team Sales: _____
Personal Sales: _____
Amount of Check: _____

September
Where I traveled: _____
Total Team Recruits: _____
Personal Team Recruits: _____
Total Team Sales: _____
Personal Sales: _____
Amount of Check: _____

October
Where I traveled: _____
Total Team Recruits: _____
Personal Team Recruits: _____
Total Team Sales: _____
Personal Sales: _____
Amount of Check: _____

November
Where I traveled: _____
Total Team Recruits: _____
Personal Team Recruits: _____
Total Team Sales: _____
Personal Sales: _____
Amount of Check: _____

December
Where I traveled: _____
Total Team Recruits: _____
Personal Team Recruits: _____
Total Team Sales: _____
Personal Sales: _____
Amount of Check: _____

Annual Total
Where I traveled: _____
Total Team Recruits: _____
Personal Team Recruits: _____
Total Team Sales: _____
Personal Sales: _____
Amount of Check: _____

August
Where I traveled: _____
Total Team Recruits: _____
Personal Team Recruits: _____
Total Team Sales: _____
Personal Sales: _____
Amount of Check: _____

September
Where I traveled: _____
Total Team Recruits: _____
Personal Team Recruits: _____
Total Team Sales: _____
Personal Sales: _____
Amount of Check: _____

October
Where I traveled: _____
Total Team Recruits: _____
Personal Team Recruits: _____
Total Team Sales: _____
Personal Sales: _____
Amount of Check: _____

November
Where I traveled: _____
Total Team Recruits: _____
Personal Team Recruits: _____
Total Team Sales: _____
Personal Sales: _____
Amount of Check: _____

December
Where I traveled: _____
Total Team Recruits: _____
Personal Team Recruits: _____
Total Team Sales: _____
Personal Sales: _____
Amount of Check: _____

Annual Total
Where I traveled: _____
Total Team Recruits: _____
Personal Team Recruits: _____
Total Team Sales: _____
Personal Sales: _____
Amount of Check: _____

August
Where I traveled: _____
Total Team Recruits: _____
Personal Team Recruits: _____
Total Team Sales: _____
Personal Sales: _____
Amount of Check: _____

September
Where I traveled: _____
Total Team Recruits: _____
Personal Team Recruits: _____
Total Team Sales: _____
Personal Sales: _____
Amount of Check: _____

October
Where I traveled: _____
Total Team Recruits: _____
Personal Team Recruits: _____
Total Team Sales: _____
Personal Sales: _____
Amount of Check: _____

November
Where I traveled: _____
Total Team Recruits: _____
Personal Team Recruits: _____
Total Team Sales: _____
Personal Sales: _____
Amount of Check: _____

December
Where I traveled: _____
Total Team Recruits: _____
Personal Team Recruits: _____
Total Team Sales: _____
Personal Sales: _____
Amount of Check: _____

Annual Total
Where I traveled: _____
Total Team Recruits: _____
Personal Team Recruits: _____
Total Team Sales: _____
Personal Sales: _____
Amount of Check: _____

As you can tell by this chapter, I believe in setting goals. Get busy setting your own goals up for your fabulous future. Spend the rest of your life saying, *"I'm glad I did"* instead of *"I wish I had."*

Boy! That's a lot of work!

Yeah, so ...

Please close this book, and take another look at the title. Do that now.

Good. The title reads *MLM Nuts & Bolts*— Right? I didn't write a book called *How To Be Mediocre in MLM,* or *How To Be an Average MLMer.*

What I'm sharing with you is how I did it, and how you can do it, too. I worked hard. I became a millionaire. If that's what you want. Roll up your sleeves. Get down and get up to work. Get busy setting your own goals for your fabulous future.

Please, please, don't spend the rest of your life saying, *"I wish I had."*

Spend the rest of your life shouting from the rooftops...

"I'm glad I did!!!!"

FIVE-YEAR PLAN

FIRST YEAR:

SECOND YEAR:

THIRD YEAR:

FOURTH YEAR:

FIFTH YEAR:

Chapter Four

35 Habits To Make You More $$$,$$$ In Your MLM Business

"Midnight Habit:
Every day at midnight, I choose to let go of the events of this day and
look forward to a brighter and better tomorrow."

Habit #1: Discover Your Values
Here's How To Have People Rushing to Do Business With You: Identify Your Top Value

One of the most important human relations ideas I know of, is to identify your own top 10 values. Then narrow those down to your top three. And then, identify your **Number One Top Value**.

Why? Once you have identified your top values and then your **Number One Top Value**, you can truly understand *why* you are so passionate about certain parts of your life.

For instance, if your top value is children, everything you do and are revolves around your children. If church is your top value, everything you do and are revolves around your church. If what you are doing is not congruent with your top values, you will constantly be unhappy, and won't be able to figure out why.

Discover other people's top values. When asking your friends their top values, you will be surprised that many of them are *identical* or very *close* to yours. If you have a struggle with people, find out what their top values are. You'll probably discover you do not share like values.

In MLM a major important habit is to identify,
right from the beginning, your upline's values,
your successline's values and your customers' values.

Discovering people's values is an important habit.

So, how do you find out what others' values are?

First, you must care. This is a master habit. Care enough to find out what people value.

How?

By asking questions, like a detective, to find out what those top three values are. Ask questions like: *What do you value in a relationship? What do you like most about people?* Remember, discover your own values first, then look for other people's values.

Now that you know about values, what do you do next?

Once You Discover Other People's Values, Present Your Product And Opportunity To "Match" *Their* Values. Speak To *Their* Values. *Not* Your Own.

The Value List

Following is a supermarket of values.
Look and see which ones are yours:

- aggressive people
- ambition
- animals
- being an American
- being on time
- boldness
- candles
- caregivers
- champions
- changing of the seasons
- cheerfulness
- children
- church

- clean air
- cleanliness
- comedians
- commitment
- confidantes
- courage
- CPAs
- democracy
- dependability
- doctors
- enthusiasm
- environmentalism
- family

- fairy tales
- football season
- forgiveness
- fresh flowers
- gambling
- generosity
- givers
- good neighbors
- fine wine
- freedom
- freedom of speech
- friends
- garbagemen
- grandparents
- good grooming
- great books
- great seminars
- great skin care
- great tapes
- great videos
- happy movies
- health
- holidays
- home
- honesty
- husband
- independence
- industriousness
- integrity
- justice
- leaders
- learning
- life-time
- long-suffering
- loyalty
- mentors
- MLM Masters
- musicals
- organization
- paintings
- parents
- people who don't hold grudges
- people who don't interrupt
- personal growth
- pictures of your children to see their growth
- positive attitude
- pretty frames
- productiveness
- quiet time
- rationality
- reading
- sales masters
- scientists
- sincerity
- singing along with songs that were hits in the '60s
- smoke-free environments
- soccer season
- soft hair
- sporting events
- surprising people and being surprised yourself
- peace
- people who can say "I'm sorry"
- pride
- quiet time
- success stories
- technology
- the ability to take risks
- the families you have met in business
- the Fourth of July
- the mountains
- the ocean
- those who help you to continue to grow
- those who you have helped who are now leading their own parade
- teachers
- transportation
- travel
- truthfulness
- trust
- unconditional love
- veterans
- winners
- winter. . .

If you didn't see all of yours, choose ones from your own list.

Habit #2 : Be An MLM Pro On The Telephone

Facts You Should Be Aware Of About The Importance Of The Telephone In MLM

When a prospect calls you and is interested in more information about joining your MLM business, take their call, even if it means stopping what you are doing at that moment. Those telephone calls have top priority. I know many, many people now screen their calls. Often times, you can't get a return call for days. Be the one who answers the phone. Be the one who returns phone calls.

In MLM, Your Most Important Tool Is The Telephone

- Always ask for the caller's number, so if you get disconnected you can call them right back. Get an address and e-mail address, too, for your database.

- Get an extra business line for your business and get the children their own phones.

- Get the "down the drain" people off the phone as soon as possible. Listen, offer a few suggestions, then tell them when they have done what you have suggested, you would like for them to call you back.

- Give elevator calls—call people all through your successline and tell them what a great job they are doing. Appreciate them. It will blow them away!

- If you have children, it's important NOT to have them answer your phone for business—*no matter how old they are!* Get professional. Children do not need to answer your phone. What if they take down one number or piece of information incorrectly and you lose the sale or the chance to recruit someone like me?

- If you're in MLM you must have call waiting- never, EVER let anyone get a busy signal, **NEVER.**

- If you pass up an opportunity to call someone back or to give your card to a prospect, you might be passing by a future champion.

- If you do not call prospects back, they will continue to call others and by the time you get back to them, they have been serviced by someone else and you've lost a sale—and maybe a future.

- Learn telephone skills, improve on those you have.

- Make sure you have an answering machine or voice mail box that will capture all those important messages you miss when you're out.

- On your answering recording, have a professional sounding message. Don't talk too fast and do not try to get too much information on your message.

Sound pleasant, not hurried. Don't have your children make your message. Cute to you, but a turnoff to customers.

- Put a smile in your voice. Be happy to hear from people. Set up a mirror beside the phone and watch yourself smile when you speak with people.

- Remember, your words must paint a picture, and people can't see your face when talking with you on the phone.

- Return your calls immediately and no more than 24 hours later— max!

And More Powerful Information On How To Be An MLM Telephone Pro...

- Use the words *"available"* or *"not available."* Example: *"I will be available Wednesday at 2 p.m. to discuss the opportunity with you."* Or, *"I 'm not available to have that conversation with you at this time."*

- When you tell someone you're going to call them back at such and such time, call them back *at that time.*

- Work on your telephone voice. If you have an accent, work on softening it. In MLM you will have people from all over the country in your successline. Don't let your accent be a distraction.

Perfect the 5 point telephone call.

Most people talk too long on the phone. Make your call friendly, quick and businesslike. Cover these points:

- ❏ Things are going great.
- ❏ Tell them of a success you have just had.
- ❏ The business is getting easier all the time.
- ❏ Offer to help them. "I'm ready to help you whenever you're _____."
- ❏ "By the way, we are having a meeting Wednesday night. We'd love to have you attend."

Say all of this sincerely and enthusiastically. Do not pressure or make the people feel uncomfortable. Convey the feeling of sharing—not selling.

Habit #3: Ask Powerful Questions *And* Listen To The Answers

An important success secret about MLM is your ability to discover information about your prospects and customers. Why? Because the more you know about them, the more you can meet their wants head on. Never sell people what they "need," find out what they "want" instead.

How do you do that? Ask questions, listen and meet their wants.

How To Surge Ahead And Go Up Your Compensation Plan—Get Information…Ask Questions.

- Ask for the hottest information on self-improvement and sales training techniques.
- Keep asking questions about the compensation plan until you understand it. Then teach the information to someone else as soon as possible.

How To Get Your Customers' Loyalty So They Keep Coming To You To Buy Your Products…Ask Questions.

- Ask questions of all your customers.
- Take an interest in your customers' lives. Keep an information card on each of them. Call them back and **follow up** on a regular basis. Don't just staple their order form to a Master Order form, file them away and forget about them. These names and phone numbers are real people and they are your business! If you aren't going to **follow up** with them, give them to someone in your successline. If they don't want them, send them to me!
- Send thank-you notes all the time.

Habit # 4: Make An "Always" List (*How To* Get Great Results After Great Results)

Be prepared at your presentations. Have a list of what you want to be, say and do. Here are some "Always" that will make a huge difference in your results. Always…

- Ask questions such as: "Have you heard of my product? May I have a few minutes of your time?" "Can you see yourself representing this product?" "Do you have the desire to make some extra income?"
- Be prepared.
- Be sincere.
- Be an apprentice.
- Listen.
- Look your best.
- Seek out the best in people.
- Tell potential customers that if they ever decide to use your product you would like their business.

Always have:

- A first class pen; I use a Mont Blanc®.

- Two pens (or refills), so you never run out of ink.

- Products with you.

- All your paperwork, catalogs and business cards available—always!

Habit #5: Perform at Your Best...Get Fabulous Results

There are very few people making an all-out effort to get to the top of the MLM businesses. Are you interested in making money? BIG money? Your presentation of your product is a gift. Practice your performance and you will get great results.

- "Tenure" in an MLM company means nothing, but performance means money.

- The great ones in this business are the ones who put ideas, ideals and ambitions into actual operation.

- The greatest motivation always comes out of performance.

- The uncommon person puts his best effort into his enterprise, for which there is no guarantee of material pay.

- The world pays for performance, production and service—not for *potential* performance, *potential* production and *potential* service.

- There is plenty of job security for performance. In fact, performance is the *only* form of job security left!

Habit #6: Buy Only A Few Items For Your MLM Business

At last, here is a list of what you really need in your office, from the beginning to being a Millionaire. Invest in only a few required supplies:

- A few three-ring binders
- A calendar
- A clock
- A computer and printer
- A modem
- A fax machine (if you don't have one in your computer)
- A journal
- A separate bank account
- A spiral notebook
- Yellow pads
- A bookshelf
- A stapler

- A big wastebasket
- An address book
- An address stamp
- An answering machine or voice mail box
- A business telephone line
- An up-to-date container for your products
- Product inventory
- Catalogs and order forms
- Files
- A filing system

That's a millionaire's office. That's all it takes! (Oh, maybe some candles, too, if you enjoy them!)

Habit #7: Invest In What You Need To Help You Succeed Fast

Take urgent action and GET the following:

- A library card, and go to a library and read, read, read.
- A sense of urgency.
- A philosophy. Mine is C.A.N.I. Constant And Never-ending Improvement (please borrow it).
- Ambition about your business.
- Books, and begin your own personal library.
- Busy.
- Busy building a future for yourself.
- Excited about life.
- Excited.
- Enthusiastic.
- Food for your mind—the single best investment you can make.
- Fiercely motivated.
- Going—quit making excuses.
- Ten percent of every check you receive in your **Wealth Account**.
- More committed.
- Motivational learning tapes and videos.
- Off the fence—stop procrastinating.
- To seminars.
- Serious about the career of sales—the greatest, most fun profession on earth.
- The attitude that your group can depend on you.
- The will to succeed.
- The attitude: I'll crawl over broken glass, live in a tent, search out the world's experts, because if it's possible for anyone in this world, it's possible for me.
- Up, put your shoes on and be thankful for a new day.
- Your foolish pride out of the way.
- That when you help enough others get what they want, you will get everything you want.

Habit #8: Get Rid Of Stuff That Gets In the Way Of Your Success

Here are two enormous secrets.

- Get the clutter **out** of your home, car, handbag and briefcase.

How? Just take a day and get some trash bags and throw out all the clutter.

- Get rid of that enormous DayTimer that makes you look so busy and that you waste all that time filling out when you really could be productive. At least take out all of those pages you aren't using.

Habit# 9: Make Choices That Will Propel You To Success

Now is the time to make some choices. If you are serious about your success, choose to pay attention to the following.

Choose to:

- Be happy, not unhappy.
- Be with those people who open doors in front of you and lead the way.
- Copy successful people.
- Control your emotions.
- Control your tongue.
- Commit, instead of just trying. ("Do, or do not, Luke. There is no try," said Yoda, the Jedi Master.)
- Concentrate on what you want, not what you need or don't want.
- Dream big, today.
- Dream bigger tomorrow.
- Be better every day.
- Learn.
- Work on solutions, not challenges.

Life can be great:

- Just make better choices.
- Look at all your choices.
- Make choices that will give you a fabulous lifestyle.
- What a high it is to have a lifestyle that gives you freedom of choice.
- Make up two new choices every day this week.

Habit #10: Take Action—Activity Breeds Productivity

Now is the time to begin a program of action. Right now. Get started.

- Act and look successful.
- Act like an achiever.

- Act as if it is impossible to fail.

- Act like a well-organized winner.

- Act fast on your dreams.

- Caution is often one of the greatest enemies of success.

- If you think you are enthusiastic, triple it, then watch your results grow geometrically.

- Indecision can be a decision, but only for a short time.

- Information without action is worthless.

- Inspire people through your personal example.

If you want your successline:

- To write newsletters—then you better be writing a newsletter.

- To recruit—you better be recruiting.

- To sell—you better be selling.

- To promote others to leadership—you better be promoting others as well as yourself.

Here Are Actions You Can Take *TODAY:*

Make:

- A big group happen.

- A decision.

- A written list of all of the advantages of your business over other businesses. Start telling others about those advantages.

- Boundaries disappear for yourself. Try new ways of doing business.

- Things happen for you, not to you.

- Decisions you can live with.

- Excellent efforts.

- Greater demands upon yourself.

- Sure you are with a company that attracts high caliber people—and leave if they aren't.

- Up your mind.

- Your own life more exciting and productive and you will have more to give.

- Your life a thrilling, productive life.

Put Action Into Your Business And Your Dreams Will Come True

- The great ones are the ones who put ideas, ideals and ambitions into actual real-life activity.

- The secret of "will power" is in building up a great love for accomplishment. "I will" is what "will power" means.

- Two little words that make a gigantic difference…

Start Now.

Habit #11: Get Organized For Success
Here is valuable advice to those who want to get rich.

- Capture important telephone calls in a spiral notebook. No need to have thousands of little pieces of paper cluttering your desk and mind.

Clean out:

- Your car.

- Your handbag.

- Your briefcase.

- Your wallet.

- Your home.

- Your office.

- The junk drawers.

- Get manila folders and file papers.

- Get rid of the piles.

- Have a pen ready at **every** telephone in your home. Never get caught with a pen out of ink.

- Make a list of what you are going to need for all your presentations. Don't be caught saying you "forgot something."

- Make sure you know where your supplies and products are at any given moment. Be organized so that you're ready for prospects and customers.

Habit #12: Creating Wealth
Here is *how to* keep the money you earn.

- Decide you are going to save some of the money you earn.

- All the world stands aside for the people who know where they are going.

- Andrew Carnegie was a millionaire. He made 38 other people millionaires.

Bill Gates has made hundreds of them. The more people you help get what they want, the richer you will be. Only help those who will help themselves.

- Be a student of wealthy people. Ask them questions, interview them.

- Believe in miracles, instead of being surprised by them. Be aware that there are angels watching over you.

- Big thinkers and big achievers have a common characteristic: They think big thoughts about themselves and others.

- Building an MLM career is a long-term gig. You don't become a rock star overnight. You don't get rich overnight either.

- Center your focus on your beginning sales force. Begin recruiting and training others to duplicate you. Start with a few people and keep training them and their successlines to recruit, recruit, recruit.

- Create your success and wealth by finding new and better ways to do everything.

- Create rapid growth.

- Creating wealth is far more exciting and satisfying than the mere possession of wealth.

- Crystallize your thinking. Think about what you will do with the money you're earning and will earn.

- Do the activities that seem impossible.

- Dream bigger than you did yesterday.

- Envision yourself the owner of a big business. Did the owners of big businesses work only part time when they were getting started?

- Establish relationships that can help you gain speed in progressing toward your goal.

- Exercise wisdom, discipline and judgment in regard to how you will spend your minutes and hours, days, months and years. That will provide you with a fabulous future.

- Expect great results.

- Make noble plans and pursue them daily.

- Financial independence does not happen by accident.

- Financial independence does not happen to be a get-rich-quick-scheme.

- Gain control of your finances.

- Go for the lifestyle.

- If you want to be rich, think rich.

- Increase your productivity.

- It's the acres of diamonds principle: the riches are inside you. Look.

- Master the savings habit. Save 10 percent of every check you get, no matter how big or how small.

- John D. Rockefeller was the world's first billionaire. He helped countless others to become millionaires. If you help enough people to get rich, you will get rich. Remember, they have to want to participate in their progression toward prosperity.

- In our country, we have a tradition that states *"Anybody can be somebody."* That statement is about you!

And More Powerful Information For You On *How To* Create Wealth...

- If you cannot save, you will never add your name to the honor roll of the financially independent.

- Keep your promises. Build your wealth on honesty.

- Know your business backward, forward and in your sleep.

- Be well organized and industrious.

- Have a great attitude, believe in what you're doing.

- Get trained.

- Follow directions.

- Learn to take risks.

- Be different.

- Go for being the best in your company.

- Go for every reward your company offers.

- Many people in MLM have reached great heights by the effective and continual use of just a few good ideas that they do over and over.

- Duplicate your upline who is getting results.

- Money isn't the primary reason to be in MLM. It's the lifestyle. The money enables you to have the lifestyle of the rich and famous. It's incredible.

- Nothing ever happens until you want something badly enough.

- Pay yourself first. When you get your check put 10 percent into a savings account until you have enough to invest it.

- Get some advice from a money manager on how and when to invest.

- Tell your mind what you see, and what you want. Paint a picture in your mind of what success will look like, feel like.
- Make a treasure map of what your life will be like when you achieve your financial goals.

"The noblest thing a person can do is to plant a seed that will someday grow into a giant tree that will give shade to people they don't even know. Make a difference in this world. That's where the true riches are. Money can't buy the letters and e-mails you will get from people you helped to get what they wanted." —*author unknown*

Habit #13: Come From Contribution

The best way to reach your goals—contribute to others. It's so true: the more you give, the more you receive.

- Appreciate those who come from contribution. Acknowledge the givers in your life. Be a "go-giver," not a "go-getter."
- Brighten the heart of every child. Not just your own child. Stop and smile or say something pleasant, just for the contribution sake of it.
- By your deeds you are known—not your philosophy. You can have all the knowledge in the world, but if you don't use it or if you abuse it, you will feel cheated in the end.
- Center your thoughts on the welfare of others, put others first and your time will always come.
- Check out the light you see in people's eyes when they make the decision to succeed, the glow on their face, the music of their voices, the inspiration of their spirit, their walk.
- Do something for others—a random act of kindness. Whatever you give, have no expectation of it being returned to you.
- Encourage the young. Take time to sit down with a teenager and get to know what's going on in their world. If you have only little children, you will be amazed to get a new perspective on parenting. If you have already been a parent of a teenager, perhaps just one word of wisdom from you will make a gigantic difference.

Give:

- A sincere compliment. Your compliment might just turn someone's life around. There is gigantic return if you can sincerely compliment another person. Put-downs or snide remarks just make you look silly. That's not the way of a champion.

- Elevator calls to give someone a lift. Call someone who is least expecting it just to say you care.

- Lots of recognition. Go overboard with giving recognition. People are starving for it. Everyone wants to feel appreciated.

- Up the need to punish. Forgive and forget. That which you can't change, endure with grace.

- Love where there was once hatred.

- People your expectations up front. Ask them for their expectations. Accommodate the other person.

- Yourself permission to reach out of your successline for support and information and be willing to pay for it. When you pay for information, it's always more valuable and meaningful.

- Of yourself, it will benefit you more than receiving. Be a giver.

Help...

...people make good choices. But remember, you are not a trained therapist. Direct people to get help if they are in need of it. Listen carefully to see if they are just sharing information with you or asking you to contribute to what they are saying. When you help people get what they want, they will come back to you for years and refer others to you.

And More Powerful Information For You On *How To* Come From Contribution...

One of the primary ways of judging the value of your life is by the contributions you make that make the world a better place. People are not born hard workers with greatness and ambition already formed. It is what they do after they are born that determines how ambitious they are. When you give, have no expectations of getting anything in return.

Habit #14: Be Prepared For Change

Here's The Fastest Way To Become Successful...
Be willing to change. If you are willing to change, you will have a great shot at becoming a millionaire.

- Change is hard but necessary—and the benefits of change are so worth it.

- Expect change.

- Go for changing yourself.

- If you are not happy in life, it's up to you to change your circumstances.

- If something isn't broken, break it. Figure out how it's going to change, because it will. Help it change.

- If what you're doing isn't working, stop it, then change it.

- Look forward to change.

- Nothing ever stays the same.

- The people who have earned a million dollars have had to learn to change and accept some major setbacks in their lives.

- Thrive on change.

- What you cannot change, don't.

- What's going on in your life today will completely change within five to seven years—if not sooner.

- You can only change and improve yourself.

- You have to change yourself. If you don't, someone or something else will. Count on it.

Habit #15: Have Fun!

Do you make these same mistakes?

- You work all day and have no energy left over for your spouse and children.

- You worry all day and have no energy left over for yourself.

- You don't want to spend any money, because there will be a price to pay.

Now is the time to take some time out for fun. Lighten up! Don't take yourself so seriously.
Here are some Million Dollar thoughts to turn into Fun Habits.

- A secret of happy living is not to do what you like, but to like what you do.

- Enjoy yourself.

- Enjoy what you are doing, and your sales reps will follow suit.

- Find a life of love and laughter—then live it.

- Find happiness in all you do.

- Give yourself away.

- Happiness is your birthright.

- Happy goals produce happy results.

- Have a gratitude attitude every day.

- If you want to be happy, think happy.
- It is much more fun to be an athlete winning the game than to be a spectator watching.
- Laugh. It's the music of the soul.
- Laugh some more.
- Let your year be filled with joy.
- Life is precious. Enjoy it.
- Make every day January 1. You don't have to start a new year only once a year. You can start over every day.
- Forget your birthday. Celebrate every day of your birth month instead.
- Play, it's the secret of perpetual youth.

Habit #16: Sell Your Products

How To Sell A Lot Of Product…Know them really well. Make everyone you present your product to want *all* your products. *Why?* Then they'll consider becoming involved with your company. Sell the sizzle.

Here is *how to* do this:
- Be enthusiastic and sincere.
- Be passionate.
- Collect testimonial letters about your product.
- Design your own presentation so it looks easy.
- Emphasize your product.
- Keep your presentations simple and less than 30 minutes.
- Know the benefits of your products.
- People need to buy.
- People want to buy.
- Put together a sales binder that shows copies of your checks or your upline's checks, people using your product, photos of you with your upline, photos of conventions, trips and rallies.
- Say that, and act like, it's an honor to work with your company.
- Stick to the fundamentals in selling. Sell the benefits to your prospect.
- Tell stories about how others use your product and how happy they are with their results.

Habit #17: Be Positive, Not Critical
- Accept your sponsor.

- Never criticize your sponsor or upline. If that person does not give you what you need, find it elsewhere. No need to say anything unkind.

- If someone is not getting results, don't criticize them. Mind your own business.

- Keep the bad news and bad ideas to yourself. You don't have to report them at meetings.

- Keep your opinions to yourself on issues that are current in our society. Do you like to be around opinionated people? Ask questions when you're with people. If you hear yourself talking, shift and begin to ask questions.

- No one is perfect. No one.

- No one knows what goes on under someone else's roof. You never know when some people are going through a crisis.

- Watch your results.

- No one does anything to you unless you permit them to. Quit playing the victim. No one can hurt you unless you permit them to. Get tough. Maybe it's time to transform yourself to the next level of maturity.

Habit #18: Be Determined To Succeed

How to be determined: Consider the postage stamp. Its usefulness consists in the ability to stick to something until it gets to its destination. Be known as a postage stamp in MLM.

- A person who can't be stopped won't be stopped.

- Business before pleasure.

- Every disciplined effort leads to multiple rewards.

- Have a recruiting attitude.

- Have a retention attitude. Let people know that you care about them and want them to continue. How? By writing newsletters filled with their names and stories about them.

- It takes just as much energy and effort to live a bad life as it does to live a fabulous life.

- Need to win.

- Duplicate the attitude of the Gold Medalist.

- Ninety percent copy is a common sales principle. Develop your business along the positive proven lines that have been effective for others. Your success will be assured if you direct 90 percent of your time and energy in this manner. Use the other 10 percent to explore other ideas.

- Opportunities never come to those who wait. They are captured by those who dare now.
- Play harder for yourself than anyone else.
- Push yourself to increase your understanding of the business. Master it.
- Strengthen your desire to achieve.
- To be great, you must be better than the best. Will you?
- Take urgent action.
- Take control of your life.

Have:

- A determined purpose to achieve.
- The attitude that you are a great recruiter.
- The attitude that you are a great salesperson.
- High expectations of yourself, and others with whom you choose to spend your time.
- The expectation that your dreams will come true. If you can dream it and are willing to work toward it, it must come to pass.
- A determined purpose to achieve.
- The courage to control your life time.
- The courage to challenge yourself with future goals.
- Stickability. Don't quit when and if the going gets tough.

If you:

- Keep your business in front of you every day, you will see progress.
- Want something badly enough—never, ever give up.
- Want something badly enough, and are willing to work for it on a daily basis, it will come to pass.
- The person who wins the MLM game is not necessarily the one who starts with a flourish, but the one who has the courage, desire and determination to stick with the goal until it is accomplished.
- With determination and a strong will, you will succeed in life. Will power is the energy that comes from expressing your determination and your strength of mind.

Habit #19: Work With Your Entire Successline

One of my secrets is to make yourself available to everyone in your successline, whether they are commissionable or not. Here's why: If people in your own successline quit, the people who were successline from them are now in your commissionable successline. If you've been working with them all along, they'll be thrilled to be direct to you and the relationship will have already been made. The transition will go so much more smoothly.

Here Is *How To* Do It

- Even if people aren't on your first level, give them first level attention. If they are ambitious and cooperative, work closely with them. Make arrangements to speak to their team from time to time.

- If there is a representative in your organization who is not supporting their successline, simply go down into the team and work with those potential leaders. The upline not working still makes money, and you will be helping those who want your leadership.

Habit #20: Work On Your Leadership Skills

There is an entire chapter on MLM leadership in this book. (But don't read it yet.)

Habit #21: Forgive Everyone Who Has Hurt You

Do you know any grudge collectors? They just don't want to work out a relationship. Through the years I have known some **major** grudge collectors. Choose not to give them any of your energy, and you'll be such a happier person.

Are you a grudge collector? Quit trying to change people. It simply doesn't work. Get on with building your own masterpiece of a life. It's okay that not every relationship you want to work out works out the way you want. When it is a struggle, let it alone. As people have time to consider all the facts, sometimes relationships can work out without you having to work it all out at all. It's exhausting to make sure everyone is happy with you. Don't try.

Here Is *How To* Start

- Forgive those who have hurt you. Just forgive them and move on.
- Forgive yourself. Stop beating yourself up about the past.
- If you disappoint a friend, apologize and get on with the relationship. If they don't accept your apology, the challenge is theirs.
- If you can't forgive, you will spend unbelievable energy on staying angry. That gets you absolutely nowhere—it becomes your life's challenge.

- In MLM you will be tested. All kinds of people will come into your life. Look at them as teachers, valuable teachers. Let them contribute to making your life better.
- Live and let live.
- Mend burned bridges if you can. If not, hold on to the good memories and forget the bad. Just let it go.

Habit #22: "Be"

We are called human beings, not human doings. We are beings. Be more, do less.
How To Be

- Be a beacon of light for others to follow.
- Be a **Big** thinker, a **Big** achiever and a **Big Brave** person.
- Be a collector of every success story you can find. Make a file of them and use them to illustrate your talks and presentations.
- Be a constant student.
- Be a **Great** thinker, a **Great** planner and a **Great** doer.
- Be a Master recruiter.
- Be a pioneer. You'll catch a few arrows, but you'll stand out in front.
- Be a student of personal growth and development.
- Be a student of personalities.
- Be a walking billboard for your products.
- Be a winning coach.
- Be all you can.
- Be ambitious and courageous and say "Yes" to being better all the time.
- Be an excellent leader.
- Be an excellent partner.
- Be an excellent recruiter.
- Be an excellent salesperson.
- Be an interesting person.
- Be available to your customers.
- Be available to your successline.
- Be better, not bitter.
- Be careful what you tell your family.
- Be careful who you allow to be your teachers.
- Be decisive, not indifferent.

- Be duplicatable.

- Be encouraging.

- Be enthusiastic and positive.

- Never be lukewarm about anything.

- Be excited about your products.

- Be forgiving.

- Be full of praise for others.

- Be grateful for the peace in your life.

- Be grateful for your home.

- Be hopeful.

- Be loving.

- Be part of the solution, not the challenge.

- Be passionate.

- Be proactive, not reactive.

- Be ready for success.

- Be the best you can be, do all you can do, have all you can have.

- Be willing to do what others will not do.

- Be willing to go for greatness.

- Be your own best customer.

- Be yourself—you are more than enough!

And More Powerful Information For You On *How To* "Be"...

- Be a student of personal growth and development.

- Be energized by those who want to improve, be the best they can be, are open to better ways of doing business and are coachable.

- Be happy for Champions, they deserve everything they earn.

- Be industrious—for industry is not a gift, it's an accomplishment.

- Be interested in hearing from those who have successfully gone before you.

- Be so busy giving recognition that you don't need it.

- Be stubborn and persistent. Refuse to let others stand in your way.

- Be devoted to your business. That will guarantee success.

- Be the beacon of what can be, what must be in the battle for improvement of your mind.

- Be the best that you can be, which may not be perfect, but focus on C.A.N.I and you will see amazing results.

- Be your best, not someone else's best.

Be Willing To...

- Break out of your boring old habits.
- Change, and be willing to pay for instruction.
- Commit to your successline. They want your leadership.
- Follow sound and proven instruction.
- Forget the past and get on with your fantastic future.
- Give more than sometimes to building your business.
- Ignore critics—they aren't talking about you anyway. (They're talking about themselves!)
- Improve your mind on a daily basis.
- Learn the business by personal involvement and study.
- Make room in your home (and home life) for your business.
- Pay little for information. Pay a lot for knowledge.
- Pay the price for success. (It's a bargain!)
- Purchase all the required sales aids and literature, which are important in your business.

Habit #23: Be A Great Listener

If you can get a person to talk to you, share with you, and you LISTEN, you will make more sales, more friends and get more kicks out of life then you ever dreamed. But really *listen*. Those who only want others to listen to them will lose!

- After you listen, be careful what you say. Many times your words are harmful when you don't even mean them to be.
- Care about what people have to say, don't shut them out.
- If you are listening to an alcoholic, know that much of the time it's the alcohol that is talking. Be careful what you make up about that conversation.
- If you give someone the power to be an expert, listen to what that person has to say and then make up your own mind about what you are going to do with the information.
- Listen, it's the pathway to understanding.
- Listen to successful motivational speakers.
- Listen to what is not being said.
- Listen without reacting right away. Put some thought into what people say (and don't say).

- Listen without thinking about what you are going to say next.
- Losers talk and never listen.
- More friendships are lost due to misunderstandings about what was heard.
- More sales are lost because of failure to listen than any other reason.
- God gave you two ears and only one mouth. Do the math.

Habit #24: Take Care Of Yourself

Advice to those who want to enjoy their future wealth: I did not take good care of myself and no one else took care of me either. I am finally taking good care of myself now. Please don't make the mistake I made by putting off time for yourself and your health and happiness for the sake of everyone else.

- Get a manicure (men, too!).
- Get some rest.
- Go to the finest plays.
- Lose weight, but only if you're overweight.
- Receive instead of resist.
- Say to yourself three times each morning this affirmation: "I feel happy, I feel healthy, I feel terrific, today is going to be a great day."
- Spend money on yourself. Quit being a victim and thinking that you're doing something wonderful because you don't spend any money on yourself. Not!
- Take vacations.
- Tighten your glasses. Make sure you have up-to-date glasses. Get rid of old, ugly glasses.
- Think positive thoughts. Really think them.
- Update your clothing.
- Update your shoes. Never wear dirty tennis shoes or sneakers, ever!
- Wear the best cologne or perfume, the very best—I wear Cartier perfume. Don't wear cheap stuff. Yuck!

Habit #25: Be On Time

Nothing is more insulting—to yourself and others—than being late. It is just that, *insulting*. It is rude to be late or to start or end a meeting late. Look at the message that being late sends to people...

- If you can't make it to a meeting or get there on time, *call*. The polite way to handle the delay or rescheduling is to accommodate the other person/people.

- Get to meetings on time—people notice.

- Quit wasting time.

- Those who do not start their meetings on time are wasting your valuable time. What are you worth?

- You only have *excuses* why you're not on time, and *reasons* why you are.

Habit #26: Be Enthusiastic

Now is the perfect time to take a look at your enthusiasm. The last four letters in enthusiasm are I A S M, which stand for *I Am Sold Myself*.

- Enthusiasm is zest for life that shines through a person's face.

- Enthusiasm is important, but you have to apply it to meaningful goals.

- Exude enthusiasm, guts and courage.

- If you can give your child just one thing, give him enthusiasm.

- If you wanted to be enthusiastic, how would you act?

- Many people work very hard, are very self-motivated, enthusiastic and have the desire to succeed. Some of these people, however, aren't successful. Why? They are busy being busy, not successful. They're all revved up just like the engine of an airplane, boat or car—but with no direction. Your enthusiasm can propel you into taking action. Let it.

- Let your enthusiasm go as high as it can and you will.

- Life happens once. Make it the best.

- Life is here. Life is now. (Life is not yesterday, nor tomorrow.)

- Lukewarm enthusiasm normally does not get you the blue ribbon.

- Maintain a good attitude throughout each and every day.

- People who know what they want and how they are going to get it are always enthusiastic. Ever noticed?

- Spark your life, recharge your enthusiasm and re-inspire your purpose.

Habit #27: Pay Close Attention To Successful People

Your business will be improved when you begin to duplicate those who are successful. You don't have to duplicate the appearance, just the methods.

- A strong basic faith is the foundation for every success.

- A pure heart is one of the greatest secrets of success. Be honest and true.

- Act and look successful.

- Ask yourself, *"What can I do that will improve my business and make me more successful?"*

- Everyone wants to be successful. Ironically, everyone can be.

- Only follow the example of successful people.

- Hang out with successful people. Most won't want to hang out with you for too long unless you're willing to give an extra effort and get big results.

- If you're brand new or been around and want to inspire your successline, seek out those at the top of every MLM company to help you find shortcuts to success.

- It doesn't take long to be successful when you dedicate yourself to succeeding.

- Much of success is determined by how a person thinks. Sooo…

- Keep thinking you're a success.

- People are attracted to successful people.

- People only fail in MLM when they don't want success enough, aren't willing to work for their success, or quit.

- People who choose to be successful usually are.

- Say *"Yes"* to an exciting future in MLM. Say *"No"* to anything less.

- Study the laws of successful salesmanship, make each of them a part of yourself.

- Success comes when you effectively focus your abilities and skills on the important aspects of your MLM business.

- Success will have an uplifting influence upon your life.

- Success hungers for image.

- Success in anything in life is available provided you want it enough.

- Success is rock climbing. Put your hands and feet exactly where your coach tells you. You will increase your success toward the top.

- Successful people experience more challenges than average people. (That's why they have more fun!)

- Successful people have fabulous pens. Buy a Mont Blanc® or Cartier® pen that states to all that you are worth it.

- Take a successful person to lunch every week or two. Ask questions and listen to the answers. Then take the actions they would take.

- Make time to work; it is the price of success.

And More Powerful Ideas For You On *How To* Pay Close Attention To Successful People...

- The first step toward any success or accomplishment is to believe in it.

- The second step is to love it.

- The third step is to do it.

- The most successful people in MLM are those who have given the most.

- The most successful people in MLM smile the most.

- You can be successful in MLM the moment you make up your mind to be successful, by thinking big.

- There is nothing as motivating to your successline as your success.

- There is nothing as inspirational as your success.

- Thomas Edison failed thousands of times trying to invent an electric light bulb. He learned a little bit from each failure, until finally there was nothing left but the bright light of success.

- To be successful, have fun with failure.

- To be successful in life, learn how to adjust to all your circumstances.

- Be better than those successful people. Blaze your own trail. Watch for people who don't want you to succeed. It's better if they're not a part of your business or your life.

- You deserve success.

Habit #28: Be Self-Motivated

Whose job it is to keep you motivated?

- Motivate yourself by reading, listening to tapes, or attending seminars.

- Motivate yourself. Who is in charge of your future?

- Motivation doesn't last very long. *Keep feeding your mind.*

- Having the properly prosperous image of yourself can be a powerful motivating force.

Habit #29: Concentrate

Discover the most efficient way to be successful: *concentration.* That which you concentrate on is exactly what you get.

- Concentrate your efforts on optimum performance. Do not be ashamed to be outstanding.

- Concentrate on your powers instead of your challenges.

- Concentrate on your strengths instead of your weaknesses.

Habit #30: Believe In Yourself

You are the most unique, special person on earth. Why settle for anything but the best that life has to offer?

- Believe more in your dreams than your doubts.
- Believe more in your dreams than ever before.
- Build up a whole-soul interest in your business.
- Courage will enable you to encounter danger and difficulty with firmness and boldness.
- Courage will enable you to follow your own convictions without being pushed aside by the thoughts and feelings of others.
- You only get to give a first impression one time.
- Your future starts now.
- And now.
- And it starts now.
- And now.
- Your future belongs only to you.

You are:

- The merchant of your own dreams.
- Going to get everything you want, if you're willing to work for it every day.
- Better than you think you are.
- Important.
- Precious.
- Unique.

You can:

- Always learn from big possibility thinkers.
- Be great.
- Change yourself and what you tolerate now, and you can change it quickly.
- Choose to be morose, miserable, negative OR constructive, positive, cheerful, radiant, glowing, dynamic. It's your choice.
- Choose to have it all.

Habit #31: Think Great Thoughts

Now is the time to change your thoughts. Read and reread this Powerful habit.

- Believing in greatness is the first step in bringing about results of greatness.
- Building your personal life is the greatest pursuit in the world.

- Consider it a privilege to live in the greatest nation that has ever existed in the history of our world.
- Fill yourself up with positive thoughts.
- If you put U and S on top of each other, you get a dollar sign.
- Make the bottom line your top line.
- Remember, the best music has yet to be composed.
- See yourself as confident, poised and successful and you will be.
- The initials of the United States are U.S., which equals us.
- The most fabulous paintings have yet to be painted.
- The only limitations are the ones you have set or let for yourself.
- The person who gets ahead is basically a dissenter, an individual who refuses to conform just for the sake of conformity.
- The tallest buildings are yet to be built.
- Think big growth for you!
- Think big growth for your company.
- Think big growth for your group.
- Think optimistic thoughts.
- Think—it's a source of power.
- Today is the first day of the rest of your life.
- We live in a era of freedom and intelligence.
- What a privilege it is to be free, free to succeed, free to win, free to love, free to laugh and free to live successfully the way you choose.
- What is truly worthwhile is something that goes well beyond your lifetime.
- What places are you going to visit?
- "Yes," is just a beginning.

The greatest:

- Novels have yet to be written.
- Opportunity of your life is to plan, study, prepare and work effectively as an expert life builder, so we all may make each part of our life strong enough to endure any strain that will ever be placed upon it.
- Salesperson has yet to be found.
- MLMer in the world has yet to appear. (Is it you?)

Habit #32: Get Busy

How to work at your MLM business every day and get results. Don't look for immediate results and you will get lasting results.

- A fair day's work brings a fair day's pay.

- Ants work all summer preparing for winter.

- Attend enough sales meetings to develop your own style. Duplicate the methods you learn at your trainings.

- Become the author of the best newsletter in your company.

- Cross bridges in your imagination, far ahead of the crowd.

- Do some in-depth planning.

- Earn the right to advance to the next position in your company NOW.

- Get a game plan.

- In football game plans, every player knows exactly where he starts and ends on each play.

- If it's gonna' be, it's up to you.

- If you are sold on your business, your product and your service, you will get busy making sales.

- Never lower your standards of integrity.

Habit #33: Set Short-Term And Long-Term Goals

There is an entire chapter in this book on *how to* set goals. Reread it.

Habit #34: Pay Close Attention To The Word "Don't"

Make a note in your journal *every* time you hear "Don't" and PAY ATTENTION. Think on what you *DO want*. To find out what you *do want*, sometimes it's easier to identify what you don't want. But remember, what you think about is what you are going to get.

This one list will help turn you into a Master. Think about the word *don't*. A Don't List is important to keep and look over to see if you are on the right track. What follows is a *Don't* list. Maybe one of the *don'ts* will change your life. Focus on what you *DO* want in life. You draw to yourself that which you focus on.

Don't be:

- A grudge collector.
- A pain to your upline.
- Afraid to play full out.
- Afraid to recognize others' successes.
- Afraid to recruit.

- Judgmental of others.
- Persuaded by group opinion.
- Too quick to prejudge.

- Afraid to be the top recruiter.
- Afraid of success.
- Average.
- Average, be a champion.
- Critical, be helpful.
- Defensive.
- Discouraged easily.

Don't fight:
- Achievers, learn from them.
- Leaders, learn from them.
- Success.

Don'ts For You To Do:
- Don't beg or talk a person into becoming a recruit.
- Don't block information to your successline.
- Don't complain.
- Don't do anything you can't delegate.
- Don't expect others to change to be like you.
- Don't fear rejection.
- Don't get caught up in a cause.
- Don't get discouraged.
- Don't hold back.
- Don't hold good news back.
- Don't let others *should* on you.
- Don't look back, only forward.
- Don't make excuses.
- Don't quit recruiting.
- Don't sit back and let life pass you by.
- Don't share your personal challenges.
- Don't *should* on yourself.
- Don't stay in an abusive, unhealthy marriage.
- Don't stroll to a goal.

And More Powerful Ideas For You on *How To* Pay Attention To The "Don't List"

- Don't feel guilty because you're working while you have children.
- Don't force people into management/leadership, if all they want is a little extra money.
- Don't get yourself into a desperate financial position.
- Don't honor, admire or recognize those who do not get results and who are uncooperative.
- Don't invest all you make back into your organization.
- Don't look for the easy way to make money.
- Don't make critical remarks about other companies.
- Don't melt when it rains. Some of your most productive sales can happen during times of "bad weather."
- Don't mistreat your heart—exercise.
- Don't permit others to hurt you. Just ignore them.
- Don't pick the wrong haystack. Life's too short.
- Don't play the victim in a relationship, pout and feel sorry for yourself. Champions don't have the energy to dwell on self-confidence challenges.
- Don't promise what you cannot or will not deliver.
- Don't run the risk of letting negative thoughts or weakness make you feel guilty or inferior. Do some in-depth planning, and never lower your standards of integrity.
- Don't say anything to anyone that can't be written on the front page of the local newspaper.
- Don't tell people what you are going to do unless you have the desire and determination to do it.
- Don't try to twist someone's arm into buying your product.
- Don't wait until you have knowledge of every product before you make recruiting presentations.
- Don't waste time talking with the wrong person.

Don't be:

- Discouraged, because you had a slow beginning.
- Lazy in getting information. Learn it and process it.

Don't think:

- About your failures, think instead of your successes.
- About the grass being greener on the other side of the fence. It's not.
- That you can't do the impossible. Go ahead! Do the activities that seem impossible.

Don't let:

- An unambitious person block knowledge from your successline.
- Others set your limitations or intimidate you, so you can't reach beyond where they are in your company. That's a myth.
- Mowing the lawn, painting your home, working on new flyers, keeping other people's children, fixing up your office or balancing your checkbook stand in the way of building your business.

And now...

Drop the word *don't* from your vocabulary.

Habit #35: Have A Great Day, Every Day

- Decide to be uplifting to others.
- Look over your goals, look over your appointment calendar.
- See if you can make at least one life happier because you have lived today.
- Start every day reading a few inspirational pages in a book.
- Your attitude of the day begins when you wake up.

Wake Up!

What New Habits Do I Need To Work On?

❑

❑

❑

❑

❑

❑

❑

❑

❑

❑

❑

❑

❑

❑

❑

❑

❑

❑

Chapter Five

You'll Love The Results You Get When You Understand The Different Personality Types

*Advice to those who want to become financially independent
and have more kicks out of life than you ever dreamed of. . . .
Become a student of human personalities.*

Your business will dramatically improve when you learn about personality types. When you recognize how people mentally process information differently, you simply speak to their unique personality type. Each personality type makes their decisions based on how information is presented to them. Your business will grow in leaps and bounds, when you began to recognize and tailor your presentation to each person's personality type.

How To Identify All Kinds Of Personalities

There are *several* kinds of personalities who get involved with MLM.

Those who:

- Are jealous.
- Are Masters.
- Are tired of the rat race.
- Watch people make things happen.
- Give, they love to give.
- Just try, they are just always trying.
- Never ever quit until they succeed.

- Make things happen.
- Quit
- Succeed.
- Take.
- Give.
- Empower.

Those who look for:

- A reason.
- A purpose.
- A way.
- An excuse.
- An opportunity to teach.

Those who want:

- A better way of life.
- Residual income.
- Retirement income.
- Financial freedom.
- To belong.
- To make a difference.
- You to agree with them.
- You to be their leader, their mentor.
- You to like them.
- You to listen to them.
- You to do it for them.

Do You Want To Improve Your Relationships?
Do You Want To Sell More Product?
Do You Want To Recruit More People?
Do You Want To Have People Respect You?

Here's How To Do All Of The Above: Study Personalities

It doesn't take long to figure out a person's personality type. Once you do, you simply tailor your conversation to appeal to their personality.

Use the person's words. Use their body language, too. People want you to be like them. So mirror them. Figure out what your successline's, upline's and family's personality types are. You will improve all your relationships when you learn to talk to, listen to and understand personality types other than your own.

It's interesting that I've had people tell me this is an insulting thing to do. That's not what I've found to be true. I have found people respond in the exact opposite way. You magnetize people to you when you appeal to their distinct personality. You show them how much you care for *them*.

Here's Information For You About The Four Basic Personality Types

- Identify which categories you fit into best.
- Identify what category or categories you don't fit into.
- This study is critical to becoming an MLM giant.
- When you find the specific categories you're not strong in, that's great! That's exactly where you can work on yourself for the greatest improvement in the least time. Begin to develop that part of your personality. This is one great secret of my success. Study this, learn this. Because you will be studying, learning and improving yourself.
- We are all part of all of the following personalities.
- You are mostly dominant in one or two of the categories.
- You need all of the personality types in your successlines.

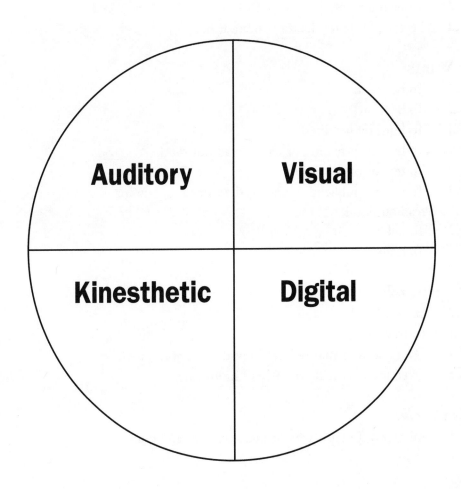

Auditory

Facts You Should Know About The Auditory Personality
This is the person who needs to hear.

Here's What The Auditory Personality Says:

- "Do you hear me?"
- "I heard you say that before."
- "That sounds great!"
- "I'm tuned into this idea."
- "Tell me that one more time."
- "Just tell me what you want me to do."
- "That doesn't click with me."
- "I hear what you're saying."
- "Describe it to me in detail."
- "Tell me your plan."
- "That's clear as a bell."
- "Read that to me."

Here Is What The Auditory Personality ...

Doesn't Want:
- ❑ To be distracted by noises.
- ❑ To be interrupted.
- ❑ People to talk too loud or shout at her.

Does Want:
- ❑ To be quiet.
- ❑ To be heard.
- ❑ To learn by hearing.
- ❑ To have information or letters read out loud.
- ❑ To repeat jokes he's heard.
- ❑ To receive public recognition; she listens eagerly for her name to be read out loud.
- ❑ To talk.
- ❑ To train.

Needs to be told:
- ❑ In detailed description.
- ❑ Instructions.
- ❑ Over and over that he/she is loved and appreciated.
- ❑ Over and over that you believe in him/her.

Needs to *talk:*
- ❑ All night, if that is what it takes to solve an argument.

- ❑ And share and wants you to do the same.
- ❑ And tell you how he feels.
- ❑ On the phone a lot.
- ❑ With others who will listen to her.

Needs to *listen* to:
- ❑ Audio cassettes.
- ❑ Music.
- ❑ A presentation.
- ❑ You and talk to you.

Visual

Facts You Should Know About The VISUAL Personality
The Visual is the person who needs to *see*.

Here Is What The Visuals Say:
- ❑ " I see."
- ❑ "We do not see eye to eye on this."
- ❑ "What I saw was…"
- ❑ "It isn't clear to me what you're saying."
- ❑ "Now I get the picture."
- ❑ "I can't picture this."
- ❑ "I can picture that."
- ❑ "I envision . . ."
- ❑ "I can see myself doing this."
- ❑ "Look at it this way."
- ❑ "Let's take a look."

They are:
- ❑ Well groomed.
- ❑ Image-conscious.
- ❑ Neat.
- ❑ Caring of how you look.
- ❑ Organized—desk, wallet, briefcase, purse.
- ❑ Apt to wear accessories and ties.

Here Is What The Visual Personality Needs:
- ❑ Whiteboards, overheads, power point presentations, blackboards and flip charts for writing on or drawing.
- ❑ Stories and examples that create mental pictures.
- ❑ The meeting room to be well organized, to look right for the occasion.
- ❑ Their upline to look nice.
- ❑ To go to beautiful restaurants and nice meeting rooms.

- ❑ To look and be organized.
- ❑ You to paint the picture of the future.
- ❑ You to tell them they look nice, that their home is neat.

They need to see:
- ❑ How your product looks and works.
- ❑ Photos, clip art, statistics, graphs in newsletters.
- ❑ Presentations/demonstrations, which show them how to use your product.
- ❑ Slide presentations.
- ❑ The Top Achievers in their company recognized in ways they can aspire and work towards. They can "see" themselves getting the same recognition.
- ❑ Their names in print in newsletters.
- ❑ Videotaped presentations and trainings.
- ❑ Your information before they will join you.

They need to watch:
- ❑ You making the presentation, so that they can copy you.
- ❑ Your presentation as many times as they need, so they can see how they will be duplicating it.

They can:
- ❑ Visualize earning company promotions.
- ❑ Visualize going on trips.
- ❑ Organize their purse or wallet with money all turned in the same direction.

They have:
- ❑ Difficulty relating to unorganized people.
- ❑ Framed photographs out in their homes.
- ❑ Goal tracking sheets to see their progress on their computers, refrigerators or bulletin boards.

Kinesthetic

Facts You Should Know About The Kinesthetic Personality
The Kinesthetic personality is the person who needs to feel.

Here Is What You Will Hear the Kinesthetic Say:
- ❑ "I have a gut feeling about this."
- ❑ "I am so happy to be with you."
- ❑ "Your presentation was great."
- ❑ "I know how you feel."
- ❑ "I'm touched by that."
- ❑ "Let's explore this."

- ❏ "I appreciate your feelings."
- ❏ "It feels right to me, let's do it."
- ❏ "I just don't have a sense of what you mean."
- ❏ "Thank you for including me."
- ❏ "I'm passionate about that.

- ❏ "I can handle that."

Here Is What The Kinesthetic Personality Needs To Feel:
- ❏ Loved.
- ❏ Special.
- ❏ Safe.
- ❏ Supported.
- ❏ Constantly in touch.
- ❏ Your enthusiasm.

They need:
- ❏ Group activities.
- ❏ To have handshakes or hugs.
- ❏ To be heard.
- ❏ To be included. To belong.
- ❏ To be invited to parties or meetings, even if you know they can't come.
- ❏ To be physically touched.
- ❏ To go to meetings.
- ❏ To have question time.
- ❏ To receive recognition for even the smallest activities.
- ❏ To touch the product.

They are:
- ❏ Normally the cheerleaders, full of energy and loving to be leaders.
- ❏ Very good friends.
- ❏ Very sensitive to others' feelings.

They:
- ❏ Crave recognition and appreciation, because they feel important if someone recognizes their contribution.
- ❏ Cry easily, get their feelings hurt very easily and look to find other kinos as a source of support.
- ❏ Have a hard time communicating their feelings to others who do not feel the same way.
- ❏ Hate conflict.

- ❑ Hold on to grudges longer than any other personality.
- ❑ Love to eat. Eating makes them feel full and satisfied.
- ❑ Love to go to monthly or weekly meetings, because they feel best when they're part of a team.
- ❑ Normally struggle with organization, but when organized feel so much better.

Digital

Facts You Should Know About The Digital Personality

The Digital is the person who thrives on statistics, numbers and organization.

Here Is What The Digital Personality Needs:

- ❑ Maps.
- ❑ Graphs.
- ❑ Receipts.
- ❑ Computers.
- ❑ Calculators.
- ❑ Newspapers.
- ❑ Current events.
- ❑ Computer printouts.
- ❑ Instruction booklets.
- ❑ Written statistics.
- ❑ Stock market quotes.
- ❑ A Day-Timer.
- ❑ Calendar.
- ❑ To know the bottom line.
- ❑ A copy of the compensation plan.
- ❑ Punctuality.
- ❑ Facts and figures.
- ❑ Dates and deadlines.
- ❑ Agendas.
- ❑ Menus.
- ❑ Organization.

They:

- ❏ Thrive on order.
- ❏ Want you to be on time.
- ❏ Need to understand.
- ❏ Can calculate numbers in their head.
- ❏ Will help you crunch numbers.
- ❏ Will help you with agendas.
- ❏ Have great memories.
- ❏ Are the CPA type.
- ❏ Can create order.
- ❏ Need newsletters with statistics.
- ❏ Pay attention to detail.

Now, Here's *How To* Increase Your Monthly Check

Have all of the different personalities included in the meeting planning.

When designing meetings, present information in a way that includes all four personality types. This means:

- Adjust your presentation to include all their learning styles.
- Allow enough time for questions.
- Be organized.
- When analyzing your audience, try to get clues about their overall personality traits.

Have...

Auditories:

- Supply the music.
- Give the introduction and closing at meetings.
- Give testimonies.

Digitals:

- Take notes.
- Think out the cost.
- Investigate and explore all possibilities.
- Offer great ideas on ways to improve.
- Price products, and make sure the budget is correct for meetings.
- Use statistics and stories.

Visuals:

- Visualize meetings.
- Prepare flip charts and overheads.
- Make sure the room looks right.
- Be in charge of decorations, lights, stage, props, signs.

Kinos:

- Be the greeters to make everyone feel welcome.
- Be in charge of room temperature and refreshments.
- Make sure everything feels right.

Your Bottom Line Will Dramatically Increase
When You Discover That All Four Personality Types
Are People Who Fall Into The Following Four Categories:

Leaders, Responsible People, Responsives and Inerts

Facts You Should Know About Leaders

- When you find them, they are wonderful.
- Leaders get out in front of others and people do what they do.
- Leaders are less than five percent of the MLM population.
- Leaders take action.
- Very often you will recruit people with leadership skills they didn't even know they had.

Facts You Should Know About Responsible People

- They are extremely valuable and a bit rare.
- They make up 25 percent of the MLM population and are willing workers.
- They need direction from leaders.
- They will actively take part in your program.
- They will join MLM, but if they are not given direction and training they will soon drop out. Eventually some of these people might rise to the top if they're shown how to do it.
- They write newsletters and make phone calls.

Facts You Should Know About Responsives

- They are not active business builders.
- They are not very responsible.
- They do not have the ability to lead and have to be continually motivated.
- They make up 40 to 60 percent of the MLM population.
- They make good customers but poor representatives.
- When you get these people in your team, they can really disappoint you— especially when you are first building your organization and you counted on them.
- They will buy the product and respond to the presentation.
- They will sign up if they are told to.

Facts You Should Know About Inerts

- They actually do nothing to build your organization and try to prevent anyone else from becoming successful.
- Avoid these people; never accept or believe the ideas they try to impose on you.
- They will blame you for a breakdown in communication.
- They make up 10 to 30 percent of the MLM population.
- Motion upsets them. You upset them.
- They have negative attitudes and are damaging to the growth of your organization.
- If you don't do things their way, they criticize you to everyone who will listen.
- Realize what category they're in and move on with searching for leaders.

Your business will grow in leaps and bounds, when you recognize the needs and wants of each person's personality type. You can design your communications in the ways that best suit each type. Also, when you know what kind of personality you're dealing with, you can more easily learn the best ways to make use of that individual's strengths and minimize their weaknesses, to build your organization.

Jan and Tony Robbins
Los Angeles, CA 1992

Tom Hopkins and Jan
Phoenix, AZ 1994

Jan and Muhammed Ali
Los Angeles, CA 1996

Aspenglow, Jan and Bill's residence
1995

Jan and Clayton
1995

Clayton breaks 4 Colorado
state football records, 1995

Jan and Bill with children in Aspen,
Colorado, 1990

Sarah, Clayton, and Ashley
Clayton graduates from Aspen High School, 1996

Sarah
Kenya, Africa, 1996

Ashley, Clayton, and Sarah
Hawaii, 1985

Clayton, Sarah, and Ashley
Vail, CO 1985

John Milton Fogg and Jan
Austin, TX 1989

Russ DeVan, Jan, Richard Brooke
Phoenix, AZ 1996

Sarah, Clayton, and Ashley
Aspen, CO 1996

Sarah and Ashley
1985

Jan and Bill   Nashville, TN 1996

Notes

Auditory

❑

❑

❑

❑

Kinesthetic

❑

❑

❑

❑

Visual

❑

❑

❑

❑

Digital

❑

❑

❑

❑

Chapter Six

How To Be A
Master MLM Leader

"Great leaders are not born.
You develop yourself into a great leader."

How To Be A MLM Leader

Great leaders search for *every* bit of knowledge they can get on being a great leader. They don't want to miss one idea that can help them be even greater and more effective.

Leaders:

- Are readers.
- Are servants.
- Are always growing.
- Are masters of recognition.
- Have goals.
- Are not afraid of confrontation.
- Are genuinely interested in others.
- Blaze a trail for others to follow.
- Bring about accomplishment.
- Can see the big picture.
- Consistently strive to be better and better.
- Follow the example of leaders.
- Give up guilt.
- Get more information.
- Launch forward before success is certain.
- Lead.

- Lead by example.
- Lead every day.
- Lead others to information.
- Make others better.
- Pull, don't push their network.
- Take others up with them.

Leadership:

- Cannot be bought.
- Cannot be inherited.
- Demands image.
- Is fun.
- Is a responsibility.
- Is only obtained by individual mastery.
- Takes courage.

"Effective leaders bring out the best in people by stimulating them to achieve what they once thought was impossible."

Leaders:

- Are magnets and attract people.
- Are passionate promoters of the vision of the company.
- Become personally and financially free.
- Champion the success of every other person, organization and company in MLM.
- Do not order or demand.
- Grow in person and spirit, expressing that there are no limits to the nature of the human spirit.
- Have a powerful relationship with their own vision; incorporate their values, gifts, passions and life purpose into these relationships such that they empower and contribute to others.
- Have fun. The world is their playground.
- Instill others with gems of thought, motives and ideas to start accomplishment.
- Lead. Period. They don't lead part of the time. They lead all of the time.
- Powerfully listen to and know that which others value and is missing in

their lives.

- Respect the experiences, values and beliefs of others.
- Responsibly tell the truth—say what is so and are honest with themselves.
- Talk about their own mistakes before pointing out the mistakes of others.

Make:

- Ethical decisions such that they serve everyone included.
- People desire to do things on their own.
- People feel important by listening carefully to them.

How To Be A Leader In MLM

❏ **Step One:** Declare Yourself a Leader

❏ **Step Two:** Act Like a Leader Before You Are a Leader

- Do not let anyone discourage you.
- Set a powerful, positive example.
- Study those who are getting results.
- Study leadership, it can be learned.

❏ **Step Three:** Here's What To Work On First...

Be a:

- Master recruiter.
- Master at selling.
- Master at learning MLM.
- Do not let anyone discourage you.
- Set a powerful positive example.
- Study those who are getting results.
- Study leadership, it can be learned.

❏ **Step Four:** Work On Your Leadership Skills. (In fact, NEVER stop working on them.)

Read *this chapter* many times before you begin to train your leaders. Read this chapter over and over again while you are working on becoming the leader you are meant to be. Be the best, the very best leader you can be. You must have the ability to convey the value of being the best you can be to your established leaders as well as your future leaders.

Timing Is Everything

- Always keep the door to leadership open for any sales rep anywhere in your successline.

- Let your successline know that the opportunity will always be available, and that you will support them whenever they are ready to become a leader.

- Be ready to become a leader and develop a leader at any time.

- Support people wherever they are in your lineage.

- Support what your successline's wants.

- What's really important is your level of commitment to creating a financial future that will set an example for every would-be leader in your successline

How To Build MLM Leaders

Sometimes You Have To Recruit 20 People To Get A Leader.

- How well you communicate with others.

- How well you listen to people.

- The strength of your leadership skills.

- Your beginning level of success will be based on you and how attractive you are to other people.

The degree to which you are willing to put yourself into personal growth and leadership development will determine the success you achieve in MLM.

That's so important. I'm going to write that again, bigger:

The degree to which you are willing to put yourself into personal growth and leadership development will determine the success you achieve in MLM.

Advice To Those Who Are Building Leaders

Commit to your leaders' success to the same degree that they are willing to commit to their own success. Create a relationship with all your future leaders, so they feel supported and safe, and view you as a friend and true business partner. You may already have accomplished this in your prospecting and recruiting conversations. If not, you might say something like I have said to my leader:

"I'm committed to you and to your success and to your leadership development. You need to know that I am not committed to your comfort. When you begin a new business and when you put yourself into development, there will be things you will be doing that may be uncomfortable for you. Beginning an MLM business is no different from starting any other business. There are growing pains and I am committed to supporting you through those times. So, do I have your permission to speak to you as a leader out of my commitment to your success?"

There is really only one right answer to this question ... .

Here's Where To Begin To Be A Detective, Ask Questions And Listen To The Answers:

Find Out What Your Future Leaders Want And Help Them Achieve It

Find out:

- About their family.
- Any concerns they may have.
- Are they a match or a fit?
- What their commitments in life are.
- What contribution they will make.
- Whether they will go for leadership.
- What their life is like at present.

- What they're passionate about.
- What's important.
- What's missing.
- What they want.
- What they do.
- What they are.

How To Create A Partnership— A Very Important Step In Building Leaders

- A partnership is a two-way street.
- You will be asking your potential leader to commit to supporting their own success.
- They will need to know what your commitment is to them. You can say:

  "My job is to support you in accomplishing whatever it is you want to accomplish. What's exciting is, this business is fun and duplicatable. I am going to teach you to support your leaders in the same way."

Here Is A Conversation To Have With Your Future Leaders

Say to your future leaders: *"There are some parts of becoming a leader in my organization that I will ask you to do in writing. I may ask that you fax some answers to me or information to me before our next conversation. Your first homework assignment is to help me get acquainted with you. Please fax me the top three values you prize in a relationship before our next call. Let's talk about some of them now."*

You're on the hunt to discover what your future leaders value. If you can help them identify their top three values, you'll be able to work effectively to help them reach their goals. Just keep speaking to *their* values, not your own.

To support your leaders in their progression up the compensation plan, create an accountability structure, and request that these written exercises be faxed or e-mailed to you prior to your next call or meeting. This will insure that they have completed the steps, and many of the exercises will provide you with insight into their values and goals.

Say to your future leaders: *"It's important for you to know what you are committing to, and also to know what my commitments are to you as a leader in my business."* This statement informs your new recruits that they will work together with their sponsor and helps them feel that they are not alone.

Say to your future leaders: *"One specific agreement that I will make to you is that I will support you in building your business and will teach you how to present our products to your prospects. One way I will do this is to teach you the benefits of all the products and how to explain these benefits to others. I will also explain how to offer the opportunity to others. I'll teach you and then you'll tell me back what you've heard. I'll listen while you present the business and then provide you with feedback. This will be valuable in your own training, so you can teach your successline what I've taught you."*

There are reasons why people are successful— and excuses why they are not.

How To Develop Customers And How To Duplicate This Action In Your Leaders

If, in your prospecting, you find 10 new customers a month who purchase $30 of products per month, there's an additional $300 in sales volume you'll be adding every month from now on. You don't have to wait until a home party, trade fair or big meeting to get 10 people to order $30 each a month. If you support your leaders in doing the same thing you just did, your volume can grow very quickly indeed.

Sometimes, distributors are so intent on recruiting, they forget to have a conversation with their prospects about becoming customers, even if the prospect has said *no* to the business.

There are only three answers to your offer of the opportunity: "Yes... No..." Or "No, I'm not interested in a business, but I'd like to try some of your products. They sound great." Many times your prospects will actually want to support you by buying and trying some of the products. Since they said "No" to the business opportunity, they may feel obligated to say "Yes" to something. Hey, if that makes them feel good, terrific! Many representatives lose sales simply because they get an opportunity "No," and forget to ask for a "Yes" about the products.

If you duplicate this approach with your leaders, and all of you are identifying 10 new customers a month, your volume will increase dramatically and so will your immediate cash income. You can also use this increased volume to move to the next level in your compensation plan, which will enhance your income even more.

Think for a moment: $300 in increased volume. Duplicated by two people is a total of $600. By four people, comes to $1,200. And if 10 of the representatives in your commission line do that, your volume would climb by $3,000 a month! Remember duplication of effort. Even more, go for duplication of results!

> ## "Successful leaders have the courage to take action where others hesitate.
> ## The great paradox of life:
> ## The more you give of yourself, the more you receive."

Future Leader:
- How many prospects will you be contacting per month?
- How many of those do you want to become customers?

Plan out your goals in both these areas for each month:
January February March April May June
July August September October November December

Facts You Should Know About Creating an MLM Leader
Should You Make a Leader? The Pros...
- Absolutely, the more people you help become successful the better.
- Many times people find the leader within themselves and take off. Why not help them to get those first two to three new recruits? It's worked for me.

So, **who do you help?** Help *only* those representatives who:
- Are selling a minimum of $300 per month in product consistently.
- Are selling and duplicating what you are doing.

- Are really working the business.
- Attend self-improvement and company conferences and seminars.
- Get their own first two to three recruits.
- Have no expectations of you.
- Never say they're putting the business on the back burner.
- Are the "doers", not the "talkers".
- Go with you and have you show them how to recruit.

Should You Not Make A Leader? The Cons...

- If you start making leaders, everyone will expect you to make them a leader.
- If you give away recruits, you won't hit your goal of being the top recruiter for your company.
- People will be stronger leaders if they do it themselves.
- When you put recruits under people in your organization, you model to them that they need to do the same for their people. They think that they must be a sponsoring superstar like you to do the business effectively.

My Secrets On *How To* Make a Leader (I Hold The Record For My Company—13 In One Year!)

First, a word of caution: It is **not** a good idea to give away recruits until you first have your own 20 to 30 recruits in your personal team. Only make a leader if you have 100 or more people in your successline. Until then, build your future leaders through training, having them go with you on prospecting calls and meetings. Have them get some prospects together in their home and give a presentation to their prospects until they can duplicate you.

Step One

Keep personally recruiting. Never quit recruiting. If you choose to create leaders, only build those who are direct to you.

Step Two

Take a look at the statistics of everyone in your organization who is direct to you.

Step Three

Look for those who have consistent monthly sales of over $500 and have from one to three new recruits. Call the person and have a conversation. Ask them questions such as:

Are you interested in making more money?

If we decide to do this, what are your expectations?

How are you selling this much product month after month?

How did you get your first one to three recruits?

What do you like best about the business?

What is your favorite product?

Who are you selling to?

Would you like to partner with me and let me work with you to help you get to the next level in the compensation plan?

Are you coachable?

Step Four
Establish Your Expectations

Here Are My Expectations For My Leaders:
You will:

- Attend the seminars I suggest.

- Be a future leader in my organization.

- Keep me informed of your team growth.

- Participate in our team meetings, trainings and rallies.

- Read at least 1 book each month and send me book reports.

- Return all my phone calls within 24 hours.

- Write a monthly newsletter—no matter what—every month.

- At any time that I see your interest wavering I will have only one discussion with you. I am looking for leaders and plan to work with several at a time. I will simply quit helping you if I see that you have lost momentum or in any way do not want my coaching.

Step Five
Make a commitment to help that future leader.

Here Is My Commitment To You:

- I am going to help you train your next five people (Get my *Duplicatable Training System*).

- I will be responsible.

- I won't let you down if you won't let me down.

- You can count on two to three new recruits this month from my efforts.

- You can count on me. It's going to happen. You will not fail as long as you let me coach you and you do not quit.

- Together we are going to get you to the next level of the comp plan in the next three months.

Step Six

Identify the future leaders' values, personality style and level of commitment.

- Be on the lookout for real leaders.
- How many people become representatives is not as important as how many representatives become leaders.
- **Leaders are different. They lead. They don't manage.**
- Many people think they are leaders when they get to the first level in your program's management. Not!
- When you identify someone as a potential leader, ask questions about their goals. Find out what they want. Get detailed information. Help them to get what they want through working your plan.

Step Seven

Set a Goal: "*Let's make a goal to get you three to six new people in your organization this month.*" Tell your future leader, "*I 'm going to work for you this month. Every lead I get we are going to call together. The first three, you will listen in on three-way calling. After that you will do the next three with me listening in. I will coach you after each call and may even jump into the conversation if I feel I should.*"

Step Eight

Go to work finding a new recruit for that future leader right away. Establish trust. Do not disappoint your future leader. When you recruit someone under one of your leaders, here is what you say to that new person: "*I want you to know that I'm not presently sponsoring anyone personally, and I will be partnering you with one of my top leaders. I want to make sure that you have the greatest amount of support possible in building your business. In this way you can be supported by (name of the person you are signing them under) and also by me. This is how we support the leaders in our business and it is duplicatable, so (name of the person again) will be supporting you in the same way that I am supporting her.*"

How To Get $3,000 A Month In Total Team Sales

- Feed your mind with books, tapes, seminars.
- Have an open house for all your local customers at least once a month.
- It's just ten people doing $300 in sales. That's it.
- Set that goal.
- Get the goal.

"I'm sick and tired of teachers
who don't want to teach,
and preachers who don't want to preach,
and salesmen who don't like to sell
and workers who won't work.
But the one thing that makes me sickest
are the leaders who won't lead!"

— Charlie Brower

How To Make An MLM Leadership Commitment

- Be consistent. Make your decision and see it through.

- Be prepared to do what most others in MLM are not willing to do. That is, get on the telephone, meet with people, continue to improve yourself by attending personal growth and development seminars, conventions, etc., **for as long as it takes.**

- Before you make the commitment, you must be prepared to work.

- Determine your level of motivation and interest in becoming a leader.

- You might need to create the income necessary to commit to investing in your future. If your commitment is genuine, you will be treated as any other leader and supported with ideas for creating that income as quickly as possible. The fastest way to create that income is to sell the product and get others to sell the product.

- Have fun becoming a leader and have more fun watching others become leaders, because of your contribution to them.

- If you only look to your upline to put programs together and to motivate your team, then, of course, you are not the leader.

- If you take off the first half of the year, you are not a leader.

- If it's time to make the commitment—just make it.

- Make the commitment. Make it to yourself, your successline and your upline leader.

- To be a leader, simply declare yourself as one. Just say, "I am a leader."

- The first two to four weeks in this business are very important. Work really closely with your new recruits to provide them the best leadership you can in the beginning.

- There are those of you who are very committed to becoming leaders. And there are the others.

- There is no Get Rich Quick Way. If anyone in an MLM company tells you otherwise, know this: Not true! Have them show you copies of their checks. Not their upline's.

- Where someone starts isn't as important as where they end up.

- Your determination is what you intend to do, and how committed you are to doing what you say. I was so determined, I searched all over America for teachers to teach me, and I paid them. Be willing to pay for the knowledge you need. Invest in yourself.

- You know you are a true leader when you begin to recruit, sell, attend trainings, attend personal growth and development seminars, and begin to tell your upline and successline about the books you are reading and audio cassettes you're listening to.

- Your contribution of working with others to help them become leaders will not go unrewarded.

"If one advances confidently in the direction of his dreams, and endeavors to live the life which he has imagined, he will meet with success unexpected in common hours."
—Henry David Thoreau

Here Are The Qualities Of A Success Partner

- Able to Bond with Others (vs. no friendship or relationship, even after a lengthy conversation)
- At Peace with Self (vs. nervous and ill at ease)
- Authentic (vs. slick salesperson)
- Believable (vs. phony)
- Charismatic (vs offensive)
- Committed (vs. undecided)
- Compassionate (vs. not caring)
- Confident (vs. wimpy and whiny)
- Empowering (vs. disempowering)
- Enthusiastic (vs. negative)
- Focused (vs. distracted)

- Genuinely Humble (vs. arrogant)
- Good Listener (vs. dumping information)
- Good Self-image (vs. beats self up constantly)
- Happy (vs. sad)
- Has Physical Energy (vs. meek, mild, not energetic)
- Inspirational-shifting people in conversations (vs. gloomy)
- Interested in Others (vs. all about me)
- Intuitive (vs. easily misled)
- Organized (vs. disorganized)
- Persistent (vs. gives up easily)
- Positive Expectation (vs. self-sabotage)
- Positive, Upbeat (vs. negative)
- Powerful (vs. wimpy and whiny)
- Sensitive (vs. insensitive)
- Supportive (vs. not available)
- Visionary (vs. lost in details)
- Vulnerable (vs. cold)
- Works in Partnership (vs. all alone)

How To Develop Your Leadership Plan For Success In MLM

Make A Decision Today On a Single Piece Of Paper:

1. What do I really want?

2. How will I get there?

3. What help tools do I need?

4. How will I measure what I've accomplished?

Here Are The Three Next Steps For You To Take

❑ **First Step:** Invest every single future day toward the realization of your goal.

❑ **Second Step:** Declare yourself a student of leaders.

❑ **Third Step:** Declare yourself a leader of future leaders.

You can do it. Just begin.

"From the little spark may burst a mighty flame."
— *Dante*

How To Be An MLM Leader

- All successful MLM organizations are built around a few outstanding leaders.

- Any worthwhile accomplishment is preceded by a worthwhile mental image.

- As much as you want your group to look to you as a leader, look first at your example. Do you look to your upline as your only mentor?

- Blaze a trail to get that knowledge from the Masters of our industry. Bring it back into your own organization and watch the explosion begin!

- Choose to be a leader.

- Choose to dream big, today.

- Clothes that you have been wearing for five years do not add to a successful image or appearance. Get up-to-date clothes.

- Do you attend MLM seminars outside of your own company?

- Develop your own leadership style.

- Enthusiasm is zest that shines through a person's face.

- Fire Up! every day.

- Form a group called your Top 10. These are those leaders who get your information first, are team players, are easy to get along with, want success and are determined to advance in your organization.

- Get dissatisfied with your status in life.

- Get out of the rut you're in. Hey, a rut is just a grave with both ends kicked out.

- Have a self-improvement program all your life.

- Have a gratitude attitude every day for your spouse and/or children.

- Ignore leaders who won't lead.

- Ignite your own passion.

- If you continue to do what you are doing, you will continue to get what you are getting.

- If you take a risk and do only the things you love, your life will become a powerful, rich and prosperous love affair.

- If you don't lead your successline, who will?

- It takes just as much energy and effort for a bad life as it does for a fabulous life.

- If you are over the age of 40, only you are responsible for your face.

- If you are hesitant to be a leader, perhaps you're a pessimist.

- Keep moving people up into your Top 10. Make it a very prestigious club, full of praise, recognition and admiration. These are the people who are your future leaders.

- Let go of whatever makes you stop.

- Learn how to make your work pay off.

- Listen to those who have developed the ability to train, motivate, inspire and lead others in a successful manner.

- There is a wealth of information flowing out there.

- There is a sharing of ideas that's real gold.

- Your successline is not psychologically tied to you.

- Your successline will follow you and get more knowledge to bring back. That's exciting!

Here Are Ten Duplicatable Steps To Take To Become A More Effective MLM Leader

❏ **Step One:**

Identify what qualities you need to develop to become: a more attractive, charismatic, effective business partner and recruiter. Develop yourself so that:

- You attract quality people to you.

- You project everything in a positive way.

- People like being around you.

❏ **Step Two:**

Identify the key areas for you to work on in your leadership development. Take a look at how attractive you are as a recruiter and the energy you give off. Would you be attracted to you if you were on the other side, if you were the person you are trying to recruit?

❏ **Step Three:**

Write down the reasons you would and would not be attracted to yourself. This can be a challenging exercise and it will be very valuable for you to do. Create a structure for yourself to work on one quality at a time. Read 10 pages in a positive book every day. Work on yourself daily.

❏ **Step Four:**

Listen to up to 10 recruiting presentations with those successful MLMers who get results—hopefully your upline. Go with your upline to prospect. Learn this.

❏ **Step Five:**

Audio tape your own calls, let your upline or someone you respect listen to them and give you feedback. Practice your presentation.

❑ **Step Six:**

Call your upline once a week to check in and to share what you're working on in your personal growth and development.

❑ **Step Seven:**

Teach others what you are learning. When you teach it, you internalize it.

❑ **Step Eight:**

Set monthly goals. If you run into a situation that has you completely shut down, ask for help getting through it.

❑ **Step Nine:**

Be a top seller and recruiter in your company three months in a row. Then do it again.

❑ **Step Ten:**

Write a dynamic, recognition-packed newsletter, send it to your upline and ask for feedback. (Go to *www.fireup.com* and click on *"The Network Flame."*)

How To Manage A Huge Organization

In MLM once you have a huge organization you have great leaders who manage their own successlines. *It is not hard to manage a huge successline.*

Voice Mail: You can use voice mail to get your information out. Use voice mail, however, if you are the only person who controls the information that goes out to your successline. I used it for awhile, but got off of it when some people out of my lineage began calling my successline making announcements that were none of their business. In fact, they interfered with my business. Be careful.

E-mail: Use e-mail on a daily basis. Start your own loop. Put someone in your successline in charge of it. You can control what information goes out on your own loop. It's so inexpensive and your successline can go to it several times a day. They can also print your information out.

Telephone: Stay accessible to your successline via phone. Be available. Stay in touch with your leaders.

Newsletters: Write a newsletter to keep in touch. Some people believe you should put emphasis on communicating to the last level of each leg, so you get maximum growth. However, that's not necessary if you have leaders who value your leadership. Just get the information out to your leaders. If you do not have a working relationship with your leaders, it's difficult to get information down your organizational legs.

National Conventions: At national conventions, make sure that you meet with your leaders. Ask them questions and listen to them. Make your business a team effort. Make sure all your leaders feel very safe, that they can give you input.

Borrow My Team-Building Leadership Philosophy:

T.E.A.M.
Together,
Everyone
Achieves
More.

Readers are leaders and leaders are readers.

What I need to do to improve my leadership abilities!

❑

❑

❑

❑

❑

❑

❑

❑

❑

❑

❑

❑

❑

❑

❑

❑

❑

❑

Chapter Seven

Vital Facts You Should Know About Being A MLM Upline

Here's What A MLM Upline Is:

An upline is identified differently in every company. The upline is a person who has gotten into the business before you and is "up line" in the organization you joined, or…the person who recruited you, or…the person who recruited the person who recruited you, or…it's the person who has gone to the very, very top level in your company.

There is only one thing you'll need to become an upline…

A successline.

How To Make Money In MLM…

Be an upline.

How To Make More Money In MLM…

Be a good upline.

How To Make Much More Money In MLM…

Be a great upline.

How To Make the Most Money In MLM…

Be the greatest upline.

What if you don't even know who your upline is?

- Find the first person upline to you who is working the business, who is getting results.

- Get involved in your company.
- If your immediate upline is not available or is not getting results, go to the next upline, and the next, until you find a leader to work with.

Most upline leaders who are **really** successful—notice I said *really* successful—talk to their successlines almost on a daily basis at first. They train their recruits and show them duplicatable ways to do the business. Ultimately, the new recruit goes on to build a successful network.

Attention Uplines!
How To Be A Master Upline...
Set The Example

Master upline leaders are Masters of MLM.
They work the business and get results.
There is no other way.

Here Is *How To* Be A Great Upline

- Become an upline yourself as soon as possible (which means, get a successline).
- Call your upline, don't expect your upline to make all the effort.
- Communicate with your successline via e-mail.
- Communicate with top producers, Peak Performers or leaders, by phone, voice-tel, e-mail, meetings at conventions. Somehow someone is available.
- Communicate by phone with your upline. Call your upline, don't wait for your upline to call you.
- Concentrate on duplicating your recruiting results.
- Continue to get education on how to improve and become better.
- Continue to recruit.
- Delegate.
- Develop goals that are challenging, pushing beyond past performance.
- Listen.
- Do the most important things first.
- Duplicate your upline's method only if they get results.
- Establish deadlines.

- Get up and get to work.

- Get an uncluttered work space.

- Help your successline become independent of you by encouraging others to build their own network.

- Hold special meetings at national conventions.

- Make every minute count.

- Pay attention to detail.

- Provide leadership.

- Partner.

- Read your upline's newsletters.

- Realize that you don't need your upline for long.

- Realize that you cannot duplicate your upline's personality, just her methods.

- Return calls promptly.

- Set weekly priorities.

- Write all your questions down on a yellow pad by your phone, so that you'll have your thoughts organized when you call your upline.

- Take a few minutes each day to be creative.

- Think of new ways to improve your performance.

- Use a spiral notebook or have an organized, duplicatable system.

- Utilize small chunks of time.

- Work the business: recruiting, selling and helping others to leadership positions.

- Write fun, informational, fact-packed newsletters with lots of recognition.

More Powerful Ideas For You On *How To* Be A Great Upline

Great uplines know how to be:

- Available to contact.

- A pipeline of information to their successline.

- An example of a Master of MLM.

- Detail oriented and well organized.

- Reasonable.

- Responsible.

Great uplines do not:

- Allow others to steal their valuable time.

- Arrange or attend unnecessary meetings.

- Become slaves to their mail. They open it over a trash can.
- Gossip.
- Make snide remarks.
- Spend time worrying.
- Waste time on unimportant activities.
- Whine or complain to their successline, ever.

Here's *How To* Become A Great Upline *Fast*

- Begin a program of consistently selling and recruiting.
- Get to the first level of your compensation plan. Hurry.
- Go to all product and opportunity trainings.
- Invest at least $1,000 a year as soon as you can into self-improvement, including tapes, books, seminars, travel to conventions and telephone consultations.
- Make a goal to be a great upline.
- Study this book.
- Study those who are great uplines, those who have gotten great results in MLM.
- Make sure you praise, recognize and appreciate your leaders.

How To Handle Conflict With Your Upline

- In MLM, the upline makes money off the successline. That does not mean the upline owes you anything. That's just the MLM business. If you want to make money, build a successline.
- Just because you have a person in your life called an upline, gives you no right to begin to demand anything of that person.
- Realize that you and your upline might have different values or goals.

What if you have had conflict with your upline?

- First, take some time to consider what has happened.
- Take time to listen to what your upline has to say. Seek first to understand and then seek to be understood.
- Maybe you just have a personality conflict and neither one of you is willing to change. Or it might even be a misunderstanding. Communicate.
- Normally, it's a power struggle. Your upline wants your respect. Also, your upline probably wants you to duplicate him and you aren't doing it.
- If it can't be resolved, oh well, bummer. What you can't change you must endure.

What do you do if someone signed you up in your program and you never heard from them again?

- My recruiter quit the day I joined. Oh, well.

- Go to the next upline up in your compensation plan and duplicate what that person is doing.

Want your upline to respect you? Do you want more recognition?

- Have a conversation with your upline and talk about each other's expectations.

- Get busy. Out-sell, out-recruit, out-perform your upline.

What if you don't want to resolve the conflict? What if the truth is you don't respect or like your upline?

- Always leave the door open for the relationship to bloom again.

- Ask your successlines what their expectations are of you. Be so busy giving recognition that you don't need any yourself.

- Figure out what your expectations were of your upline and make a list of them. Be the person you wanted your upline to be for you.

- Get your own successline.

- Have a conversation with your upline such that you thank her for training you and getting you started, but that you are now ready to go on your own.

- It's time to be an upline yourself.

- Provide your own trainings.

- Write your own newsletters.

Advice To Those Who Have A Long Distance Upline

Oh, so what. Big deal. If you're sold on your product, read the company literature, call and get product training, get to a Leadership Conference or Convention, you will **see** your upline. With today's technology, don't let this one be an excuse for you not being great. I'll never buy it.

For the first six months in this business, I didn't know I was supposed to be recruiting people to join me. My recruiter, my upline, had quit. The sales rep who trained me had not said *anything* about recruiting. She quit! Finally, in August 1980, I read the company manual, which clearly stated that this was a business where I was to **Recruit and Sell**. Heck, I didn't even know what MLM was!

During the remainder of my first year, in the six weeks from August to September, I recruited 13 people. At this point I still had had **no** contact with an upline. I lived in Texas, my nearest upline now was in California. The company was only two years old and my upline was long distance. And those 13 people had recruited at least one recruit each. By the end of 1980, I had 26 people in my successline. I was the only upline in my company in the state of Texas. My upline was still long distance. You don't have to have your upline in your city, or even your state, to succeed in MLM. Believe me.

Here's What Happened To My Upline

My upline was in California, I lived in Texas. Her organization had spread across the country. Although she had helped me in so many ways at the beginning, she was not a mentor or a role model to me. She was having tremendous personal challenges of which I was completely unaware. She made some difficult choices and left our company in 1989. A few months later, she made her most difficult choice. She committed suicide. As of the writing of this book, I have not had any upline leader in over six years.

Facts You Should Know About Not Having An Upline

- It's all in what you attach value to.
- If you're great friends with your upline and the upline quits, the friendship should continue. Notice, I said *great* friends.
- If you are only shallow friends, as long as your upline is in your company, then that's a relationship, not a friendship.
- Seek out other leaders at your level who are like minded and begin to network with them.
- Not every upline wants to be close friends with you. Just because you are in their successline does not necessarily mean you now can attach the word friendship to that relationship. Some uplines are not open to you being their best friend when you first join. They are building their business and want you to work the business. As your business develops most likely so will the friendship.
- Not having an upline is only hard if you choose to think that way. **You Don't Have To Have An Upline Leader To Succeed In MLM. I didn't.**

How To Handle Not Having An Upline

- Be a student of the upline who is getting results.
- Don't get into a power struggle with someone who is a Master. Respect what he has accomplished.
- Duplicate the Master upline's methods.
- Invest in your mind. Practice brain gain.
- Most importantly, go to seminars of pros, the Masters and *be willing to pay for information.*

Why?

Masters have spent a lot of their time, money and energy learning what they know. Why should they share what they have paid for in time, money and energy for free with you if you're not in their successline? Do you think Masters in any endeavor should share for free?

Here's what I suggest to those of you who believe that knowledge should be shared freely by Masters:

You go take years of your lifetime, invest your money, expend your energy, internalize some valuable information, come and share your time, money spent and energy teaching that information with my successline for free. Make a difference, for free in my successline. And I mean make a huge difference.

How's that sound to you?

You see, I did that for a long time and my experience was this. It did not come back. I was expected to spend money, share freely and motivate an entire sales force. It wasn't right. I have invested **years** in my life and **thousands of dollars** in seminars, tapes and books and most importantly my **energy** into gathering this precious knowledge. Now, if *you want my knowledge* you can **invest** in my books, tapes and seminars or telephone consultations. **My experience does not come for free.** If you happen to be in my successline, you get all this information because you are an investment of mine. If you are not in my successline, but want to take an hour of my time, that is fine. It will cost you. I only charge $250 an hour for a one-hour telephone consultation! (My friends say I forgot a zero!)

Here's what I suggest to those of you who are working on becoming Masters.

Have the attitude that you will crawl over broken glass to get the knowledge that the Masters have…and be willing to pay for it.

Am I A Great Upline?

- ❑ Do you give tons of recognition?
- ❑ Are you recruiting?
- ❑ Are you selling?
- ❑ Are you training people to become great trainers?
- ❑ Are you writing a monthly newsletter?
- ❑ Are you online?
- ❑ Are you investing in yourself by buying books and tapes and attending seminars?
- ❑ Are you committed to helping your successline move up the compensation plan?
- ❑ Do you earn all company incentive trips?
- ❑ Are you listening to your leaders?
- ❑ Are you empowering others?
- ❑ Are you making your own list of what you could do to
- ❑ improve as an upline?
- ❑ Are you leading by example?
- ❑ Are you promoting leaders and making <u>them</u> successful?

Chapter Eight

How To Be A Master Recruiter in MLM

"When the Why gets clear, the How gets easy."
—Jim Rohn

Would you like to sponsor more people?
Would you like to have more people in your organization?

This chapter is full of recruiting thoughts, ideas,
knowledge and actions to take—
starting TODAY!

How To Build An MLM Successline And Show Others *How To* Do The Same Thing ...

- Duplicate what you are doing with three or four people, then three or four more, then three or four more.
- Help others succeed. Show them how to recruit. Go with them. Show them. Show them.
- Move product and get a few others to move product, too.
- Move product and get several others to move product, as well.
- The more people you recruit/sponsor, the quicker your Network will grow.

How To Get Started Building A Giant Network

- Duplicate your recruiting/sponsoring methods.
- Duplicate yourself, show others *how to* do it, too.

- Have a lot of people each selling a little bit.
- It's much, MUCH easier to have many people moving the products than to do it all by yourself.
- Recruit several people and teach *them* to recruit. Simple—yes?

Here Is Who Should Be Recruiting
Those who:
- Desire financial independence.
- Like to help others succeed.
- Want to earn a lot of money.
- Want to make a difference in this world.
- Wish to live a lifestyle of which they are worthy.

Here Are Ideas That Will Help You Get Confidence In Recruiting
- Every person has the ability to be an outstanding recruiter.
- One potato brought to England by Sir Walter Raleigh in the 16th century multiplied itself into food for millions.
- One tomato seed multiplies itself a million times in a single year.
- Only through the practical process of explaining your MLM business to others, will you ever really know this business.
- Reap rewards through others.
- Ten forests can grow out of one acorn.

How To Teach Geometric Progression That Will Help You Have The Biggest Successline In Your Company
This is the most powerful business concept in *any* business. In MLM numbers grow geometrically.
- When you are by yourself, starting out you are the number one, then you get a recruit and that makes two.
- Then you both find another recruit, which makes four. Then all four of you find one each and that makes eight.

Your MLM grows like this: 2, 4, 8, 16, 32, 64. The numbers double every time.
- The first numbers are low. However, when you get into the next levels, the numbers skyrocket: 128, 256, 512, 1024, 2048.
- Build strong in your first few levels, since those leaders will be the ones leading their own powerful, geometric organizations.

- Don't become discouraged in the early phases of your business, just because the numbers seem so low.
- Every business grows differently based on the leaders you find, the time they are spending and their leadership ability.
- Find someone just like you.
- Find someone better than you.
- Find someone who is ready to take the steps necessary to be successful and someone who is as committed as you are.
- Geometric progression begins slowly. At first, you have to look hard to notice. So you must plan long term for the massive growth.
- The toughest and slowest part of your business is in the beginning, so you must prepare for it.
- You are not responsible for all of the distributors in your business, only your top leaders. That's why duplication is so critical. In fact, when your business gets to the growth stage, you won't know most of the people in your business. You'll simply receive a commission every time they purchase products. It is very powerful!

A Commonly Asked Question Is: "When Will I Make Money?" Here Are Some Answers...

You should make some money right from the beginning. To make the big money you have to be patient. It takes time. In MLM it is necessary to give yourself some time. It might take up to three years to see a **huge** return on your investment of recruiting others and selling your company's benefits.

What if you recruit 20 people a year? Think about what would happen if you recruited 50 people in a year.

I know a lot of people say it's too hard to build a MLM organization by yourself. Find three people and work with those three to get a leg going. However, if you are a recruiter and can't help yourself, try recruiting 50 people in one year. I did. My MLM business exploded. So did my check.

After recruiting people, I spent a lot of time training them on the product and *how to* recruit. Sure, there were times during the first couple of years when I wondered if I was ever going to make any money. A few times, I felt discouraged, but I never, ever gave up. Keep the power of your dream. *The vision of a better life.* Have a passion for what you are doing. You are changing lives and you will see evidence of that every day. Love your products, and believe in them. *Be true to yourself. Don't represent a product you don't believe in.*

Your big checks will come when you start bringing a huge volume of sales into your company. A lot of people doing nothing will not bring you a fat paycheck. You will begin earning more than $100,000 a year when your team brings in huge volumes in sales annually to your company. Count on it. Count on it! The more leaders you have, the faster this will happen. You need leaders. **Be patient, keep recruiting and duplicating yourself over and over. The money will come.**

Finally, Jan Ruhe's Secrets On *How To* Recruit

One of the most often asked questions is "*How To* Recruit?" As if there is a magic **one** WAY. After many years in this business, I can tell you that there are **tons** of ways. You might have to try several until you find what works for you. But do you quit if you don't get your first recruit in your first 24 hours or your first six weeks? It takes some people a whole year before they get their first recruit. I didn't even know what recruiting was until I had been in the business for six months!

- You can make a great recruiting presentation, but you must **ASK** the prospect to join you.

- All the great and polished recruiting presentations will go down in your history book of why you didn't make it great in MLM, if you do not close (or open) by asking the person to join you.

- Always be honest.

- Be bold. Be brave.

- Get over the fear. If you have fear, get it gone as soon as possible.

Remember, you are not selling drugs or something harmful to people. Right? You love your product. Well, then let others have the same excitement! Are you being selfish?

- Believe in your product.

Believe in the Network Marketing Industry. This is the Time to be in MLM. Millions of People are Looking for a Home-Based Business.

- Design your own recruiting presentation so it looks easy.

- Earn while you learn.

- End your presentation like you are slamming a car door shut—give it your all!

- From the beginning, the more demonstration/presentations you do, the more you will sell and the more recruits you will get and the more money you will make.

- Eliminate fear in your presentation. Some MLM companies have a reputation for being tricky. Always tell people what they can expect and what your company name is.

- Every day, anyone who comes within three feet of you, tell them what you do for a living.

More Powerful Success Secrets On *How To* Recruit

- Getting a check for a product kit is easy. Here's how. Present your opportunity and say, *"So how does that sound? Are you ready to join?"*

- Give your recruiting presentation at every demonstration and at every opportunity.

- Go shopping for people.

- Go with your upline to several (maybe even 10) recruiting presentations, or at least listen to them on the telephone. Millions of recruiting presentations are going on right now in MLM.

- Have your thoughts and your recruiting materials all organized for recruiting.

- If a person can fog a mirror, tell them about the benefits of your company.

- If you give a fantastic presentation, but you forget to close and ASK the person to join you, most likely the person will not sign up with you.

- Joining needs to be a commitment on the part of your recruit.

- Make your product presentation so fabulous your prospect will want ALL of your products. They will want to sign up with you, if you show them how all the products will benefit them or their family.

- Most people only want reassurance that you think they will succeed.

- Many people start out just wanting to make a little part-time income to help with family expenses, help pay off credit cards, buy new clothes, pay school expenses, buy gifts and holiday presents, but soon they start to expand their dreams.

- If you use the right words in recruiting, you get results.

- If what you are doing doesn't work, try something else. Something simple, like changing your words.

- If you don't believe in what you are doing and you're not enthusiastic about it, you're not going to be able to share the opportunity effectively and honestly with others.

- Whatever is holding you back, get over it.

- If your upline isn't recruiting, they're probably complaining about the lack of money they're making, which keeps their group from recruiting. Ignore this kind of upline. Ignore the person *completely.* Go seek out the people who *will* help you in your organization!

- It's in your eyes. Sincerity. If you don't believe it, neither will your prospect.

- In recruiting, sometimes you may feel like you are beating your head against the wall and getting nowhere. Yet suddenly, it will all start to fall into place. Do not give up.

- It is sad when MLM sales reps say they are fearful of recruiting. It comes, for the most part, from their initial training and their upline's lack of a clear and powerful example.

- Just selling beginning kits of products does not constitute being a Master Recruiter.

- Know that if you personally recruit 50 people in one year and train them with my *Duplicatable Training System*, you will have unbelievable growth.

- Know your products' features and benefits.

- Look and act the part of success.

- Make your recruiting presentation when you feel enthusiastic and positive. There were times, however, that I made my presentations at the height of distraction and even tragedy. I never canceled a home party, not ever—and I did over 500 of them. Get you and your challenges out of the way. F.A.Y.C. *Forget About Yourself Completely*. Hard to do? Sometimes, but the results are worth it, believe me.

- Master recruiters practice their closing skills until they become natural. They internalize what works for them. Find two or three closes that feel right for you and learn them backwards.

More Powerful Success Secrets On How To Recruit

- Make a goal—public or private—to be the top recruiter in your company, your state or your city. If you are saying, "No way, I am just trying to get my first recruit," back up, make a goal to be the top recruiter, it works!

- Your own abilities multiply fastest when you are sharing with others.

- One of the biggest misconceptions in MLM is that you personally need to sponsor thousands and thousands of people to make any real money. This is a myth.

- People who need you and your services are riding in elevators, are at the malls and are in the parks—they are everywhere!

- Put **Ask** into your life. Ask, Seek and Knock. What does the Good Book teach? Ask and you shall receive. Seek and you shall find. Knock and it shall be opened unto you.

- Project a professional and confident appearance.

- Recruiting is fun. Act like it.

- Recruit and train others to recruit. Duplicate your efforts.

- Recruit and train a minimum of 20 people, three years in a row. Watch what happens to your business!

- Rise to the top level in your company by being the top recruiter.

- Start today controlling your words.

- Take an interest in your prospect. Look them in the eyes. Blink, do not stare. Smile. Do not be bustling about, do not seem busy. Be relaxed.

- Talk about the future and how your company can help others achieve extra income, independence and self-assurance.

- Talk to people every day, explain what your business is, why it's different, how it operates and the benefits of the products.

- The first rule of successful recruiting is to have energy. Use it, sustain it.

- The best way to become wealthy in MLM is to build an organization of people through which you multiply your efforts.

- There are people out there who want to do business with you. They need to do business with you. They are waiting for you to recruit them.

- There is no need to have pre-approach packets or any other crutch. This works for some people, but it's not necessary.

- The new recruit is responsible for their own success and the only way to fail is to quit.

- The big step is to get one recruit, sponsor just one person. The next goal is to get five recruits. Then get 10 and then 15. Once you've reached this point, your MLM business will be off and running.

- There are all kinds of reasons people want to join you and your company.

- When giving your presentation, find out who the decision maker is.

- To be a Master Recruiter you must learn how to become a Master Prospector.

- Triple the number of phone calls and presentations you are making.

- Use the magic words "happily involved," instead of sponsoring or recruiting.

And More Powerful Success Secrets On *How To* Recruit

- Want a recruiting explosion to happen? Sponsor one or more new representatives each week.

- What is necessary is that you believe so much in your product that people just have to have it.

- Words you say at the end of and during your presentation get you the new recruit and make it look so simple that almost everyone will think… "I can do that!" Say something like, *"If you've liked what you've seen today, perhaps this might be a business for you to consider. Before you leave, if you're interested please tell me. Let's set up a time so that you can see if this is a match for you."*

- Share with your new recruits from the beginning that MLM is not a get-rich quick scheme.
- You have to get focused and organized to be the number one recruiter in your company.
- You need people just to sell and buy the product.
- You will be successful if you keep working on improving your presentation.

Practice:
- Drilling and rehearsing your presentation. Adjust it as you make more and more presentations.
- The three-foot rule. To anyone who comes within three feet of you, present your opportunity.
- Your recruiting and product presentation over and over every day.

Sell the benefits:
- Of joining you and your company.
- Of working with you. You are the best.
- Of your company, not the details.
- Of your products.

Sometimes:
- It's easy to spot winners; like you.
- It's hard to spot winners; ask everyone to join you.
- You have to reach deep down for that something extra. Some call it extra effort. Call it what you like, but be prepared to give it. Make up your mind that you will hunt for the knowledge you need, so that you can become a great recruiter in MLM. It's just a game. You're just a winner.

"It is too hard to do this business by yourself. It's much more rewarding to have a productive successline. Once you start recruiting, your successlines will duplicate what you are doing and your recruiting explosion will begin."

How To Get Your Recruits To Sell, Recruit And...
Get Your Network To Explode:

- Prior to taking the prospect's money for the initial investment, have a quality conversation with them. Don't be in a hurry to get their check for the kit. That will surprise them and they will trust you more **and** listen to you.

- Have a conversation with them on *their* expectations.

- Have a conversation with them about *your* expectations.

- Train your recruits yourself and from the beginning about sharing the opportunity every chance they get. Share the opportunity with people over and over. Every day, every way.

How To Set Expectations That Make It Clear To Your New Recruits That They Are To Move Product And Recruit

For a new recruit to get my attention, leadership, partnership and support, there are a few expectations I have of them from the beginning that I make clear **before** I take their check and signature:

I say: *"You understand this is not a get-rich opportunity and you're going to want to invest some time in your business. Who are the first three people you will present the product and the opportunity to?*

After they answer, say: "I expect you to... "

- Attend a mandatory training to learn all about the products and the opportunity.

- Remember, you not only represent our company, but also me.

- Attend the national convention every year.

- Feed your mind.

- Study. I will be recommending books, tapes and seminars for you to attend.

- Hold a minimum of six presentations in your first six weeks.

- Attend at least one presentation of the products and opportunity with me.

- Not criticize our company.

- Read the company literature and any publications that come from my office.

- Recruit and feel confident in recruiting from the first presentation you give.

- Return my calls promptly.

- Represent me in a professional way.

- Attend monthly meetings.

Now, you ask, will anyone sign up if you have too high expectations for them?

Well, I think my success speaks for itself. Many of the leaders in my organization have been with me for over a decade. They have duplicated the above list and have many people who are successful in their organizations. Make up your own expectation list to fit your own wants and style. If you don't give people your expectations, you have no right to be disappointed in their results.

Here Are Some Powerful Recruiting Fundamentals

- Build your network wide for income, build it deep for security.
- Do not recruit just for your own sake—you will struggle.
- It's your job as a leader to recruit and teach others to recruit.
- Keep looking for those who understand the value in recruiting.
- Not everyone will want to recruit. That's okay. But get this clear, lots will.
- Once you start recruiting, get some success, begin to train your recruits to recruit. Then watch what happens! Be prepared for success. If you can't recruit, hang out with your upline and learn how! Master this one part of the business. Master it—you can.
- Once you understand how extremely critical it is to your financial success, the desire to recruit will become huge and your momentum will begin.
- People are being recruited by the thousands, so hurry up and join the successful recruiters. Why not you and why not now?
- The MLM business is a recruiting and sales business.
- The MLM business is built on the foundation of many people moving a product or service.
- The more products/services are moved, the more everyone benefits.
- Think of what's in it for others and you will soar with the eagles.
- Until you are committed to your product and your opportunity and your future and the future of your prospect, the recruiting part will be a slow process for you. Want to speed it up? Change your attitude. Get more knowledge.

How To Begin A Recruiting Explosion That Will Make You Rich

- Get that first recruit. Find someone who sees the benefit and value of your products. Show them your opportunity. Then turn it on, turn it on, turn it on!
- Just act like someone is Xeroxing you and copy yourself over and over and over.
- Recognize those people in your organization who recruit and train their recruits more than anyone else.

- Run an **Each One Reach One** contest: Get out a flyer to your organization, however big or small. Have everyone reach just one person by month's end. Have two or three prizes. Books and tapes work great (and twice!). It doesn't have to be all that much.

- Run a **Star Search** contest. Let everyone in your organization know that you're looking for 10 Super Stars for the year. I call mine the Top 10 Club. Set your expectations for them high. Give them tons of well-deserved recognition.

- Reward them often.

- Remember, your network will only grow as fast as you do. For your group to explode, you must EXPLODE FIRST!

The Better You Get At Prospecting, The More Recruits You Will Get Recruiting.

What Is Prospecting?

Prospecting is finding out, by asking questions, if someone is interested in discussing the possibilities of buying or representing your products. Prospecting is sharing your enthusiasm and passion for your company. It's not trying to convince people of anything or signing them up on first contact. You want to discover what's missing in their life, what their needs are, what they value most.

The next step is that you want to see if there is a fit or a match for them in your business. It's simply sorting through the public, asking questions, presenting your information to find people who are interested in your opportunity.

How Many Times Do You Prospect?

Offer the opportunity to as many people as possible. Only through continual and frequent offering of the opportunity can you build your MLM business.

Although your product is an integral part of the opportunity, many more people will be interested in the business of sharing the products with others. In fact, 10 times more people will want the opportunity of sharing the product than will want to merely use the product. Always offer all of the benefits of your opportunity. Let your prospect decide the size and scope of their involvement.

What Do You Give A Prospect?

Not much. Remember, when you give a prospect anything, that's what you are role-modeling that they need to give to people whom they prospect. It's not necessary to spend a lot of money on giving prospects anything but your time and personal attention.

Here Are Some Questions To Ask Your Prospects

Begin by asking questions that build a relationship. To the degree you don't know them, ask:

Where do they live?

What do they do for a living?

Their family?

Their special interests?

Here Is What To Listen For

Listen for what is missing in their life, what's important to them, what they value. With your family and close friends, you will probably already be clear on the answers to these questions. Ask questions until you believe you are completely clear about their answers.

The next step is to repeat back to them their answers using an introductory phrase, such as: *"I've got an idea on how you could…"*

For example: *"I've got an idea on how you could stay at home, be with your children and make extra money."* Or *"I've got an idea on how you could make some extra money to retire your credit card debt."* Or *"I've got an idea on how you could increase your income and retire early."*

Make sure you read about How To Handle Objections in Chapter 8.
Make sure you read about How To Handle Rejection in Chapter 2.

Follow Up!

The single most valuable action you can take in the prospecting process is to **"follow up."** Without this single activity you are wasting your time in MLM. If you have 100 "hot" leads and you wait to call them, they become "cold" and are wasted. Shift your paradigm and get clear on the concept. **Follow up!** Call your prospects within 48 hours of their receiving the material. Find out if they've read it; they won't retain interest or the information for much longer. Ask questions about the possibilities they see for themselves with your opportunity. Listen carefully. Be a detective. Discover what is important to them. Your objective with this **"follow-up** call" is to schedule an opportunity presentation.

Prospects are only suspects until you REALLY prospect them and ask questions!

How To Be A Master Prospector

Here Are Three Powerful Results You Will Get From Prospecting

1. You sponsor the prospect, they become a distributor.

2. The prospect becomes a customer—retail or wholesale.

3. The prospect is not interested in either the business or the products.

> **"Do not waste your high energy hours.**
> **Invest them where they yield the highest payoff.**
> **The best place to use your time in the beginning of MLM is**
> **to become a master prospector and master recruiter.**
> **Your next step is LEADERSHIP."**

Here Are Some Prospecting Secrets That Will Help You Become a Master Prospector In Your Company

Ask questions of your prospect. Gather information. Ask: *Have you heard of (your company)? Have you heard of home-based businesses?* Take the information that you gather and take the facts and features about your company and turn them into benefits that make prospects want to get involved right now.

Always:

- Be honest and up front with people. This is a personal commitment as well, if you are working directly with me in my life.

- Carry business cards, catalogs and company literature with you for any unexpected encounters you will make. Never pack your business cards in your suitcase.

- Arouse curiosity. You've got to if you choose to magnetize people to yourself.

Ask:

- Everyone if they might be interested in your opportunity. Pass out business cards and flyers.

- **Everyone** for referrals.

- If your prospect would like to join now.

- Your prospect questions, be a detective, and listen carefully to see if you have a match.

- The prospect to join you. Just ask.

- Questions and meet your prospect's wants.

- Questions to see if the prospect is a potential leadership candidate.

- *"Would you like to take a look at my opportunity and see if this is a fit or a match for you?"* It's critical here that you, the prospector, fully understand what your commitment is in our industry. Do not pressure people in any way, or try to convince people to do anything. You're simply looking to see if there is a fit. If there is a match, then you're looking to contribute to people in their success.

- Lots of questions and find out what your potential distributor requires to be successful.

Become:
- The person who makes that person want to be around you.
- The person who just sorts through the public. This is the process of providing people with some information to review, showing the products, so they can determine if they want a full- or part-time business or even to join at all.

Call:
- All referrals immediately.
- Back people you meet or whose name and phone number you get and follow up A.S.A.P or sooner.

Don't:
- Give out too much information. Just find out if there's interest and provide people with just enough information to make a decision.
- Lead with the product, lead with the opportunity.
- Prejudge anyone.

Give:
- A person enough information to determine if your opportunity is right for them.
- People the opportunity to look at your business opportunity.

More Powerful Ideas For You On *How To* Prospect
- Concentrate on your prospects' lives, concerns, commitments, hopes and dreams. If you can create a sense of freedom for people, it provides them with a chance to really take a look at your opportunity to see if there's a match.
- Deception is lying. Always tell the truth.
- F.A.Y.C. stands for *Forget About Yourself Completely.*
- Great prospectors do not dwell on the products. When you do that, you

attract all the objections around the product and only get product purchasers. We all know that our products are quality products and people will see the value once they have tried them.

If:

- A prospect is not interested in the business, they may still be very interested or at least open to trying some of the products. And you know once people start using these products, they'll fall in love with them, because of their quality and uniqueness.

- A prospect says *"No,"* so what? You haven't offered them anything that would hurt them, have you? It's their decision to say *"No,"* for whatever reason. Ask them if they could they help you understand *Why it's not the right decision for them?* Ask them if something about your presentation made them think this was not for them. Do that to get feedback to help you perfect your presentation for the next time.

- You create pressure for people, they will not feel the desire to even take a look and they certainly won't want to be in business with you.

- You leave a message and the prospect does not return your call, that's not a clear communication that they're not interested. It's never okay to harm or in any way jeopardize a relationship. When people feel the total freedom to say "No" to you, without disappointing you or you continuing to try and convince them, then your relationship cannot be harmed.

- Just keep asking—and passing your name out into the world.

- Let others know that you're proud to represent your product and believe in what you are doing.

- Let people know within the first one or two sentences that you're involved with an MLM company.

- Make a list of your friends, relatives, business associates, neighbors, members of organizations you belong to and begin to call them. If they're not interested in being recruited, ask them for referrals.

- Many people will say they are interested! Just ask!

- Network every day in every way.

- Make prospecting fun.

- Never assume a person will call you back.

- Offer such an abundance of support that they know, when they do decide to join, it will be with you.

- People must never be deceived.
- Prospecting is a great way to practice, drill and rehearse (PDR) your presentation.
- Remember, some people become customers first, out of support for you, and then they join you because they love the products and the opportunity.

And Even More Powerful *How-To* Prospect Ideas

- Review your list of friends and share with them what you're doing.
- Say, *"This may be the most unusual request you've heard, I know you're not interested in my MLM opportunity, but many people are. I'm wondering, who would you know that I could call that MIGHT like to take a look at the benefits I'm currently enjoying?"*
- Say *"I'll be asking you questions and listening to you to see if my MLM business is a fit for you."* If the conversation is about you, you can be guaranteed that it will be perceived by your prospect as pressure, as if you have an agenda for her. This does not honor people. It takes some practice to be able to separate your conversations with prospects and your own goals.
- Seek to improve everything about your presentation. Practice, practice, practice.
- Speak directly to your prospect's values.
- Speak about the products, you get product users.
- Speak about the business and that you are looking to partner with powerful leaders, and leaders and business partners will show up for you.
- Talk, talk, talk about your business, all the time to everyone you meet.
- Prospect. The more prospects you have, the more recruits you'll have. Prospect every day, every way. If you ever get a chance to ask a Master Network Marketer a question, or to interview him, ask him how many ways he has prospected and recruited people.
- Until your prospect realizes she can turn her dreams into reality with your company, she won't join.
- Tell people you will be asking them questions, supporting them in creating their goals and having conversations about them. Such as, *"What is it that you're looking to find that appeals to you about my business?"*
- The more you share the opportunity and product, the more opportunities will come to recruit.
- The rewards you will reap will be worth all the sorting of people you went

through.

- Wear an *Ask Me About* button.
- Wear your company logo on a T-shirt.
- Whatever you speak about is what will show up for you.
- Word-of-mouth works.
- Until the prospects make the decision, every conversation is simply a conversation for possibilities. Try to get to the point that you really don't care if any one person comes into your business and all people get from you is the freedom to choose.
- Your words must paint a picture for others to visualize in their minds what you are talking about.

You:

- Don't have to contact anyone you don't want to contact.
- Have nothing to hide. Hiding does not honor people and honoring people is something that you must be very committed to.
- Have to sort through hundreds of people and the least expensive way to get recruits is word-of-mouth.
- If your hands get all sweaty and you feel sick, stop. Become more committed to the other person. Get *you* out of the way. Begin to think about what benefit the prospect will gain by using your product or service.

How To Prospect During Trade Shows And Get Lots Of People Happily Involved In One Day

- Ask everyone who comes to your booth if they would like to join you or if they will be an ambassador for you and take some literature to three prospects who might be interested in your opportunity.
- Ask tons of questions of people who come to your booth.
- Don't just be trying to get your money back on your investment from the booth.
- Get everyone's name and number on a list for future mailings. Add the names to your data base.
- Have a dynamite display.
- Have giveaways.
- Practice your recruiting presentation. If your product is great, tell the world.
- Smile.

- Trade shows are mainly for presenting your opportunity.
- When prospecting during a trade show, you're role modeling to those people that if they join you, they will prospect through trade shows. They will duplicate what you are doing. Remember, most people will want to approach others in the same way that they were initially approached.

How To Advertise And Get Results, Prospects And Recruits

When your budget allows, advertising is a great idea.

- Advertise in many yellow pages. Get your name out everywhere.
- Always put enough information in the ad to help the prospect pre-qualify themselves—so you don't have to. You don't want to just put out an ad that will make your phone ring needlessly.
- Answer your phone.
- Get people's phone numbers as they call in, so that if you get disconnected you can call them back and so you can keep their names for the future.
- Lead organizations that give you excellent service and up-to-date leads that are great, but only if you **follow up**.
- Many people have found tons of different ads that work. Check them out.
- Put enough information in your ads so that the prospects will have an idea of why they're calling you.

How To Do Direct Mail And Get Big Results

One time during the Christmas holidays, I sent out 800 flyers to my data base to ask people to come to an open house at my home. I had my products displayed, a special cake baked, the house was spotless and I was ready. Well, sad to say, no one showed. Not one person!

What to do? I got on the phone that night and called 10 of my best customers. I told them they had missed a wonderful open house at my home and that, because they missed it, I would have the product displayed the next morning until noon available for them to pop by to view them and to place their order. The next morning eight of those prospects came and guess what? I got orders totaling over $1,000. Of those who came, not one had read my flyer.

The point: **Follow up.**

Here Are Some Powerful Ideas For You On *How To* Do Direct Mail

- Direct mail works for tons of MLM people.
- **Follow up** with phone calls. It's critical.

- The only way direct mail works is if you send out enough of your literature and you **follow up**.

- You must have a decent mail-out piece of literature. I know I throw away thousands of dollars worth of horrible junk MLM mail.

- Tom Hopkins says to *"follow up until they buy or die."*

- When I've sent out direct mail, I've found if I follow up, I get results. If I don't **follow up**, no results.

How To Handle Objections

What are objections? Objections are *questions* that the prospect needs to have answered before she can make a decision. The Master Recruiters have all figured this out: Questions are not *objections*. The new person is just seeking more information, so he can make a decision to join or not.

Replace their objections with your facts.

Objection: *"Oh, I already know many people doing your MLM in my area."*
The real question is: How many people are in the area involved in selling the product? I am fearful that it is saturated with MLM and no one will buy from me. Please address my fears.

Answer: *"There are people joining our company every day. With people moving in and out of cities on a daily basis it is difficult to ever know exactly how many people are selling our product in a given area. There are not many aggressive salespeople in any sales organization. There's room for many, many people to share our opportunity."*

Objection: *"I don't have enough time."*
The real question is: How much time does this take? I work full time and don't have any time left over. How can I possibly do one more thing?

Answer: *"Many people begin their business with limited hours. Many of my customers are busy working people who appreciate the convenience, personal attention and leisurely pace of buying from their own personal sales rep. If you're able to do one presentation a week, you can get your business off and running. The more you put into your business, the more you will get out of it. Who do you know that you can pinpoint that you could tell all about the products tonight if you got started today?"*

Objection: *"I have no desire to get involved with MLM because I don't want to recruit others."*
The real question is: I am scared to death of recruiting and I know that's some of what MLM is all about. Not for me, no way. Unless, however, you will help me.

Answer: *"Many people succeed in recruiting. If you like and believe in the product, your self-confidence and enthusiasm will build and grow. You'll receive positive feedback from your customers, friends and family. You will make remarkable progress in a short time. All you have to do is to share the products with others. Use them yourself, get sold on them and your enthusiasm will take off."*

Objection: *"Oh, this sounds like Amway®."*

Answer: (Always ask a question for more information before jumping to answer this question. They might love Amway®, their parents might have been or still are involved. Be careful how you answer this. I always answer this question with, *"Actually, I believe Amway® is a great company. Yes, it's very similar. Please tell me a little bit about why you would ask that question, I'm curious."* This is an easy one for me.

> Help people get clear information on your business.
> Once they get enough information, if it is right for them,
> then say, "So how does that sound?"
> Try to get to the real objection as quickly as possible.
> Normally, it's the money.

How To Get To The *"Yes, I'm Ready To Join"* Stage And Help Your New Recruit Get Started

- Ask your prospect, "So how does this sound, are you ready to join?" as soon as you have completed your presentation.

- Be a Monster Closer. Be the best one in your company.

- Choose a close for the benefits of your product or service.

- Go for the close, it's a game you must master to be the best, the very best.

- It's fun and rewarding when you learn to close the sale.

- Learn one or two closes.

- Learn verbatim champion closing techniques taught by top leaders in your industry.

- Make up your own close, just get it down pat and use it.

- Reread some of my scripts and seek out other closes.

- Write down your close, then memorize it. Practice it in front of a mirror.

> **"As time has gone by, I have found the most important part about starting a recruiting explosion is for you to be the catalyst. It doesn't matter where you are in your organization. If you want your people to duplicate you, then you need to be doing the business."**

How To Explain The Benefits Of Joining Your Successline To a New Recruit. Sell Yourself. Here's How:

- Explain how and why you joined your company.

- Explain to your friends that you are expanding your business, that you are the best upline they can possibly join under and you think they would be an excellent person to represent your company.

- Have scrapbooks and photo albums prepared.

- Share with people the kinds of prizes you've won.

- Share with your prospects your career possibilities.

- Tell new recruits about the benefits and incentives and show them how you're getting (or going to get) yours.

- Explain that you attend personal growth and development seminars.

- Show how you are a committed Network Marketer.

- Tell them you love the product and how much you have sold.

- Share with them that you are committed to being a master prospector and will teach them how.

Jan Ruhe's Words To Say To Recruit People Into Your Organization

Start Today, Call Someone Right Now And Actually Read The Words And See What Happens... Say The Words Like You Mean Them.

"I've just gotten involved in a MLM business and I am looking for some business partners. I don't know if you have an interest in looking into this and if not, that's okay with me. However, I do want you to know when I was thinking of who this opportunity might be perfect for, I thought of you. I respect you and you are truly someone I would like to partner with in this business. In looking into this company I found that it is just perfect for me. I want to be in business together. So, what do you think?"

Here's *How To* Build A Nationwide Network...It's The Key To Long-Term Security In MLM

- Always return calls within 24 hours.

- E-mail your prospects regularly.

- Go to the new recruit's city to train them if you can.

- It's very hard to "untrain" or retrain.

- If people keep saying "no" about joining you or using your product over the phone, perhaps you're giving them too much information—or not listening.

- Your job is to use words to alleviate pressure, so that people aren't scared to death of you, but are so excited that they can barely wait to begin.

- Run a Break-a-State contest in your successline to see who can get an out-of-their-state recruit in a certain time frame. Very effective!
- Send videos of yourself giving a presentation.
- Start a National Ambassador Program, call everyone you know in another state. Offer them free product or $25 to help you sponsor someone in that state. Tell them you're building a National Network.
- Study the pros, and I mean study. Learn to use their words, exactly. Keep it simple.
- Tell long distance people they can call you every day or better yet, that you will call them.

Why To Build $$,$$$ Security With Out-Of-Town Groups

If you only recruit in your own town and there's a disaster, all your efforts could be demolished. Just think, if you have worked for five years in one state and a disaster hits, you could be out of business overnight. However, if you have a national network, your residual income will continue to come in. I worked harder on building a National Network than on anything else.

How To Set A Powerful Recruiting Goal

Fill In This List And Begin Today Contacting Your Prospects

My Next 20 Recruits Will Be:

1. Name, _____ Date Joined _____ .

2. Name, _____ Date Joined _____ .

3. Name, _____ Date Joined _____ .

4. Name, _____ Date Joined _____ .

5. Name, _____ Date Joined _____ .

6. Name, _____ Date Joined _____ .

7. Name, _____ Date Joined _____ .

8. Name, _____ Date Joined _____ .

9. Name, _____ Date Joined _____ .

10. Name, _____ Date Joined _____ .

11. Name, _____ Date Joined _____ .

12. Name, _____ Date Joined _____ .

13. Name, _____ Date Joined _____ .

14. Name, _____ Date Joined _____ .

15. Name, _____ Date Joined _____ .

16. Name, _____ Date Joined _____ .

17. Name, _____ Date Joined _____ .

18. Name, _____ Date Joined _____ .

19. Name, _____ Date Joined _____ .

20. Name, _____ Date Joined _____ .

Here Are Some Ideas To Use For Your Advertisements At Fairs And In Flyers

At demonstrations, conferences and fairs, cut out pictures from your company literature and attach them on bright poster board.

Here is what to write at the top of the poster board:

Discover a Career With (Your Company)
Part-time Sales Reps Needed. No Experience Necessary.
Low Investment. Ground Floor Opportunity.
Fast-Growing, Successful Company Offering
Flexible Hours, Unlimited Income Potential,
Huge Tax Advantages and Fun!
How To Join Today? Just Ask!

Here Is What To Write On A Recruiting Flyer:

Successful Company Seeks Sales Reps For Quality Product.
What's In It For You?
Fun, Great Income Opportunity, Flexible Hours.
Full or part-time career opportunities.
Call 970-MLM Pro For Information.

How To Talk To People And Eliminate Rejection

Ask Questions:

Learn to use the following questions and watch your results.

- Are there any questions you would like to ask me so I can answer all your questions?

- Are you ready to make your selection and begin enjoying the benefits of this great product?

- Can you see yourself presenting these products?
- Do you have eight to 10 hours a week you could dedicate to building your MLM business?
- Have you heard of MLM?
- Have you heard of my company?
- Hi, may I give you my business card?
- How does that sound?
- Is there anyone else besides you who needs to make the final decision of your getting involved with our company?
- If this makes sense to you, can we go ahead and fill in some paperwork that our company requires? You can go ahead and get your checkbook out and make out a check for only $25 to get you started. What's your middle initial and to what address would you like your mail from my group and our company to be sent to, so it can reach you right away?
- I love what I do. For 17 years I've represented an excellent company. If you want to travel, make new friends, make money and get more kicks out of life than you are presently getting, please tell me. How does this opportunity sound so far?
- If I can show you a way to make $200, $500, $1,000 or more a month. Would you like to hear about our company and product? I just need five to 10 minutes of your time.
- If what I share with you in the next five to 10 minutes makes sense to you, could I assume we can move forward and get you happily involved in our company?
- May I show you our compensation plan and a few of our products and share with you the benefits of being associated with my company and me?
- My company has given me the responsibility to build their presence in your area. May I tell you about this exciting opportunity? Let's see if it would be a fit for you.
- What happens if you say "Yes," and what if you say "No" to joining me? If you say "No," everything stays the same as it is right now, but if you say "YES" to this opportunity, you can begin immediately to enjoy the benefits of being with our company and enjoying these products.

Here Are My Actual Recruiting Scripts You Can Use In Your Recruiting Presentation That Will Get Your Prospect To Say 'Yes' To Your Opportunity

- I'm anxious for others to meet you, you will add so much to the value of our team.

- I am so anxious for you to begin to enjoy the benefits of these products.

- I love what I do. I'm home every day when my children come home from school. I easily work around my family's schedule.

- I want to answer all of your questions, so that you have nothing to think over.

- I will help you. There are two trainings a month in our area, where you can attend over and over. This is a fun job to have!

- Congratulations, you've chosen to join a group of successful people who set goals and achieve them. We'll see to it that you do great.

- Let's talk about the benefits of your being a member of my team.

- Let's see if this makes sense to you, and if it does can I assume you'll be ready to make a commitment to join me today?

- Let's get you happily involved right now, so you can begin to enjoy the benefits of our products.

- Our company has simple product and training manuals for you to refer to when you have questions.

- No one owns a customer. It's a courtesy to ask if the person to whom you are talking is currently working with someone else. If that person has not been contacted in a while, feel free to move ahead and work with him.

- Now is the time to get involved with our company.

More Powerful Ideas On Scripts To Use That Will Get You Recruits

- One of the reasons my group is number one in the nation is that I ask you to pinpoint three people who will help you get started right away.

- One of the great benefits of our company is that we don't encourage you to stockpile inventory.

- Our company's track record is quite impressive. We're growing fast (and cite the latest numbers if you know them). Now is the time to join.

- Our product is easy to demonstrate. If you believe in the product, you can sell it and recruit others to sell it.

- Thank you for meeting with me today. I'm hoping you're thinking about joining my company. I'm looking for people to represent our company part time. If you are interested in getting involved, please let me know now before I take up any more of your time.

- It appears to me, after some of the information you've shared with me about yourself, that this might be a great part-time business for you.

- The income opportunity in MLM is unbeatable. Are you aware that you can rise in our compensation plan as fast as you want? Building a business does take time. You will receive big checks when you have a successline of people each selling only a little bit.

- **The next step is** to get out your checkbook or credit card and authorize the paperwork. Welcome to our company!

- We have monthly or weekly meetings in our area where you can come and get product knowledge, recognition and continued training on our compensation plan. You can come to see and be with your new friends and share any information you have.

- Welcome to my group and to our company.

- What are your expectations of me?

- You will be an independent contractor and not an employee.

- I will not be your boss. I'll be your coach.

- The company does not treat you as an employee. You're a partner.

- You will fit in great in our company.

Here Is The Worst Mistake You Can Make In MLM

Stop Recruiting!

There are several reasons for making this mistake:

- You think that you have made it.

- You think that you really should just sit back and manage your organization.

- You think you can keep it going by just motivating your existing people.

If you stop, here's what happens:

- Your group sees that you do not recruit, that it is not important.

- Your group sees you concentrating on training.

Next: Your group duplicates you, so they quit recruiting and just train their existing people. If you want an active, growing, dynamic organization, set an active, growing, dynamic example.

How To Get 1 To 5 Recruits Today

Get on the phone. Call everyone you know. Say, *"I am so excited about my MLM business. I am looking for from one to five people to join me today. Who do you know whose names you can give me to call—smart people who might be looking for a better way of life."*

"Here is who I am looking for: (S.T.E.A.M.) Sales people. People who sell anything. Teachers. Teachers are great Network Marketers. Enthusiastic people. Who is the most enthusiastic person you know? People with a good Attitude. Who has the most positive attitude of anyone you know? And Money. Who do you know who could use some extra money?"

Announcing A Proven Way To Recruit: Sell Them The Benefits Of Joining Your Company

Always sell the benefits of your company in all presentations. Be knowledgeable about the benefits of your product and company. (Get my *Duplicatable Training System*.)

How To Have People Choose Your MLM Company

There are many MLM companies for people to choose from today. You must sell the benefits of your company over the others. Yet never, ever, say anything unkind about another MLM company.

Why?

You only hurt our industry when you do. More and more people want to join Network Marketing today. Don't disparage them by criticizing individual companies. Simply focus on the benefits of your company.

Why Should Someone Join Your Company?

Make a list of clear statements of benefits about your company. It's imperative in MLM to join a company that you feel and believe will be of benefit for others to join. You have to believe that and be sincere about it, before you can be an MLM giant, a Master.

Your Recruiting Will Be Improved When You Can Share The Benefits Of Your Company With Others.

Build Credibility By Sharing The Answers To These Questions:

How long has your company been in business?
Has your company earned a reputation for integrity and performance?
Is your company…

- Linked synonymously with quality?
- Totally computerized for better service?

- A recession/depression-proof business opportunity?
- Represented by enthusiastic salespeople?
- The epitome of the American free enterprise system?

Here Is What A Great MLM Company Does:

- Advocates the advantages in life of selling your product to others.
- Allows you to work today and be compensated for your efforts the rest of your life.
- Attracts people from all walks of life.
- Believes that the founder of your company was an inspired man or woman with a mission in life.
- Engages in qualitative measures to produce consistently high standard products.
- Establishes regular goals and expends their focused energies to attain them.
- Gives you gems, pins, rubies and diamonds, for awards.
- Gives you the opportunity to double your annual income each year for years.
- Supports your having no time clock and no set hours.
- Guarantees product satisfaction or your customer's money promptly refunded.
- Helps you develop the talents and skills necessary for success.
- Holds that you can be successful regardless of where you live.
- Instills within you the concept of thinking big.
- Motivates you to great accomplishments.
- Pays your monthly check promptly and accurately.
- Prospers during hard times, recession and inflation.
- Protects your interest by not selling their products through retail stores or mail order.
- Radiates the prestige that you would like to have if it were your business.
- Represents a worthy cause.
- Rewards you financially by paying you exactly what you're worth.
- Stresses hard work and smart hours as opposed to gimmicks.
- Takes people seeking to change careers after age 40.
- Views your business as a lifetime career.
- Welcomes and accepts aggressive and progressive ideas from the field representatives.

A Great MLM Company Encourages You To:

- Become financially independent.
- Get information from anyone in your company.
- Help others help themselves.
- Operate out of your home to maintain a low overhead.

A Great MLM Company Has:

- An outstanding credit rating.
- Products that sell themselves through repeat business.
- The reputation of pioneering various concepts of products.
- The reputation of keeping their top sales leaders for a lifetime.

Here Is What A Great Company Offers You:

- A monthly newsletter or magazine.
- A people-to-people business.
- An unlimited territory to build your business.
- Annual achievement trips to breathtaking places like Hawaii, the Caribbean, London, the Far East, Mexico, the Bahamas, Canada or other exciting places.
- Challenges to make you a stronger individual.
- Everyday variety in your work.
- Great material benefits early in the business.
- Great success without going door to door.
- Individuality.
- Numerous business tax deductions.
- Opportunity to compete.
- Opportunity to build a nationwide sales force.
- Opportunity to earn money 24 hours a day.
- Prestigious titles to keep you going and growing.
- Products that are used every day by people everywhere.
- Products that enrich the lives of users.
- The opportunity to purchase your own products wholesale.
- Special seminars to help you further your education on your industry.
- The ability to take time off and still have a growing income.
- The finest quality products in its field.

- The same promise of success to people with disabilities.
- Free trips to the home office if you are a sales leader.

The Opportunity:

- To become a millionaire in your own business.
- To become renowned in just a few years.
- To build your own business empire.
- To determine your own income.
- To earn money the very first day in your new business.
- To make more money than you ever dreamed possible.
- To meet hundreds of new friends each year.
- To travel and the chance to see America and the world.
- To train at seminars and workshops for Sales Leaders.
- To work full time, part time, spare time or any time at all.
- To make a powerful, positive difference in the lives of hundreds and thousands of people.

A Welcome Letter

Just imagine the impact on your new recruits when they receive this a day or two after they start their new business.

Dear (Your new recruit's name),

Welcome to The Greatest Business in the world!

As your partner, I'm anxious to help you reach the level of success you desire in our fantastic business. I am happy to have you in our organization.

The first thing I can do for you is to refer you to a fine repeat customer. You! Begin selling yourself on the value of our products. When you have succeeded in selling yourself, you will have no trouble with others. Sell yourself our product all over your home. Make a special commitment to your new business by converting to as many of our products as possible beginning today.

This first big personal purchase is your business "kick-off," and it will be an exciting experience. You're saving money by buying from yourself, and your enthusiasm for our product will lead you to sales profits.

Another step to take immediately is setting your goals: Why did you become a sales representative for our company? What level of success do you have in mind?

Let's review some of the benefits of your being excited about your business:

1. We offer you an unlimited financial opportunity.
2. You can enjoy association with ambitious, enthusiastic, superior, fun people.
3. In our business, you work with superior products.
4. Rapid advancement is possible. You work at your own pace.
5. There are no territorial restrictions. You may build in your own community or expand nationwide, even grow internationally.
6. You can share this tremendous discovery with others!
7. We offer you the independence of owning your own business and being your own boss.
8. We offer you a rewarding personal challenge. When you excel, you will enjoy widespread recognition. As an independent contractor, we offer you the opportunity to grow and surpass your previous success.
9. We offer tons of bonuses and incentives, all-expense-paid incentive trips, annual conventions, high-level leadership meetings. And much much more.
10. A successful MLM business is free from most of the "headaches" that plague other businesses: no employees, no fixed hours, very little bookkeeping, no major investment, no previous experience or special education required. It really is quite simple—and powerful. You must decide how fast you want to advance and how many hours per week you will regularly devote to your business. Everyone has the same opportunity in our business.

Nothing this good comes without work. Fortunately, the "work" is very exciting…it's never seemed like "work" to me. Do you think you'll enjoy "playing" for a living?

You'll be happy to know that you've joined the most dynamic group in our company in the entire country! We have a proven success plan and a winning attitude. So, begin now by spreading your enthusiasm amongst all your friends. Give them all the exciting information you have, set a personal example they will want to copy. You will be greatly rewarded.

Enthusiastically yours,

And, sign your name.

What Do I Want To Say In My Welcome Letter?

❑

❑

❑

❑

❑

❑

❑

❑

❑

❑

❑

❑

❑

❑

❑

❑

❑

❑

Chapter Nine

How To Be A
Master MLM Trainer

*What Matters In MLM Is Not Who Recruits You...
It's The Training You Get.*

So You Don't Have A Duplicatable System And Want To Start Your Own Trainings In Your City...Here's How

- If there is no upline for you to duplicate, start your own duplication program.

- If you want to succeed in MLM, you need to get properly trained.

- Make your trainings work around your family and business. It's one of the benefits of your business.

- Most of the time, people will take off work if they really want to attend your training. New recruits are expected to come to a one-day training and are asked to commit to that before you take their check and signature.

- Start and end all training with upbeat music. Hint: use *Fire Up!* Music.

- When people are excited about getting the information you don't have to browbeat them to come. They see the value!

- When your recruits get a new recruit, they have to come to the training with their new recruit and do a portion of the training. The more they train people, the more they internalize the information and the better they get at recruiting and training their own people.

- Write down what you do that works. Duplicate yourself. Show and tell others *how to* do the same.

Here Is The Location:

- Always have the same location.
- I held trainings in my home for years. So can you.

Here Is What To Bring:

- A calculator.
- A student's attitude.
- A lunch, including a drink of your choice.
- A spiral notebook.
- Two pens (in case one runs out of ink or doesn't work).

Here Is What Not To Bring:

- A sour attitude.
- Babies over three months old; you must make sitter arrangements.
- Sickness.
- Video camera or tape recorder.

Here Are Facts You Should Know About Daytime Training; Here Are Facts You Should Know About Nighttime Training

- Time: 9-2 pm and we work through lunch.
- Day: Always on the second Tuesday of every month.
- I wanted the trainings in my home, because I did not want to leave my children.
- You can have trainings while your children are at school and people don't have to pay for sitters.
- You can get people when they are fresh instead at the end of the day.
- Night-time trainings never worked for me.
- I wanted to do my product presentations at night.
- I didn't want to be gone one more night if I didn't have to.
- I couldn't commit to night trainings. I worked other parts of my business at night.
- Many people can come at night.
- Many people would prefer to come at night, they are busy during the day.
- Many people have sitters at night and want a night out.

Here's What To Do If People Can't Come To The Training When You're Available
Plan A:
- They rearrange their schedule to fit yours.
- If you can rearrange the training to fit the schedule of the person who works, go ahead. If not, go to Plan B or Plan C.

Plan B:
- Your training might be short enough to meet with them over a lunch break.
- Let them know that it will take them longer to get all the knowledge.

Plan C:
- Let them know that they would have to get their training out of the company manual.
- Make yourself available to them by phone.

Here's An Agenda For A Great MLM Training
Welcome
- Have them say their name, how and when they joined your company.
- Have nametags and use first names.
- Tell them they are to take notes.
- Tell the purpose of the training: So they will succeed in their MLM business.
- Tell them that you're going to give them so much support they can't help but succeed since they are in your group.

Announcements
- Day/time of the next training.
- Day/time of the next meeting.
- Any company announcements, such as regional meetings, trainings, trips, new products or policies.

Product Knowledge
- Give them so much information about the benefits of the products that they can barely wait to get started.

Paperwork

- How to organize it.
- How to take orders.
- How to get the products to the customers.
- How to take MasterCard and Visa.

Customer Service

Rule #1: The customer is always right.

Rule #2: When the customer is wrong, refer immediately to Rule #1.

Product Guarantee

- Make sure everyone knows they can stand behind the product 100%, because the company is standing behind them.

Recruiting

- Train people to be so excited about what's in it for them to recruit that they **know** they can recruit. Have them believe so much in themselves and the product that they **cannot wait** to get out of your training to go recruit. Tell them the words to say. Role play. Talk about objections. Talk about rejection. Talk about MLM being a BIG numbers game. Talk about their dreams.

Goal-Setting

- Sell xxxxx in product a year—no less—and recruit three to five people every month.

Expectations

- When they get a new recruit, they're to come to the very next training and they will participate as a trainer.
- Everyone must attend monthly or weekly meetings.

The Opportunity

- Have a wipe-off board.
- Draw the circles. I don't care who tells you that's old news. Draw them! It works. Show your new recruits what's in recruiting for them.

Here's how to do it:
Show And Tell Your New People *How To* Start Making Money...

Be up front, explain where the new recruit needs to be to increase their percentage. Don't hold that information back.

Money Comes In Two Ways In MLM:
Selling product

You make XX% of everything you sell. If you sell $10,000 in product x 25% you will earn $2,500.

Recruiting

Show them the possibilities when they begin recruiting. Have them feel confident to begin recruiting from the first presentation they make. Many people just need encouragement to face and replace rejection. Have them begin from today on offering the opportunity.

Be sure to direct your new recruits to this information while you train on recruiting.

If you sell $10,000 in product x 25% and begin recruiting, you make the $2,500 plus (whatever percent it is for your company) of their recruits' efforts. And when the new recruits begin to recruit they earn a percentage of that person's sales and so forth.

Ask: "How long will it take you to sell $10,000 in product all by yourself? Let's talk about the reality of that."

"To present your product to 500 people in a year, here are a few ways to do it: 50 people who buy $200 = $10,000. 100 people who buy $100 = $10,000. 500 people who buy $20 = $10,000." Pick one. And have your recruits help you.

"How can you learn to earn $100,000 a year
from someone who is earning $30,000 a year?"

You Can't.

Should You Have Inventory? Pros and Cons

- Absolutely, there are many people who want your product right then and there. If they have to order it, they will not do it.
- If you buy inventory you get a discount and make more money.
- No need to tie up your money. Just have the customer place the order.
- In many MLM companies the customer can just call an order directly in to the company.

One of the all-time MUSTS is never let anyone train you to do something they have not done themselves. Hearing information someone shares on how to do something makes no sense, unless he has gone out, carried in products and gotten results that are better than yours. How can someone possibly train you when they have not experienced what you are getting ready to experience? Beats me!

It reminds me of a question I was asked one time. If you had to have brain surgery, would you go to someone who has experience and gets results all the time, or someone who gets results sometimes, or who tried it for a few months, didn't like it, but thinks that they can do it? People who are not experts in MLM do not fool me, not one bit.

You are well on your way to earning the big dollars when you learn to learn from the best. Write everything down that Masters tell you to do and then do it. What are the people you listen to doing? Are their actions in agreement with their instructions? Watch closely the results those who are instructing you are experiencing. Many people want to be teachers, but before you let them train you check out their results.

Get trained by someone who gets results. Someone who has done what they are training you to do. Why would you want someone to teach you how to be average?

Train your own successline as soon as you feel confident. Why? That way you will internalize the knowledge. When you train your own new recruits they will respect you more.

Facts You Should Know About Being A Master MLM Trainer

- A great place to begin is to train yourself about your products, your opportunity and the MLM industry.

- Being a master trainer is fun and rewarding.

- Get some recruits, get some sales, use your product, get some results, contribute to trainings.

- The teacher always learns more than the student.

- To be asked to teach or train, just be a top seller or top recruiter. People will be very interested in listening to you. Until that time be the one who listens.

- Train for the benefit of contributing to others.

How To Be A Master Trainer

- Be an example. Do that which you are training others to do.

- Be unsatisfied with the status quo.

- Create and articulate a vision of your goals and help others set their goals, so they can see all that they can achieve.

- Communicate the purpose of the training.
- Encourage others to duplicate you in the beginning and then improve on what you teach them.
- Favor taking risks and making changes, improving on how things get done.
- Get to know the person, take an interest in your new recruit. Once you get to know them and have a sense of their values, train toward those values.
- Read every tip you can get on MLM training.
- Go to a training yourself and listen closely.
- Stress relationships with others, values and commitment.
- Understand that once your recruit signs the application, your real work begins.

Here's Some Great Information For You On Training New People

- As soon as you see the new recruits duplicating your efforts, ask them to begin to train others. Let them know you are training them to become the trainer and leader.
- As soon as they get on e-mail, have them send you their e-mail address, so that you know they are up to date with information from you.
- As time goes by and you get some experience, you will want and need further training. Ask for direction.
- Ask questions of your new people. What's working for them and what isn't?
- At least one training is mandatory. This is the most important part of our business. After you recruit someone, it is your job to train them or get them to a training.
- Be open to people having new ideas on how to do the business better.
- Be coachable yourself. Get advanced training.
- Be teachable, listen for success tips to use in future trainings.
- Be available for day-to-day training.
- Becoming a leader might begin slowly. It begins with lots of support and partnership and your being there to give it to them. **As long as they are coachable.**
- Don't give too much information in the initial training.
- Call your new recruits every day until the product kit comes in.
- Commit to all applicable conference calls.
- Have your new recruit continue training until you get all of their questions answered.

- Continuing training is a must for yourself and your successline. (Say: "I will call you and be there for you for six weeks—plan to take my calls and be prepared for them with no interruptions.")
- Create a partnership promise at the training and during your recruiting presentation.
- Have a training scheduled the same day of the week every month, same day, same location. People are welcome to come, over and over again. Encourage new recruits to bring their hot prospects.
- Have conversations with the trainer and others after the training.
- Have special meetings to train only on the product. Share ideas on how to demo each product.
- Have your recruits call you when they've gone over the products.
- Take new recruits with you on prospects and recruiting presentations. On-the-job training is critical.
- If they need immediate income, inform the recruit that THEY must go out and sell the product. Train on the value of your product. There is SO much money to be earned. You are an American, living in the most prosperous country in the world. Get out there and make a huge difference in the rest of your life and the lives of thousands of others! You can do this.
- Train with passion. Ho hum training gets ho hum results.

"When the student is ready the teacher appears. All sorts of teachers will appear."
— Tom Hopkins

And More Powerful Ideas For You On *How To* Train New People

- If your recruits are long distance, you'll be the one to spend the time and money and tell the long distance recruit that you will train them over the phone. I **never** sent my new recruits to be trained by someone else. Never. I took total responsibility for my own recruits. I would not trust anyone else to teach my recruits to do the business. I had a duplicatable plan that I wanted to make sure they learned. (Get my *Duplicatable Training System*.)
- Make the trainings fun. Remember why you love your product and opportunity and let that passion ignite others' passion.
- No one does this business on their own. It's all about teamwork and partnership.
- Order the recruits' new kit **the day they join.** Don't put it off, even one day.
- Personally sponsor and train a minimum of 20 people, three years in a row,

and help those people to begin to recruit, if you desire a large network.

- Presentations can be called presentations or demonstrations, home parties, workshops or private showings, whatever **they** wish to call it. They must feel comfortable in calling it whatever **they** want. Guide them, but don't demand they call the presentation a demo if they don't want to call it that. It's okay.

- Separate people into "leader/business builders" and "wholesale buyers." Have special meetings for future leaders only.

- Set up a time and place where you can be uninterrupted, go over the product and the opportunity with them. Encourage them to bring a prospect along.

- Start by training a handful of people and teach them to train others.

- Emphasize the importance of attending the next national convention.

- The initial training is the most crucial to the success of the new recruit.

- The only way a new recruit will become one of your important legs in your successline is to train them to recruit. There is no other way. Train people who are long distance by telephone, video, e-mail or audio cassette.

- The person who does the training gets the respect.

- Train everyone you personally sponsor or recruit.

- Train new recruits before they ever walk into someone else's meeting.

- Train on the product **and** the opportunity. Show them how to show the product and the opportunity, so that they can duplicate you.

- Train the new recruit within the first two weeks after you recruit her.

- Train your new recruits to recruit from the very beginning.

- When you relinquish training to someone else, your recruit believes they should conduct their business that way, too.

- Train your own people. Why? What if your new recruit is trained by someone who is not an aggressive recruiter? Most likely they'll follow that lead.

"The people who succeed are those who have the self-discipline to develop themselves."

You put so much time into recruiting people for your MLM business and then they take no action, won't return your calls, don't sell product. A lot of valuable time is wasted in this process.

Here's a strategy to begin today: Set up expectations with people prior to taking their check. One of those expectations is that they will attend one product and opportunity training.

A Message To All New Recruits

Please know that you might have a desire to do things bigger, better, faster. You might think you can redesign your upline's training. Do yourself a big favor. Copy what your upline is doing. Most likely, he is copying what he has been trained to do and keeps doing it that way, BECAUSE IT GETS RESULTS!

Messages For Existing Networkers

- You might be bored, tired of the same meetings, making the same presentations.
- You might think a different type of training is needed. If this describes you, please know that you are a challenge to your upline. When you get away from the basic way that your upline has built her organization, the basics begin to get lost. Eventually, the further you get from the basics, the quicker all of **your** MLM group growth will grind to a halt. You might think you're smarter. Look at your upline's results. If you're doing better than your upline, more power to you; your upline should pay attention.

Here Are Some Powerful Ideas For You

- Don't lose sight of what made your upline successful.
- Find a training that works and don't change it.
- Keep your training simple.
- Stick to the basics.
- Work with people, train them and don't get lost trying to create shortcuts or skip steps.

Here Is Where To Put Much To Most Of Your Training Efforts: Product Training

- Teach the benefits of your products. Have your successlines so sold on their products that if another opportunity comes along they will be loyal.
- Train on the product. Have your successline know all about the products.
- Make sure you get my *Duplicatable Training System*—it's a super place to start! You can order it from my website-www.fireup.com.

Chapter 10

How To Have Meetings And Events Where Your Successline Will Be In Action Before The Meetings Are Even Over...And Get Results, Too

The first meeting I held for my company was in my den. It was 113 degrees outside and I was nearly nine months pregnant with my third baby. After a phone call from the VP of my company, who encouraged me to start my meetings, low and behold, I set one up.

With no idea of where to begin, I just decided to call my new recruits and tell them that I was having a meeting in my home. Would they like to come? I set a date and a time, and everyone came! And, by the way, we all had a ball.

Our meetings got so big we ultimately had to go to a hotel for everyone to fit. We had over 100 people show up to those monthly meetings...for years.

The real key to getting people to come to a meeting is for them to be getting results. When you get results, people will come to meetings to hear how to do it so that they can get results, too. They will drive across town, across state, even fly. Results are the best way to get people to meet with you.

I never held weekly meetings. I was too busy building my business. I had three little children and a new career. There just wasn't any time to plan them. I was on the phone hours a day as it was.

My MLM Business Took Off...
When I started having monthly meetings in my home.
When I started recognizing my people's accomplishments.

Here's When To Start Your Own Meetings

- Keep going to the bigger meetings, always.
- Start your own small meetings. Start on your kitchen table. Start when you have sponsored your third person.

Here Are Powerful Ideas For You About MLM Meetings

As you get a group of people recruiting a group of people, all of a sudden your business will explode. You don't have to be an established leader to start your own meetings. I wasn't—yet. And those meetings helped me become a leader.

- Be the last one to leave your meeting.
- Be the person who controls the monthly or weekly meetings.
- Bring people together to help them help themselves be better Network Marketers.
- Meetings build relationships.
- Call your successline and give reminder calls at first, then send postcards until everyone knows about the meetings. Watch your voice on the phone. Be enthusiastic.
- Create a meeting of your own. Small meetings around kitchen tables are going on every day and night in MLM around the world. That's how large networks begin.
- Delegate ahead of time two or three people to demonstrate the product.
- Do a slide show—pictures say a thousand words.
- Don't mix your new recruits with those who have quit. They begin to think maybe they should quit, too.
- Figure out what works and how you could improve on making a great meeting even better.
- Get yourself **Fired Up!** for the meeting; do not share your personal challenges. Keep the focus on the meeting.
- Go over the initial compensation plan, where they need to be setting their goals to achieve the results they want.

- Go to other leaders' meetings. Do not criticize, just quietly take notes.

- Go to successful Network Marketers' meetings.

- Have the meeting at the same location every month.

- Have your product displayed.

- If there are no meetings in your area, be the one to start one.

- If there is any part of MLM that scares you, like speaking at meetings, conducting meetings, trainings, recruiting, being the best, etc., the way to overcome that fear is through courage.

- It is more fun and exciting to have team meetings where you go together with other like-minded people in your company.

- Know that meetings are necessary and important in MLM.

- Make your meetings easy to get to, always on the same day (first Monday night, second Tuesday morning, etc.) and at the same time and location.

More Powerful Ideas For You On *How To* And Why To Have Meetings That Get Results

- Many people are "belongers"- they want to come to meetings.

- Meetings should be from 7 to 9 pm.

- Month, after month, after month, as you have this meeting, people will begin to value your leadership. Sometimes it takes a few months to get the respect you want and deserve.

- Never have people who are no longer involved in your company at a mixed meeting with new motivated people. The new people are negatively influenced by those who have quit.

- New programs can be announced.

- Pay attention to details.

- Pay attention to how the room is set up, the refreshments, the greeters, music, what the opening words are, the lighting, the energy, everything.

- Product knowledge is covered; the more product knowledge people have the more secure they feel in explaining it to others.

- Set the stage in the beginning that it will be a successful meeting.

- Start and end on time.

- There are all kinds of meetings: weekly meetings, quarterly meetings, leadership meetings, before-the-meeting meetings, after-the-meeting meetings, regional meetings and national meetings. **They are all important.**

- There's much excitement in synergy.

- Up-to-date information can be shared.

- The leader should be the pipeline of information.

- When you have one monthly meeting, everyone can come together and it cuts down on time on the phone.

Here's What To Have At Your Meetings

- Enthusiasm.

- Greeters at the door.

- Handouts.

- Others to do product demonstrations.

- Plenty of bottled water, juice and sodas. Ask someone to bring them.

- Plenty of pens and paper and a wipe-off white board for presentations.

- Someone to take pictures. Put the pictures in your newsletters.

- Someone to tell their success story.

- Tons of recognition. Go overboard.

- Upbeat music playing as they walk in.

Start Monthly Meetings In Your Home.

- Have it at a home while your group is small. It won't be long until you out-grow it. Home meetings are less expensive.

Here's *How To* Have A Monthly Meeting Where People Will Come And Can't Wait To Come Again

Step One: Setup and Purpose

Start with refreshments. Stand up in front of your group, little or big. You will be the facilitator. Say this: *"The purpose of this meeting is to share ideas, give information and announcements, get recognized and socialize. If you have anything negative to say, please keep it to yourself. This is going to be a great meeting. Let's all share as much as we can, stay on time and go out of here with one great new idea. Right now we are going to start with recognition."*

Step Two: Meeting Agenda
1. Welcome Everyone
Make sure you welcome the new people and their guests.

2. Recruiting
Ask, *"Who has gotten one or more recruits? Please come up and tell us how you did*

this, and let's welcome the new person to the meeting..." if that person is there.

When the new person comes up **You Say**, *"Now let's all show how happy we are for (person's name)"* and start the clapping.

3. Sales

Ask, *"Who sold product this month? Stand up and tell us how much and how you did it. Let's capture some great stories right now."*

4. Sharing

Say, *"The next part of the meeting is to go around the room and everyone, please, give your name and say something positive about your business this last month. No negatives allowed. If you are having a challenge, please ask it as a question. Someone here might have the answer for you."*

5. Compensation Plan

Say, *"Tonight, (name) is going to present to you what we're all shooting for."* (Always have someone different explain the basic comp plan.)

6. Leadership

Ask, *"Who is going for leadership? Please come up and share with us about what you are doing so we can cheer you on."*

7. C.A.N.I. Constant And Never-Ending Improvement

Ask, *"What books, tapes or seminars have you experienced lately?"* Have those who have read books or listened to tapes or attended seminars share a couple of great ideas.

8. Goals

Say, *"Everyone, share your goals for the next month. Who's first?"*

9. Team Calendar

Pass around a calendar and have everyone put a check on the date that they have a presentation scheduled for the month.

Step Three: Call to Action

Say, *"Here's what I want everyone to do before the next meeting ... (now **You** set the team goals).

For example: *"Everyone needs to bring at least one person to the meeting. It can be a new recruit or a prospect. How many of you are excited about the information you got tonight? Let's go around the room one more time and everyone say your name and what action you are going to take before our next meeting."*

Always end your meetings on dancing feet. Put on the *Fire Up!* music and turn up the volume.

What If No One Comes To Your Meeting

You have meetings scheduled and month after month no one comes. First of all, do you have a decent product? Is anyone selling or recruiting? You should not have to beg people to come to your meetings. Look at the value of your meetings for your people.

If no one is coming to your meetings, make sure that you try all of these ideas:

- Delegate. Ask everyone to bring something, whether it be drinks, product, ice, their smile as a greeter or whatever.
- Don't have meetings just for the sake of having a meeting. Be productive.
- If you are too intense, no one will want to come to your meeting. Lighten up.
- Make sure your home does not smell like smoke or any other bad odor.
- Get a surprise speaker to come and talk about sales or recruiting or duplication.
- Get some mega results yourself. When you are successful, people will want to hear what you have to say.
- Give everyone a job to do.
- Give more recognition.
- Have nice prizes that your successline can only get if they come to your meeting, such as books and tapes.
- Have something of interest to share.
- In your newsletter say something about a surprise announcement to be made at the next meeting.
- Put a time for the meeting in your newsletter. Make reminder calls.
- Set up 10 chairs at every meeting. Say to your group, we are going to fill these chairs next month. Visualize it. Expect it.

How To Propel Your Own Business Into High Gear: Get To A National Convention.

Here Are The Benefits Of Attending The National Convention Or Leadership Seminars

- If you total up your phone bills, all your time on e-mail, and all of the efforts you put into trying to figure out how MLM works, you could have learned it all in just a few days at this big meeting.
- It confirms that what you are doing must be worthwhile.
- It provides you access to business and leadership development training and

most importantly you will get to experience who your company is.

- It will change your entire perspective, for the better. Even if it's already sky high.

- People shift how they communicate about their company and the opportunity, once they have been to a national convention. And since you're going to be out there talking to people every day about your product, you need to be as powerful as possible.

- The leaders you will meet are committed to people's personal development, which is needed for those who desire to become the leader of a million dollar business.

- The national convention provides information on new products and support materials.

- This is a critical step in your leadership development, training and success in your business.

- There is excitement when someone attends a big meeting and sees many people doing what they are doing.

- This one meeting will speed up your process of understanding the big picture.

- You need to be at the next national convention or leadership seminar.

- You get the big picture of where they want to go with the business.

- You get product knowledge.

At Your Convention You Will:
- Learn more in one three- or four-day period than you will in three years.

- Have an opportunity to meet your leadership, your uplines—and they get to meet you.

- Have the opportunity to meet and network with other company leaders.

How To Respond If People Say No To Attending Meetings, Especially The National Convention Or A Leadership Seminar
- Those who do not attend the national convention, for whatever reason, do not get as much of your attention as those who make the investment of time and money.

- Those who come and don't put into action what they learn, don't get your attention. If you go to the convention, go to learn and take action. You're making a clear statement that you are a serious business builder. Go for yourself and your future—not for your upline.

- Your attendance is a good start in showing your upline that you are a serious business builder.

- What is most important is the understanding of the importance of attending a convention. If you cannot commit to the next convention, are you willing to commit to the next event? If you're not willing to commit to attending a convention, the upline must use his/her own judgment, and strongly consider the possibility that you are not yet ready to commit to being a leader in the organization.

- When you're ready to be a leader, wild horses can't keep you away from this one grand meeting!

How To Hold A Big Event

I've been doing large events (100-400 people) for years. It's very apparent to me, when I go into a meeting that size, whether the people planning the meeting know what they are doing.

Step One
Make Some Decisions.

- Decide you're going to have a large meeting.
- Decide what results you want.
- Decide what town.
- Do not use a cheap hotel.
- Establish a price, date and time for the event.
- Find out how much the hotel sleeping rooms cost.
- Find out how much a meeting room will cost.
- Gather dynamite knowledge to share in an organized system that will benefit your successline.
- Get the details of the information out in your newsletter on white paper, so that your successline can copy it and put it into their newsletters. Make sure the information is correct.
- Give more value than expected.
- Go and look at several locations and negotiate with the hotel.
- Have only those who are getting results give input on the planning.
- Many hotels will give you a free meeting room if everyone at the meeting eats in the hotel.

- Plan the date and time of the event.

Step Two
Delegate.

Here's *how to* **set up your chairpeople.**
Set up chairpeople and delegate as much as you can, make the event a team effort. Lots of people love to be part of planning an event

Here are the categories you'll need chairpeople for:

- Music.

- Registration, to collect the money and to pay meeting room expenses out of that money.

- Starting and ending on time.

- To bring and set up products.

- To be responsible for a group of greeters.

- To decorate the room.

- To plan the menu if you choose to all stay in the hotel for a luncheon or dinner.

- To sell books and tapes at the back of the room.

**Here Is *How To* Get More Information
On *How To* Have Meetings That Get Results**

Read *Fire Up!*
**Here's *How To* Get It.
There's an order form in the back of this book.**

What Do I Need To Do To Have More Productive Meetings?

❑

❑

❑

❑

❑

❑

❑

❑

❑

❑

❑

❑

❑

❑

❑

❑

❑

❑

Chapter 11

How To Handle Conflict And Discouragement, So You Can Get On With Your Success

"We are supposed to be happy. God created us to be happy—remember the birds—they sing after the storm—why shouldn't we?"
- Rose Kennedy

"When you are successful,
there will be very unprofessional people who are silly,
who will question how you became successful.
Let those people motivate you, not discourage you.
Separate yourself from them. Have nothing to do with them.
They will bring nothing to your life. They are a total waste of your time."

That which you resist will persist.

Find opportunity in obstacles.

Only you put obstacles in your path
to the fabulous future that awaits you.

How To Be Successful in Handling Conflicts

When you're in MLM, you will be meeting and working with lots and lots of people. Some share many of your values and some do not share your values at all. Some have like goals, and some do not. How do you handle all of these different personalities without conflict?

When you are working in any industry, you will come in contact with people who are not like-minded. They do not have the same top 10 or maybe even top 20 values you have. They are in your successline, they are in your company, under another successline, they are corporate people, salespeople, customers and more. Each with their own agenda. You begin to build an organization and conflict happens.

Where do you go?
What do you do?

Always dump up, to your upline. What if you can't reach your upline or your upline won't or can't help you and you have to help yourself?

Here is what to do:
The First Step
Choose not to react right away.

The Second Step
Never go to anyone else with your conflict, except your upline for counseling. Never ever go to your successline. Go to the person the conflict is about first, if you can.

The Third Step
Seek out information, first to see if you have all the knowledge you need to help resolve it. Get both sides before you react.

How To Handle Personal Conflict In MLM
- Do not blame yourself.
- Do not let anyone discourage or intimidate you.
- Feel sad for the people who tried to start rumors about you.
- If you choose to listen to the criticism, keep your sense of humor.
- Let conflict motivate you.
- Make choices of what you will tolerate and what you will not tolerate.
- Most people just make things up, that's all it is. Just stuff made up that's not even true. Silly, but human.
- Never let conflict stop you from pressing on toward your goals.

Ask yourself these important questions:
Are you willing to make powerful choices, will you do it?

Are you willing to take charge of your own time left on earth?

Who is holding you back?

Why are you listening to them?

What do you want out of life?

Secrets of How Jan Ruhe Handles Conflict

Here are my thoughts, straight out of my journal. Every time I had conflict, I turned to this information.

- All the sorrow, fear, anxiety, frustration, jealousy and worry in the world cannot sink you, unless it gets inside your mind. To keep it out, fill your mind so full of happiness, positive constructive thoughts, desired outcomes and helpful ideas, that there's no room for the negatives to seep in.

- All the water in the world cannot sink a ship unless it gets on the inside of it.

- Appreciate and value your life time.

- Are you flying close to the ground with the turkeys?

- Are you aware that you could be soaring with the eagles?

- Ask yourself, can this person help me solve this challenge, or have I now simply created a new challenge?

- Avoid conflict.

- Avoid phony pep talks.

- Detach yourself from negative people.

- Do not share your precious life time with people who do not respect you.

- Dump the slump.

- Eight hundred million Chinese don't know what you are doing and don't care.

- Evaluate what's holding you back.

- Give no one person, no one event, the power to threaten the peace and love that live in your heart.

- Give up guilt.

- Handle the pain of change.

- It's not a good idea to talk too much about work with your family. Join in other interests together. If you complain all the time, what kind of support do you expect? If you are complaining, your spouse will encourage you to quit.

- Let go of people who want to struggle with you, detach yourself from them.

- Learn from failure.

- Learn to ignore the critical people, do not value them.

- Learn from negative people, find out what they read and don't read it. Find out what they do and don't do it.

More Powerful Ideas For You On *How To* Handle Conflict

- Life is not meant to be a struggle.

- Look for ways to improve situations, instead of ways to keep the tempest brewing.

- Look for new people to come into your life to show you how to improve yourself.

- Nobody is lucky or unlucky.

- No one can hurt you. You let yourself be hurt.

- Nothing is more irritating to customers, uplines and successlines, or peers, than to hear someone complain constantly about how hard they work. Stop doing it—it doesn't work!

- Optimists are seldom surprised by trouble.

- Only jealous people have unkind things to say about those people who earn large incomes.

- Part of the fun in life is asking questions of the person who is having a conflict with you and listening to what others find so important.

- People who are not successful will question how you became successful.

- Put your recommendations in writing and send them to someone who can solve the challenge.

- Realize that in five years nobody will care.

- Realize that not everyone will agree with you—so what? Wouldn't this world be boring if everyone agreed with you?

- Realize that not everyone will like you or respect you and that's ok with you.

- Refuse to play "Ain't it awful."

- Release those people from your life who are a struggle, and your life will be more peaceful.

- Say *"challenge"* or *"an interesting situation."* Drop the word *"problem."*

- Steer clear of the negative-thinking experts. Say what you need to say and drop it.

- Take control of your situation.

- The main thing is to keep the main thing the main thing.

- The more successful you are, the more criticism you will receive. Just keep moving forward. Say to yourself, *"Oh, well."*

- There are always two sides to a story.

- There are people in your audience who are just waiting for you to say something that can be misconstrued, so they can make an issue of it. Ignore them.

- 35 percent of people don't want to hear your challenges, and 65 percent will be happy the challenges are happening to you.

- Toughen up.
- *Thrive* on chaos.
- Turn from those who say no to you. Think *"Yes."*
- Turn off gossips. Get away from them.
- You get either bitter or better in life. Pick one.

And More Powerful Ideas On How You Can Handle Conflict

- When you are successful, many who are not will criticize you. Don't give them any power over your life.
- Your MLM business is too important, the potential too great, to be wasted by conflicts and distractions from uninteresting interests.

Get:

- Dissatisfied with your status in life.
- Out of a bad relationship, now. This very minute.
- Uncomfortable with losing. It's a lot easier to lose than to win.

If:

- People are not successful, over a period of short as well as long time, they will quit.
- What you are doing just clearly isn't working, change it.
- You get in a relationship that isn't going anywhere, be bold. Get out.
- You have a complaint—take it to someone who has the power to solve it.
- You tell your family about your business, sometimes they won't understand and will discourage you.
- You want to stay away from conflict, stay away from the people who bring you conflict. Have absolutely nothing to do with them.

Never:

- Choose to quit because someone does not agree with you.
- Share your challenges with someone who can't solve them.
- Call anyone a liar.
- Call someone and say, *"I have a problem."*
- Communicate that someone is wrong.

Quit:

- Blaming other people.
- Blaming your circumstances, your I.Q., your parents and spouse for your challenges.
- Blaming your situation, your upline, your company, spouse or children for your lack of success. Ask yourself, *"Just who I am permitting to take control of my time and energy."*
- Letting others hurt you.
- Trying to please everyone. That's one guaranteed formula for failure.
- Starting and stopping your business.
- Wearing your feelings on your sleeve.

Stop:

- Faking it, start making it!
- Having pity parties.
- Beating yourself up and allowing others to beat your self-esteem up.

THE CRITIC

"Dare greatly, it is not the critic who counts,
not the man who points out how the strong man stumbled
or where the doer of deeds could have done better.
The credit belongs to the man who is actually in the arena,
whose face is marred by dust and sweat and blood;
who strives valiantly; who errs and comes short again and again,
who at worst, if he fails, at least fails while daring greatly;
so that his place shall never be with those cold and timid souls
who know neither victory nor defeat!"

—*Theodore Roosevelt*

How To Handle Discouragement

Don't let anyone or any event discourage you. When you think about quitting, that's the time to start all over again.

- Accept personal responsibility for yourself.
- Accept the challenges of life.
- Believe that you will have a fabulous future.

- Beethoven was deaf.

- Break off the rearview mirror of your life and look forward.

- Build up your opportunities; don't magnify your challenges.

- Challenges make you a winner.

- Change challenges into opportunities.

- Depart from your past.

- Detach yourself from your old self.

- Develop will power instead of won't power.

- Discover the difference between merely trying and doing whatever it takes.

- Do what you fear the most and you will overcome it.

- Enjoy every precious moment.

- Enter every day without giving mental recognition to the possibility of failure.

- Even the failures are remembered, because they at least tried.

- Failure is the fertilizer of success. So pour yourself a cup of ambition, jump off the planet earth and let people see that you have mastered habits of those who have earned one million dollars.

- Fear is the biggest obstacle to getting on the road to being a champion.

- Focus your attention where you are weak, then work with that weakness to build up a reserve of self-confidence and strength.

- Grow instead of die.

- Help others overcome their fears by your confidence.

- Improve your weaknesses, seek out help.

- In planning for success in your MLM business, include some will power.

- Isn't it strange, with so many wonderful ideas and great ambitions, people allow themselves to be victimized by terrible weaknesses that make them quitters.

- Keep your chin up.

- Let go of whatever makes you stop.

- Life is too short for us to make all the mistakes personally.

- Lincoln was unhappily married.

- Mentally walk through a gate, look back and say, *"I'll never go back to where I was before!"*

And More Powerful Ideas For You On *How To* Handle Discouragement

- No one *makes* you feel discouraged.

- No one makes you feel inferior without your consent.
- Nothing worthwhile ever comes easily.
- Only those who never try, never fail.
- Only those who do not expect anything are never disappointed.
- Reprogram yourself.
- Risk rejection.
- Sometimes it's hard to keep on going, but you must keep yourself motivated.
- Sometimes it's one painful step at a time.
- Stay away from those who can't make decisions.
- Stay away from those who distract you.
- Start over right now, if you are ready to quit.
- Take opposition and hardships in stride.
- The easiest decision is to quit.
- The future is ahead of you, not behind you.
- The majority of people take the negative view of life and are easily discouraged. The ambitious work to not let this happen.
- The time that you doubt your business is probably when you are neglecting it.
- The prizes go to the person who can stick it out and finish what she started.
- The traps you're experiencing might be put in your path by you.
- Those who can confront mistakes and rise above them are the champions.
- Those who wait get run over by those who do not procrastinate.
- To get approval, give approval.
- Tune out selfishness and focus your mind on the best interests of each other.
- Tune out the shallow.
- Turn obstacles into opportunity.
- When you have the attitude of a quitter, you are always headed for disappointment.

We:

- Need negative feedback. Negative feedback is good.
- Need to make mistakes.
- Rise or fall, succeed or fail, based on the image we hold in our own mind.

You:

- Can work your way to the top against all the adversities that you have. Just make a decision, walk through that mental door and tell the guard at your brain, goodbye, forever.

- Deserve the best life has to offer, it's up to you to get it.
- Have: control over your future, the key to the ignition and the combination to the vault.
- Have choices and options.
- Must believe in yourself and the power of your dreams.
- Were born to succeed, not fail.

And More Powerful Ideas On *How To* Handle Discouragement

Every:

- Challenge is an opportunity for personal growth.
- Ending is a beginning.
- Journey begins with a single step.
- Person who has ever accomplished anything, could have found excuses for quitting short of his goal. Many had good reasons for not beginning in the first place.
- Time you even have a thought of quitting, start over again.

Few:

- People ever quit while they're ahead.
- People ever get discouraged while they are winning.
- People want to sign up with someone who lacks self-confidence.

If:

- Anyone is making money in your MLM company, there is an opportunity for you to make money, too.
- You have initiative, that's a big part of success.
- You lack self-confidence, try to get over that hurdle in a hurry.
- You don't give up, you can be successful in MLM.
- You want to be successful, think successful.

It's:

- A show of great character strength when one keeps on in a good cause in spite of distractions, difficulties and other unforeseen events.
- Always too soon to quit.
- Better to have a few great people than many doing absolutely nothing.
- Not what happens to you; it's your attitude toward what happens.

- Not acceptable to call yourself a failure.
- Not what you have, it's what you do with what you have, that makes the difference.

Most:

- Real success is actually built on failure.
- People fail because they don't know how, or don't try hard enough, or don't stick to what they are doing long enough.
- Successful people fail forward.
- People fail, because they don't understand they must duplicate themselves.
- People have negative minds, because they focus on negative things.
- People who are busy enough to tell you how busy they are, usually aren't very busy.

Never:

- Ever give up.
- Ever quit, *No Matter What.*
- Never, ever quit MLM, if your product and company are sound. **Never!**
- Allow anyone to make you feel unhappy.
- Let anybody make you feel angry.

And More Powerful Ideas on How To Handle Discouragement

You are:

- Better than you think you are.
- Either growing or shrinking.
- In control of your life.

You can't:

- Always depend on other people to show you the way.
- Beat a person who can't be beaten.
- Change others. Quit trying.
- Soar with eagles if you hang out with turkeys.
- Change what happened five minutes ago. You can only change the present and the future.
- Get to second base with your foot on first.

You don't have:

- To have great ability to get ahead and become financially independent.
- Time to do too much mental wavering.
- Time to grow old.
- To psych yourself up when you live a positive attitude life.

You might:

- Have to detach yourself from others and go on.
- Have to do activities when you don't want to do them.
- Have to sort through more people than most people to find the people you want. While stewing you could be doing a million dollar habit that would bring you money, fame and fortune in the future.
- Take two steps backwards before you get a break and surge forward.

How To Handle Your Disappointment When Someone You Recruit Quits

When you first begin recruiting, most people are so excited that they have the expectation if they can just sell a person a kit of products, the person will go out and start selling. When that doesn't happen, the recruiter gets discouraged.

When you recruit someone, **take time to train them**. Show them how to duplicate you. Just selling them a kit of products and talking with them two or three times on the phone doesn't mean they'll be sellers or even stay with you. **If you have not trained them to sell and recruit and train others how to do the business, then most likely** *they will quit.*

Here's a big reason people quit: They think they know how to do the business. They stay in for years, going up and down, with major emotional swings. Some months they take off and some months they work really hard. Ultimately, their MLM business doesn't take off, they get discouraged and quit. You scratch your head wondering why.

Quit worrying about it. It's not you. Most people sabotage themselves in MLM. They think they have all the answers. They get a title with an ego and quit listening. They set themselves up as pros, want to manage, quit selling, quit recruiting and wham. It doesn't take long before they get discouraged, begin blaming the company, you and everyone and everything else, *except* for the fact that they quit working their business too soon.

Here's *How To* Handle It

- Ask your successline for input on why they're **really** quitting.
- Become clear on your expectations for people in the future right from the beginning.
- Decide to train people much better to duplicate your methods.
- Let them know that the door is always open for them to come back in the future.
- Or say: *"I trust your judgment to do what is best for you and your family"* …and then, let them go.

"It's always too soon to quit."
–Jan Ruhe

Chapter 12

Here Is A List Of Music, Books, Poems And Stories That Will Ignite Your Passion

Music

Music is a tremendous influence for millions of people in this world. Motivational, upbeat, positive music is used at all of my seminars and meetings. I love music.

Why?

Changing people's state of being is critical to being a great leader. It's a feeling created by movement and emotions. When you are a Master, you've learned to not only teach people, but to change people's emotional state of being. The person who just talks away, sentence, after sentence, after sentence, who thinks they are a Master or the "expert" in their field and doesn't move people's emotions, is missing a great opportunity.

Take three minutes out of your presentation and put on some music. Feel what happens in the room. Watch what happens to the people.

People have difficulty listening to someone talk for hours at a time. During the breaks, fill the meeting room with music. Change the music. Never have the same music on during every break. When the room is filled with music, many people are moved to move, dance, sing along. It brings back memories and that's called changing people's states.

People have such learning differences, it's important to know that music in a meeting is imperative for those who have to have a break from listening to talk. Music is a great benefit in meetings. It is a must. When I attend seminars where there is no music during breaks, I don't pay attention to what the speaker is saying for long. Make sure the music in the room is filled with a positive message, through music.

"Music speaks louder than words"
-Glen Yarborough

Music is an anchor.
When there's music at your seminar or meeting,
and people hear it again,
memories of being at your seminar
come flowing back.

Here Is A List Of Music That Inspired Me To Use It At Seminars And Monthly Meetings Or To Just Listen To

All I Wanna Do, Sheryl Crow
Aspenglow, John Denver
Back in the High Life Again, Steve Winwood
Best Woman Wins, Dolly Parton
Cadillac Ranch, Bruce Springsteen
Can You Feel the Love Tonight, Elton John
Can't Keep a Good Man Down, Alabama
Chariots of Fire, Vangelis
Christie Lee, Billy Joel
Dreamland Express, John Denver
Eagle When She Flies, Dolly Parton
Easy Money, Billy Joel
Eternal Flame, Bangles
Even the Nights Are Better, Air Supply
Fast Movin' Train, Restless Heart
Fire Up!, Jan Ruhe
For the Longest Time, Billy Joel
Forever Young, Rod Stewart
Get on Your Feet, Gloria Estefan
Give Me All Night, Carly Simon
Going Home, Kenny G
Hero, Mariah Carey
Hungry Eyes, Eric Carmen
Hungry Heart, Bruce Springsteen
I Wanna Dance With Somebody, Whitney Houston
I Will Always Love You, Dolly Parton
I'll Be Home for Christmas, Elvis Presley
Life Is Eternal, Carly Simon
Lost in Love, Air Supply
Making Love Out of Nothing at All, Air Supply
My Home's in Alabama, Alabama

New Attitude, Patty Labelle
Nine-to-Five, Dolly Parton
Oh Heart, Baily and the Boys
Olympic Hymn, Leonard Bernstein
Out Of Africa soundtrack
Power of the Dream, Celine Dion
Rocky soundtrack
Rope the Moon, John Michael Montgomery
Some Days Are Diamonds, Some Days Are Stone, John Denver
Sound of Music soundtrack
Silver Threads and Golden Needles, Linda Ronstadt
Streets of Philadelphia, Bruce Springsteen
Stuff That Dreams Are Made Of, Carly Simon
Take It As It Comes, Steve Winwood
That's My Job, Conway Twitty
That'll Be the Day, Buddy Holly
That'll Be the Day, Linda Ronstadt
The End of the Innocence, Don Henley
The Greatest Love of All, Whitney Houston
Think About Love, Dolly Parton
Two of a Kind, Garth Brooks
Walk a Mile in My Shoes, Elvis Presley
Welcome to Our World of Toys, FAO Schwartz
When Will I Be Loved, Linda Ronstadt
Wild Women Do, from *Pretty Woman* CD
You Don't Own Me, from *The First Wives Club* CD
You'll Never Walk Alone, The Righteous Brothers
You Can Depend on Me, Restless Heart

Advice To Those Building Huge MLM Networks...

Read

"Somewhere there is a map of how it can be done."
— *Ben Stein*

Do You Know That You Speak About 3,000 Words A Day?
That is the equivalent of a small book.

Make Today A Best Seller.
Instead of, *"Hand me another soda,"* try saying *"Hand me another book."*

Here's A Way To Become An MLM Success Story:
Read And Collect Success Stories, Lots And Lots Of Them

Read, it's a fountain of wisdom. When you become ready, you will search for information on *how it's done.* Many times just one sentence in a book, or one chapter, will get you so excited that you'll get on the phone and make more calls than ever before…and get huge results!

Through the years, I outlined more than 300 books. Buy books before you can afford them. Outline books and teach someone else what you have learned. **This is powerful!**

Do You Make These Mistakes?

Do you say you don't have time to read?

Do you say you don't retain what you read?

Well, here's what you might want to consider…

- Always have a book to read.
- Change your attitude, you have as much or more time.
- Come on. You can find a way to read.
- Feed your mind.
- Keep a book in your bathroom, a book in your car, a book in the kitchen, a book by your bed, a book in your handbag, a book on your desk.
- Make a commitment to read a book a month—how 'bout one book a week?

The Results of Your Reading Could Be…

The more you read: the more you share powerful information at meetings, the more confident you become, the bigger your monthly check becomes, the more your lifestyle improves, the more success you attract, the more knowledge you retain.

At meetings, practice speaking by giving book reports. The more you give book reports out loud, the more you retain the knowledge. The more you teach what you've learned, the more you internalize it. Teach it, and the more you want to read. The more you read, the more educated you become, and respect will began to overflow into your life in abundance. And ultimately, your successline will began to read, too. Their self-confidence will began to soar, their checks will become bigger, which makes **your** checks bigger.

Here's what to do next…

Buy your leaders and future leaders books, and give them books as prizes for your contests. Encourage your successline to read. Feed your mind. Invest in books and audio cassettes.

Discover The Wealth of Information In Books

Are you hungry for success in MLM? I'm telling you, I read tons of books. I was going to find a way. I would not be denied the lifestyle. READ.

Only When You Are Hungry For Knowledge, Will You Go Hunting For It.

A Word Of Caution:

Be careful about randomly giving books and tapes to your successline. Sad but true, until *they* are ready to read what it takes to help *them* get from being average to being a Master, all the tools in the world won't help them get there. There has to be desire. Give them books that get you excited for prizes, activities and for results. Recommend books. Center your contests around personal growth and development. The attitude of being a student is what separates the Masters from the average. When you are ready, you will grow personally, by leaps and bounds…and so will your income.

"Keep Focused And Hungry!"
— *Ray Pelletier*

Here Are Important Ideas For You About Reading

- Begin a program of reading and never ever stop.
- If you don't read great books, it will be obvious to those who do.
- Once you believe you know it all, watch out!
- Some books are rare …when you follow the knowledge in these books you will find yourself on a fabulous path that is certain to lead you to a better life.
- The more educated in MLM you become, the bigger your checks.
- The more you read, the more educated you will become.
- Words, quotes, stories and examples in these books will contribute to your success.

You will:

- Develop your leadership skills.
- Gather stories to tell.
- Increase your confidence.
- Increase your knowledge.
- Increase your vocabulary.
- Learn time management skills.

Here's Powerful Information On What To Read

- About Champions.

- About Masters.

- At least five pages a day of positive material on building your business.

- Be the student. "When the student is ready, the teacher appears."

- Books written by successful people.

- *Every book* on MLM that's been written.

- *Fire Up!*

- Good stuff—good stuff in, great stuff out.

- How others took themselves out of their pitiful situations and made a future for themselves.

- Lots of magazines, including the advertisements.

- Magazines pertaining to current events.

- Motivational books.

- Newsletters.

- Powerful books.

- Powerful newsletters.

- Search out books written about successful people in your industry and learn from them.

- Success stories.

- The *Wall Street Journal* and the *New York Times*.

- Upline® Magazine.

Here Is A List Of The Books That Inspired Me. What Would One Great Idea Be Worth To You? (Check Off The Books You Have Read.)

❑ *A Passion for Excellence*, Tom Peters
❑ *Act Right, Feel Right*, Dr. Salvatore Didato
❑ *Angels Are Forever*, Esther Beilenson
❑ *Ann-Margret—My Story*, Ann-Margret
❑ *As A Woman Thinketh*, Dorothy J. Hulst
❑ *Atlas Shrugged*, Ayn Rand
❑ *Awaken the Giant Within*, Anthony Robbins
❑ *Barbra Streisand*, Nellie Bly
❑ *Be Happy, You Are Loved*, Dr. Robert Schuller
❑ *Big Al Series*, Tom Schreiter

- *Being the Best You Can Be in MLM*, John Kalench
- *Beyond Selling*, Bagley Reese
- *Beyond Success*, Brian Biro
- *Breadwinner, Breadbaker*, Sandy Elsberg
- *Buddha's Little Instruction Book*, Jack Kornfield
- *Building a Champion*, Bill Walsh
- *Call Your Office*, Robert Mankoff
- *Cash Copy*, Dr. Jeffrey Lant
- *Changing Channels*, Dr. Robert Gordon
- *Changing the Games*, Larry Wilson
- *Chicken Soup for the Soul*, Jack Canfield & Mark Victor Hansen
- *Choices*, Dr. Shad Helmstetter
- *Claw Your Way to the Top*, Dave Barry
- *Closings for Dummies*, Tom Hopkins
- *Comeback*, Dave Dravecky
- *Compassionate Capitalism*, Rich De Voss
- *Creating Affluence*, Deepak Chopra
- *Dear Family*, Zig Ziglar
- *Discover Your Possibilities*, Dr. Robert Schuller
- *Ditka—Monster of the Midway*, Armen Keteyian
- *Doak Walker*, Dorothy Bracken
- *DO IT!* John Roger and Peter McWilliams
- *Doing It Now*, Edwin Bliss
- *Dolly*, Dolly Parton
- *Earl Nightingale's Great Discovery*, Earl Nightingale
- *Financial Freedom Through MLM*, Kenneth Smith and Richard Walsh
- *Find Happiness in Everything You Do*, Susan Schutz
- *Fire Up!*, Jan Ruhe
- *Freedom Unlimited*, Dr. Mack Douglas
- *Future Choice*, Michael Clouse
- *Get a Life*, Philip Stills
- *Getting Things Done*, Edwin Bliss
- *Getting to Yes*, Leroy Brownlow
- *Gift From the Sea*, Anne Morrow Lindbergh
- *Growing a Business*, Paul Hawkes
- *Guerrilla Marketing*, Jay Levinson
- *Have a Great Day*, Norman Vincent Peale
- *How to Build a Large Successful Multi-level Organization*, Don Failla
- *How to Build a Large, Successful Multi-Level Marketing Organization Using a Three by Eight*, Dennis Goldner
- *How to Build a Multi-Level Money Machine-the Science of Network Marketing*, Randy Gage
- *How to Make A Whole Lot More than $1,000,000*, Dr. Jeffrey Lant

❏ *How to Master the Art of Selling*, Tom Hopkins

❏ *How To Sell Yourself to Others*, Elmer Wheeler

❏ *How to Succeed in Your Own Network Marketing Business*, Debi Ballard

❏ *I Dreamed of Africa*, Kuki Gallmann

❏ *I Lived to Tell It All*, George Jones

❏ *Illusions*, Richard Bach

❏ *In Search of Excellence*, Tom Peters and Robert Waterman, Jr.

❏ *Leadership Jazz*, Max Depree

❏ *Life 101*, John-Roger and Peter McWilliams

❏ *Life Is Just a Chair of Bowlies*, Mary Engelbreit

❏ *Light From Many Lamps*, Lillian Watson

❏ *Living with Passion*, Peter Hirsch

❏ *Looking Deep*, Terry Bradshaw

❏ *Looking Out for Number One!*, Robert J. Ringer

❏ *Love Can Build a Bridge*, Naomi Judd

❏ *Mach II With Your Hair on Fire*, Richard Brooke

❏ *Magic Words*, Ted Nicholas

❏ *Marilyn Monroe*, Donald Spoto

❏ *Mary Kay on People Management*, Mary Kay Ash

❏ *Meditations For Parents Who Do Too Much*, Johnathan and Wendy Lazear

❏ *Million Dollar Habits,* Robert J. Ringer

❏ *MLM Magic*, Venus Andrecht

❏ *Money Talks*, Dr. Jeffrey Lant

❏ *Native American Wisdom*, Dr. Kent Nerburn

❏ *Network Marketing*, David Stewart

❏ *Networking*, Sarah D'Amour

❏ *Never, Never Quit*, Mike Shields

❏ *Now Is Your Time To Win*, Dave Dean

❏ *Official And Confidential—J. Edgar Hoover*, Anthony Summers

❏ *101 Thoughts to Make You Think*, Anne Sadovsky

❏ *One Frog Can Make a Difference*, Kermit the Frog

❏ *Only as One*, Rex Dockery

❏ *Out of Madness*, Bart Andrews

❏ *Paradigms*, Joel Baker

❏ *Pay Yourself What You're Worth*, Shirley Hutton

❏ *Peak Performance Principles For High Achievers*, John Noe

❏ *Permission To Win*, Ray Pelletier

❏ *Positioning: The Battle for Your Mind*, Al Ries & Jack Trout

❏ *Power In Management*, John Kotter

❏ *Power Networking*, Fisher Vilas

❏ *Power of the Plus Factor*, Norman Vincent Peale

❏ *Power Thoughts*, Dr. Robert Schuller

❏ *Power With People*, James Van Fleet

- *Proverbs, Promises and Principles*, Vern McLellen
- *Real Moments*, Dr. Barbara DeAngels
- *Reflections on a Philosophy*, Forrest C. Shaklee, Sr.
- *Run to Daylight*, Vince Lombardi
- *Run With Your Dreams*, Maureen Burns
- *Sales Power, The Silva Mind Control*, Jose Silva
- *Secrets of Effective Leadership*, F.A. Manske, Jr.
- *Secrets of Multi-Level Fortune Building*, Debbie Ballard
- *Secrets of Success*, J. Donald Walters
- *Secrets of the World's Top Sales Performers*, Christine Harvey
- *Secrets of Winning People*, Donald Waters
- *Seeds of Greatness*, Denis Waitley
- *Seven Strategies for Wealth and Happiness*, Jim Rohn
- *Self Worth*, Dr. Robert Gordon
- *Solo Parenting*, Kathleen McCoy
- *Spirit of Leadership*, F.C. Harrison
- *Splashes of Joy in the Cesspool of Life*, Barbara Johnson
- *Succeed and Grow Rich Through Persuasion*, Napoleon Hill and Clement Stone
- *Success Through a Positive Mental Atttitude*, Napoleon Hill
- *Swim With the Sharks*, Harvey MacKay
- *StreetSmart Networking*, Robert Butwin
- *Success is Never Ending, Failure is Never Final*, Dr. Robert Schuller
- *Success Without Stress*, Guy Finley
- *Superachievers*, Gerhard Gschwandtner
- *Team Building*, Robert Maddux
- *The Art of Peace*, Morihei Ueshiba
- *The Assertive Woman*, Stenlees Phelps and Nancy Austin
- *The Athena Treasury*, Marty Maskall
- *The Best of Success*, Wynn Davis
- *The Bible*
- *The Be Happy Attitudes*, Dr. Robert Schuller
- *The Book of Be Attitudes*, Bob Baumann
- *The Book of Five Rings*, Miyamoto Musashi
- *The Boys*, Skip Bayless
- *The Dallas Cowboys*, Leonard Shapiro
- *The Edge*, Howard Ferguson
- *The Executive Deskbook*, Auren Uris
- *The Fountainhead*, Ayn Rand
- *The Gamesman*, Michael Maccoby
- *The Greatest Gift in the World*, Og Mandino
- *The Greatest Opportunity in the History of the World*, John Kalench
- *The Greatest Networker in the World*, John Milton Fogg
- *The Greatest Salesman in the World*, Og Mandino

- *The Guide to Greatness in Sales*, Tom Hopkins
- *The Magic of Thinking Big*, Dr. David Schwartz
- *Theodore Roosevelt*, Edmond Morris
- *The Official Guide to Success*, Tom Hopkins
- *The One-Minute Sales Person*, Spencer Johnson
- *The Popcorn Report*, Faith Popcorn
- *The Power of Optimism*, Alan McGinnis
- *The Power of Positive Thinking*, Norman Vincent Peale
- *The Richest Man in Babylon*, George Clason
- *The Safe Child Book*, Sherryll Kraizer
- *The Sales Survival Guide*, Judy McKee
- *The Secrets of the Master Prospectors*, John Kalench
- *The Seasons of Life*, Jim Rohn
- *The Self Esteem Passport*, Michael Krawetz
- *The 7 Habits of Highly Effective People*, Stephen Covey
- *The Seven Spiritual Laws of Success*, Deepak Chopra
- *The 17 Secrets of Master Prospectors*, John Kalench
- *The Supermanagers*, Robert Heller
- *The Tao of Pooh*, Benjamin Hoff
- *The Treasury of Quotes*, Jim Rohn
- *The True Believer*, Eric Hoffer
- *The Twelfth Angel*, Og Mandino
- *The Winner's Edge*, Dr. Dennis Waitley
- *They Dared to Be Free*, Robert Natiuk & Dale Maloney
- *Think Again*, Dr. Robert Anthony
- *Think and Grow Rich*, Napoleon Hill
- *Thriving on Chaos*, Tom Peters
- *Time Management for the Unmanageable People*, by Ann McGee-Cooper
- *Timing is Everything*, Dennis Waitley
- *Tough Times Never Last, But Tough People Do*, Dr. Robert Schuller
- *Tough Minded Faith for Tender Hearted People*, Dr. Robert Schuller
- *251 Answers to 124 Objections*, John Nelson
- *Try Giving Yourself Away*, David Dunn
- *Turning the Thing Around*, Jimmy Johnson
- *Unconditional Love*, John Powell
- *Unlimited Power*, Anthony Robbins
- *Victory Secrets of Attila the Hun*, Wes Roberts
- *Wealth 101*, John Roger & Peter McWilliams
- *Wealth Without Risk*, Charles Givens
- *Well Done! The Common Guy's Guide to Every Day Success*, Dave Thomas with Ron Bergman
- *When You Walk on Water, Take the Boat*, John Harricharan
- *Who Stole the American Dream?* Burke Hedges

- *Winning*, Michael Lynberg
- *Winning the Greatest Game of All*, Randy Ward
- *Wishcraft*, Barbara Sher
- *Why Some Positive Thinkers Get Powerful Results*, Norman Vincent Peale
- *What To Say When You Talk To Yourself*, Dr. Shad Helmstetter
- *When All You've Ever Wanted Isn't Enough*, Harold Kushner
- *You Can Heal Your Life*, Louise Hay
- *Your First Year in Network Marketing*, Mark and Rene Yarnell
- *Zen Lessons*, Thomas Cleary

Here Are Some Great Inspirational Poems, Stories And Quotes For You To Share With Your Successline

"I have kept these poems with me since I discovered them over a decade ago. The meanings are that we must make the best of our ability. We have to do the things that are right and stand up to the critics. When all is said and done, each day at the end of the day, you are by yourself and your creator. You can't fool either one."
-Jan Ruhe

Press On

Nothing in the world can take the place of persistence.
Talent will not;
nothing is more common than
unsuccessful men with talent.
Genius will not;
unrewarded genius is almost a proverb.
Education alone will not;
the world is full of educated derelicts.
Persistence and determination alone are omnipotent.
— *Calvin Coolidge*

The Man In The Glass

When you get what you want in your struggle for self
And the world makes you king for a day,
Just go to the mirror and look at yourself
And see what that man has to say.
For it isn't your father or mother or wife
Whose judgment upon you must pass.
The fellow whose verdict counts most in your life
Is the one staring back from the glass.
You may be like Jack Horner and chisel a plum
And think you're a wonderful guy.
But the man in the glass says you're only a bum
If you can't look him straight in the eye.
He's the fellow to please—never mind all the rest,
For he's with you clear to the end.
And you've passed your most dangerous, difficult test
If the man in the glass is your friend.
You may fool the whole world down the pathway of years
And get pats on your back as you pass.
But your final reward will be heartache and tears
If you've cheated the man in the glass.
—*Anonymous*

Whether You Think You Can Or You Can't You're Probably Right

If you think you are beaten, you are;
If you think that you dare not, you don't;
If you'd like to win, but you think you can't,
It's almost certain you won't.

If you think you'll lose, you've lost;
For out in the world you'll find
Success begins with a fellow's will.
It's all in the state of mind.

If you think you are outclassed, you are;
You've got to think high to rise;
You've got to be sure of yourself before
You can ever win a prize.
Life's battles don't always go
To the stronger or faster man;
But sooner or later the man who wins
Is the man who thinks he can.

— *Author unknown*

The Bridge Builder

An old man going down a lone highway
Came in the evening cold and gray
To a chasm vast and deep and wide
Through which was flowing a sullen tide.
The old man crossed in the twilight dim;
That swollen stream held no fears for him;
But he turned when safe on the other side
And built a bridge to span the tide.

"Old man," said a fellow pilgrim near,
"You are wasting your strength with building here;
Your journey will end with the ending day;
You never again must pass this way;
You have crossed the chasm deep and wide—
Why build you this bridge at the eventide?"

The builder lifted his old gray head.
"Good friend, in the path I have come," he said,
"There followeth after me today
A youth whose feet must pass this way.
This swollen stream which was naught to me
To that fair-haired youth may a pitfall be;
He, too, must cross in the twilight dim;
Good friend, I am building the bridge for him."
— *Author unknown*

Do It Now

If there were ever a time to risk, to make a difference
to embark on something worth doing, do it now.
Not for any real reason necessarily, but for that which tugs at your heart,
the innermost secret that's your real aspiration, something
that's significant enough to be called your dream.
You owe it to yourself to make your days on earth count.
Have fun, fire up, start today, the time is here, do it now.
That which is worth doing seldom comes easy.
There are good days and there are challenging days.
There are times when you will think about quitting.
Those times tell you that you are pushing yourself,
that is the time that you must not quit.
It is time to start all over again. Do it now.
With your dream, determination and commitment,
and the right tools you can achieve your dreams.

Let your instincts,your dreams and your heart guide you.
Believe in the incredible power of your mind.
Do that which makes a difference.
Of working hard. Of laughing and hoping.
Of seeing yourself living your dream.
Dreams do come true. Lift up others, help them succeed.
Forgive others. Forgive yourself.
The time is right. Do it now.
The start of something big brings the hope of a better, brighter tomorrow
for you and those you love.
Everything is possible.
There is only one you. And you will pass this way only once.
Why not you be the one to make the difference?
Why not you take the time to improve yourself?
Why not you be the one to help others get what they want?
Why not begin right now, this very minute?
It is time.
Do it now.
— *Jan Ruhe*

Two Small Words That Make A
Gigantic Difference

One evening there was a great MLM Master practicing in an auditorium for a speech she was to be giving the next morning to a group of Network Marketers. She had the room all arranged so that as people walked in they would be very excited.

She had her books and tapes at the back of the room all organized for sale.

She had her notes organized, the white board and a flip chart ready for the next day.

As she was going over her notes a janitor came into the back of the room, unannounced. He made his way down into the front of the room and sat down in a chair right under the great Master's nose.

Of course, the Master saw him and stopped her practice and welcomed the janitor to listen. However, the janitor said to the Master,

"I've been listening to you practice your speech for the last 30 minutes while I was standing at the back of the room. I think that I can give your speech in two words."

The Master laughed and said, *"Oh, sure, two words? I don't think so. You see I've been in MLM for 17 years, have lots of experience, have written three books, produced tapes, spoken to thousands of people, trained even more. I don't think you know what you're talking about."*

But the janitor replied, "With all due respect, I do think I can wrap up what you are saying in two words:"

"Gotta Wanna."

Do Random Acts Of Kindness.
You Never Know Who You Are Helping.

One night, years ago, a young man stopped on a highway late at night to help a woman in need. She had car trouble and was frantic. Her husband was dying and she was trying to get to the hospital to be with him.

The young man helped her into his car and she explained the urgency of getting to the hospital. On the way there she asked the young man what his goal in life was.

He shared with her that he wanted to be a pianist more than anything in the world, but that he was unable to even afford a piano.

As they approached the hospital the woman took out a pen and piece of paper and asked the young man to write his name, phone number and address on the paper so that she could send him a thank-you note for helping her at this perilous time.

She got to the hospital in time to hold her husband's hand as he passed away.

A few days later the young man was shocked when a baby grand piano was delivered to his address. It had a brief note attached.

Thank you for coming to my aid when I so needed a ride.
My husband did pass away. But I got to the hospital in time to be with him.
Enjoy this small token of my appreciation.

Sincerely,
Mrs. Nat King Cole

From the Master's Seminar
Phoenix, Arizona 1996
Be a magnet for magic.
Be a vortex to attract not repel.
Celebrate your imperfections, come from your heart.
Enthusiasm is more important than technique.
Every sparrow knows an eagle.
Identify the talents in others for true success.
The sacrifice of today is the reward for tomorrow.
There are special people in your life—
don't ever give up on them.
To say you are on a World Class level of anything,
you must pay a price.
Treat everyone like an eagle.
You have so much untapped creative potential.
Look at the Olympians.
Always remember the Power of the Dream.
Fire Up!
-Richard Brook, Russ DeVan, Sandy Elsberg, Randy Gage, Jan Ruhe and
Tom Schreiter.

From Merging Seas
Newsletter of Semester At Sea, Spring, 1996
contributed by Sarah White
Every morning in Africa,
a gazelle wakes up.
It knows that it must outrun
the fastest lion or it will be killed.
Every morning in Africa,
a lion wakes up.
It knows it must run faster than
the slowest gazelle or it will starve.
It doesn't matter whether you are a lion
or a gazelle—when the sun comes up,
you'd better be running.

THE CHALLENGE

Let others lead small lives,
but not you.
Let others argue over small things,
but not you.
Let others cry over small hurts,
but not you.
Let others leave their future
in someone else's hands,
but not you.
— *Jim Rohn*

PERSISTENCE

The prizes of life are at the end of each journey,
not near the beginning;
and it is not given to me to know how many
steps are necessary in order to reach my goal.
Failure I may still encounter at the thousandth step,
yet success hides behind the next bend in the road.
Never will I know how close it lies
unless I turn the corner...I will persist until I succeed.
— *Og Mandino*

ATTITUDE

The longer I live, the more I realize the impact of attitude on life.
Attitude, to me, is more important than the past, than education,
than money,
than circumstances, than failures, than successes,
than what other people think or say or do.
It is more important than appearance, giftedness or skill.
It will make or break a company…a church…a home.
The remarkable thing is, we have a choice every day regarding
the attitude we will embrace for that day.
We cannot change our past… we cannot change the inevitable.
The only thing we can do is play on the one string we have, and
that is our attitude…
I am convinced that life is 10% what happens to me and 90%
how I react to it.
And so it is with you…
We are in charge of our attitudes.
— *Charles Swindoll*

Chapter 13

How To Be A Master Of Praise, Recognition And Appreciation

The One Key To Having Your People Produce Results...

Appreciate them.

Here's The Foundation Of All Successful MLM Masters

They have all learned that the secret is not in what you have done or are doing, or how busy you are or how important you are, but that you give, and keep on giving, sincere recognition. Besides recruiting, selling, focusing on training others, duplicatable programs, going to meetings, phone calls, organization and time management in addition to being a spouse, parent, child, friend, neighbor—the underlying foundation of it all is recognition. Be the King or Queen of Recognition and you will be great.

Here Are Facts You Should Know About Recognition

- Be so busy giving recognition you don't need it.
- Being a Master of recognition is a major key to success in MLM.
- Have fun giving recognition.
- If you fail to recognize the people in your organization you are missing an enormous opportunity.

Go overboard with recognition! ! !

- Have people speak into the microphone.
- Have your own team pin and team t-shirts made. They're fun.

- Make recognition phone calls, send recognition over e-mail.
- Once you finish recognizing people begin to think of the next way to recognize them some more.
- Only give recognition if you are sincere. Recognition from the heart is critical.
- People will work harder for recognition than they will for money.
- Polish your stars. Feed your horses. Cut and get rid of your dead wood.
- Present your gifts in unusual manners, when they are least expecting it.
- Put pictures, names, statistics in your newsletters.
- Recognize all achievements.
- Recognizing others' achievements is the best way to grow an MLM business.
- Recognize people for their contributions to your team.
- Recognize people by spending your time with them.
- Smile, hug, send cards, postcards.
- Stop looking for recognition from someone who is too insecure to give it to you. Take note that they aren't able to give it to you and don't criticize them. Go a new avenue, find those in your organization who are able to recognize you.
- Take people to lunch or to dinner as a way of thanking them.
- The people in your organization need recognition from you—and they deserve it.
- When you get results in MLM, **you will be noticed.**
- The more you give it, the more you get.
- You can't give enough recognition.
- You can't buy recognition.
- You can't store recognition.
- You deserve recognition.

How To Get Recognition If You Are New To MLM
- Sell more than the minimum.
- Recruit two to three new people a month.
- Attend all meetings.
- Participate in all trainings.
- Be agreeable.
- Be fun to work with.
- Be enthusiastic.
- Call your upline every week to report what your results are, not for more ideas on how to take action. Be the one who calls the upline who isn't asking for more ideas.

Be the one who's calling reporting in that you are taking action and getting results.

Think about this:

Your upline gets calls every day, many of them. People call all day to get ideas on how to move more product, get more recruits. You call and ask the same thing and want your upline to spend his quality time with you. You feel disappointed if the upline doesn't seem excited about your call after a few weeks.

Well, try this. Get results. Get BIG results. Offer to come to the next meeting and give a 10 to 15 minute talk about how you got your results. The people who get results are noticed. It's really the only way in MLM.

A Word Of Caution To Those Of You Who Do Not Feel Recognized

If you are one of the people in MLM who will do just about anything for recognition, be careful. Are you the one who comes up with cute ways to display the product, fun jewelry with the company logo on it, incredible flyers from spending hours at the computer, and who will plan meetings for your upline for hours, etc.? However, you are not moving product or recruiting and training others to do the same. End result: You will quit MLM, not feeling recognized or appreciated.

Here's what to do. Put the same energy and time into recruiting and selling. Get some results. You will be recognized and appreciated far more.

What About The People Who Say Recognition Doesn't Mean Anything To Them?

I don't believe this for one minute! From experience, I can tell you that everyone wants to feel appreciated. Don't buy into this. Everyone who makes a contribution in your successline should get recognized, and over and over. It's a fundamental part of this business.

Here Are Different Ways Of Recognizing People

Telephone calls, faxes, post cards, e-mail, letters for personal recognition, newsletters and meetings for public recognition. Giving people a title, such as Chairperson of Meetings.

Kind Words Make A Difference

Here's a story that illustrates this:

On a trip to LA in 1997 to attend a seminar, I stood in a short line to check in to the LAX Hilton about 6 o'clock one evening. Of course, I had a reservation, I just needed to check in. I was in no hurry and waited patiently in line.

The hotel was bustling and very busy. It was pouring down rain outside, taxies were unloading and loading back up, it was pretty busy. When it was my turn to step up to the counter, a nice young woman looked at me from the other side of the counter. Her eyes were puffy and somewhat red. I said, *"Hello, my name is Jan Ruhe and I would like to check in. Here's my reservation confirmation."*

As she punched my name into the computer I said to her, "You're doing a nice job checking me in, thank you for your nice service to me."

Well, guess what? She burst into tears. Just burst into tears. Her name tag said *Nancy.* I said, *"Oh, Nancy, I am sorry I made you cry."* Nancy said,

"Oh, Mrs. Ruhe, you are the first person who has said anything nice to me all day. Everyone has been so pushy, crude or rude to me. I was beginning to think there was no one nice in the whole world. The woman before you was so demanding. It is just so wonderful that you said something nice to me. Thank you."

Nancy left me a voice mail every day that I was in the hotel, thanking me for my kindness.

Please be kind to others. You have no idea what your kind words do to help others in their daily path.

Here Are Some Recognition Phrases To Use

- *I am so proud of you.*
- *I appreciate you.*
- *Keep up the good job.*

Attention Leaders, Here Is How To Be A Master At Giving Recognition

- Keep a journal.
- Every time someone in your successline tells you something he/she has accomplished, write it down.
- Every time someone in your successline sends you a gift, make a journal entry.
- Make a journal entry for every person who calls in to your office who announces positive results to you.
- Make a journal entry for every letter, postcard, fax or e-mail that you get.
- Collect all that information and list those people in your newsletters.
- Write thank-you notes for every little thing.

Here's Who To Recognize In Your successline The Most

Your top people. Never forget your top leaders. Recognize them over and over, and more than anyone else. Why? Because that is the position people need to strive to get to.

Here's *How To* Have a Recognition Club

- Have a $400 Club for everyone who has one product workshop and sells $400 in product in one day.
- Have a $1,000 Club for those who sell over $1,000 in one month.
- Have a Top 10 Club when your organization gets big enough. It's based on their total team sales. In my organization, you have to have group sales of over $100,000 a year and promote two leaders to get to be in this prestigious club.

Here's *How To* Recognize People In A Small Meeting

Never be in a hurry. Talk about the specific results the person has.

Say, *"In this room today, we have a sales rep (distributor) who has accomplished the following: Sold in excess of.... Gotten her first recruit.... Come to two meetings."*

And then say, *"I am so proud of what this person is accomplishing. Please help me bring up front our Outstanding Sales Rep for the month... Let's hear it for (name),"* and begin the clapping.

When the person comes up front say, *"So, tell us how you are doing all of this."* (You get out of the way, stand off to the side, sit down. Let the person talk. This is true recognition. Let them have the spotlight for a few minutes.)

Here's *How To* Recognize People In A Big Meeting

Set up an annual meeting where people will work all year long just to be recognized at that special meeting.

Years ago, I started a meeting called "The PowerTeam Rally." It's held once a year at our annual convention. We recognize our Top 10 people out of thousands in the organization. We keep it a surprise until the convention.

At the convention I have a meeting in my suite for Sales Directors and existing Top 10 people. The Top 10 are invited only for the second part of the meeting. During the meeting, I spend time recognizing each top leader in my organization. It is a very special moment. We then have an agenda, and go over what worked for the previous year and what didn't, what we can do to improve our organization. This is the meeting where I listen, gather input and then make a plan for the future year. It is the most important meeting of the year for me. I value what my top people have to contribute and they feel recognized.

Here's Information About *How To* Give Recognition At A Rally Or A National Convention

Get a Chairman of the Event

Someone who is at the top of your organization. It needs to be someone the rest of your organization looks up to.

Ask for Co-Chairs for the Event

Only the Top 10 of our Team get to plan this event. They get the room, collect $5+ from everyone to help cover the room cost. Decorate it and set the agenda. Give your successlines practice on being leaders.

Sales reps want high energy and enthusiasm

We have from 300 to 500 people come every year. The meeting has some *"Nuts $ Bolts"* (knowledge) but mostly it's wild with recognition. Everyone is up on their chairs dancing to loud music until the meeting starts. We start at 9:30 PM and go sometimes until midnight.

Have this meeting late at night and here's why:

People fly in from all over the country and sometimes flights are delayed. By 9:30 p.m., most everyone has gotten to the convention. Have this meeting the night before your National Convention starts.

Recognize everyone

Welcome everyone.

Recruiting

Have a countdown for recruiting. Everyone who recruited anyone last year, or the last six months, stand up. Start the clapping. Stay standing if you have sponsored two…three…four…five…and keep going until there are only a few people standing. Bring them all to the front of the room and ask them to tell everyone how they did it.

Selling

Have a countdown for selling. Everyone who sold product last year, or the last six months, etc., stands up. Start the clapping. Keep standing if you sold $500, $1,000, $3,000, $5,000, etc., until there are only two or three people standing. Bring them to the front and have them tell everyone how they did it.

Trip

If there was an incentive trip, hear from **everyone** who went.

Car

If there was an incentive car, hear from everyone who got one.

Have the upline do only the very top recognition

Have the upline of the entire group recognize only the top people. I only recognize the National Sales Directors on my team.

How To Write A Recognition Newsletter

In MLM a monthly newsletter is a must!

When to write a newsletter:

When you have your first two to three people.

Why write a newsletter:

People will work so hard to see their name in print. Why do people read *People* magazine and the *National Enquirer*? What people are doing sells. Be smart, write a monthly newsletter. It's addicting to many people to see their name in print.

How To Write A Newsletter That Gets Results

Make sure:

- It goes out monthly, same time, no excuses, month after month, year after year.
- It's on light-colored paper, so that your successline can copy it if they want to.
- That it can be clearly read.
- That it is proof read *carefully. Three times!*
- You begin with an opening statement.
- Don't type your letters too small.
- Your name, phone number, fax, e-mail and address are clearly printed on the outside and inside.

That it has:

- A page of statistics including your own.
- A calendar of upcoming events.
- A section for C.A.N.I. (who has gone to seminars or who has read a book that has changed the way they are doing business. What you, the leader, are reading).
- Enthusiasm on every page (use quotes).
- Photos in it that can be seen. Pictures say a thousand words.
- Some product knowledge.
- Success stories (interview people, find out how they sold so much).

Do NOT have:

- Messy looking copy.

- Excuses in print why you haven't written in so long.

- One that shows you are in a hurry just to get it out.

- It come out at different times of the month.

- Statistics.

- Any photos that are black and no one can tell who the people are.

- Too much copy, or be hard to read. Leave space for the eye to rest.

Never tell your successline that writing a newsletter is a struggle for you—if it is. If you are not writing a newsletter, do you think your successline will? I doubt it. Remember, do the things that are duplicatable. A good newsletter is imperative. Work on improving your newsletter. Interview your uplines and successlines for it.

Official Team Newsletter of the Jan Ruhe Discovery Toy PowerTeam

Vol I
October 1993

Over 1,000 copies in circulation!

Happy Holidays

Thanksgiving Message from Jan Ruhe

Let me take this opportunity to thank those of you who helped make 1993 such a special year! THANK YOU TO:

My Teachers

Tom Hopkins—for your calls of encouragement and sincere interest in my family and business! We had over 300 members of my team in your audience this year and now boast over 20 Boot Camp Grads.

Jim Rohn—for our time together in Dallas and Carmel, CA., your friendship means the world to me!

Tom Schreiter—You are a remarkable friend. Thank you for contributing to my life in so many ways!

Anthony Robbins—thank you for having me as your guest to your Firewalk Seminar in San Francisco! I am very focused on leading a vital life with more energy than ever!

My Personal Support System

Georgette Klinger SPA—for my days of beauty this year.

Estella Pequeno—my trusted housekeeper of over a decade.

Mailstop—Cindy, Donna, Dee and Susan for taking care of all my mailings...what a job!

Kristi Anderson—Ashley's Soccer Coach, Lady Longhorns.

Staff at Signature Athletic Club—our family loves this great club.

My Family

Lois and Joe Kelley—the positive upbringing and ongoing support and love.

Kay Anderson—my sister, for always being there for me.

Mrs. Willis Tate, Sr.—(my aunt) for your ongoing love and support.

Sarah, 17, Clayton, 15, and Ashley 13—my precious children...your outstanding behavior, outstanding family contributions, your support, energy, encouragement, fun, charisma, love, care, team players, helpers, intelligence, high achievement in: football, piano, cheer leading instructions, driving skills, volleyball, modeling school. The stars continue to dance in heaven cheering the fact that you are alive on earth. Thank you for all the happiness you bring to Bill and me! You are so very loved.

Billy Ruhe—my precious husband, happy third anniversary. How lucky can a woman be to have a soul mate and teammate like you.

My Friends

Libby White—being my confidant and running and shopping buddy! My beautiful and best friend.

To all my dearest friends across the nation, for your gift of friendship.

To **Mimi Walker**, get well soon my friend. I'm waiting on the painting you promised me of the Caribbean.

The Ruhe Team

To all of you on my Diamond Director Team in *Discovery Toys*. Our team will sell over $10 million in toys this year, and now numbers over 7,000 people on our team and growing every day. I wish each one of you great success! *Just Do It!*

I am truly one of the most fortunate women in the world. I pray for your wealth, health and happiness! May you continue to love to grow, love to change and love life!

God bless all of you this Thanksgiving and always. My love from our home to yours!

Happy Holidays,

Jan Ruhe

Pour Yourself A Cup Of Ambition ● *Go For Greatness* ● *Don't Be Average, Be A Champion*

Page 1

Chapter 14

How To Take Yourself From Being Average To Being A MLM Champion

"How do you know what average is?
It is the top of the bottom, the best of the worst,
the bottom of the top, the worst of the best."

How To Decide On Self-Improvement

Ninety percent of your success or failure in MLM depends on your attitude. Going to self-improvement seminars, training seminars and advanced training seminars is a big, huge part of my success—and the success of every MLM Champion I've ever known.

Let's start with some questions to help you identify why self-improvement might be a good choice for you:

- How would you live if you had a $100,000 to $200,000-plus annual income?

- What would you do if you were financially independent?

- Do you think it can only be done by others?

- Do you believe you have what it takes?

- Are you willing to work to get it?

- Are you willing to live and work with no excuses—ever?

How To Begin a Lifelong Program of Self-Improvement

Start with the belief that you are going to transform yourself from being average to being a Champion. All you have to have to do is start. And to do that…

Take Action !

What Will You Do When It's Too Late To Quit Being Average? Only you can answer that question.

Now Is The Time To Make a Decision To Quit Being Average

- Being on the Masters track to becoming a Champion is a lot of fun. It is also very profitable.

- Help yourself, go over the average list and don't be average. Start today, go to work on yourself.

- In the eyes of average people, just above average is always considered outstanding.

- Real risk in life is doing nothing—look at how few real Champions there are, watch the Olympic Gold Medal winners, the practice is apparent, isn't it? Who is winning and who is watching?

- Write on a piece of paper that which is holding you back, that which is keeping you average. Make a list. If you have several, circle the main one. Now go to work on that main challenge and overcome it. You can do it. You are a Champion!

Here Is A Story About My Transformation From Being Average To Being A Champion

It was in 1986. I was sitting at a Houston's Restaurant in Dallas, passing time until it was time to go to the airport to leave on a business trip. While reading a local newspaper, I noticed a photo of Tom Hopkins announcing that he was coming to speak in Dallas.

Here's what happened:

Tom's name had been brought to my attention several years before by Danielle Kennedy, who is now a personal friend of mine. She had told me that Tom was a great Sales Trainer and that he had some special techniques that would be useful to me. I decided to go. Into the ballroom I went, all by myself. I could not believe it, as I walked in that room I was astounded, there were 2,000 people! What rock had I been under? Why had I waited so long?

Now, there I was, the student who had no idea what I was about to learn. The next eight hours proved to be the turning point in my life and career. I was ready to hear what this man had to say. It's said, *"When the student is ready the teacher appears."* I was ready!

Amazing Information Generates Breakthrough

Tom Hopkins was that teacher. I went to hear him. I walked into his seminar with old, worn out, average attitudes and ideas. I walked out of the seminar with an entire new outlook on life. Fired up! If it was going to be, it was up to me.

I now had the goal of becoming a Master Sales Trainer. Not just for MLM. A Master in Sales and Sales Training. A Champion. I began a program of being coachable. Tom Hopkins became my mentor. He talked about positive ideas, the right words to say, hope for the future, financial freedom, how to be a Master in business. A Champion in life.

Everything he had to say made sense to me. I was looking for knowledge. *If you get just one piece of knowledge from a speaker, tape or book, it's worth your listening. Some people don't value sales techniques. I do.* Tom Hopkins taught me sales techniques that changed my life. I became his student.

In 1987 when Tom Hopkins again came to Dallas, I bought seven tickets and took my top salespeople. Tom invited my children and me to meet with him after his seminar. He was very interested in what I was doing. I send hundreds of people from all over the United States to sit in his audience. One year, over 400 of my successline attended his one-day seminar. Many have attended his Boot Camp. I know the angels directed my steps. My children would have the lifestyle I secretly dreamed of having. I would not be denied.

Here Is Another Amazing Breakthrough
Meeting the philosopher Jim Rohn.

I took my children several times to hear him. I listened to what he said. I knew he was speaking to me. There were thousands of people there, but his message was for me. It was about financial independence. It was about changing yourself, about being the very best you can be. His message was to me.

Years later, my daughter Sarah and I were invited to have lunch with Jim in Dallas. We had a great conversation. He gave me his home number and told me that there was an answering machine on it and to feel free to call and leave him messages from time to time.

Well, do you know what I did? Jim had a home at that time in Carmel, California. I planned a fabulous dinner party in Carmel and called Jim to invite him to be my guest of honor. I called him **every month for one year.** He *never* returned my call.

The night came for the dinner party in Carmel. There we all were, 14 of us. My husband Bill was hosting one table and I was hosting the other. I was so proud of the winners of my contest. I had a very special, beautiful dinner planned. I had called ahead and asked for a place to be set next to me for my special guest. I still had *never* heard from Jim.

As I walked into the lobby of the hotel, there he was. Not only did he sit by me and encourage me, but one comment he made changed my life yet again. We discussed a challenge I was having with my company about the way they handled recognition at that time. I asked him to share his wisdom on the subject with me. He did.

Want to know what he said to me that night that took me to the next level of life? Tattoo this on your forehead: "**Be so busy giving recognition that you don't need it.**" Thank you, Jim. I think of that night frequently.

He not only had dinner with us, he came back to Bill's and my suite and gave a seminar for all of the attendees! I just knew he would be there. I knew it.

I was already giving tons of recognition. What happened for me was that I gave up needing recognition from my company. It simply didn't matter anymore. What a relief. I didn't know how much energy working for recognition took out of me. Give it, give it and guess what? It comes pouring back.

I vowed that night to become a better leader, a better woman and a better role model to my children. I bought this truth; I deserved success. I would become a Master. A Champion. Read this carefully: You can become a Master…a Champion.

Study this book over and over…begin today.

Facts You Should Know About Being Average
Average is:
- Any performance that's as close to the bottom as it is to the top.
- Being run-of-the-mill, mediocre, insignificant, an also-ran, a non-entity.
- Belief that you will come up with a scheme.
- Believing that one day someone will hand you a book or a bunch of leads, or wave a magic wand and you will be making thousands and thousands of dollars a day in MLM.
- Getting discouraged before you have spent some time building your network.

Building an MLM business takes time. *You will* not likely earn a million dollars in the first 10 hours, 10 days, 10 weeks, 10 months. However, you are willing to put four or more years into college. You are willing to work at the same job for over a year. You are willing to work at the same career for over 40 years. Why is it that in 30 days, if you aren't making money in MLM, you get discouraged and quit?

This is average.

- Selling products. Masters and Champions sell the idea of selling the opportunity.
- Spending hours dreaming about finding a magical get-rich-quick way of making your debt go away, and being at the top of your company's pay structure.
- The silent majority.
- The lazy person's cop out.
- Lacking the guts to take a stand in life.
- Living by default.
- The worst of the best and the best of the worst.
- To be forgotten once you pass from this life.
- To commit a great crime against oneself and humanity.
- To pass one's life away with time, rather than to pass one's time away with life. It's to kill time, rather than to work it to death.
- To take up space for no purpose, to take the trip but never pay the fare, to return no interest for the investment in you.

One of the saddest epitaphs reads:

> **"Here lie Mr. and Mrs. Average. Here lie the remains of what might have been, except that they were only Average."**
> *- Edmond Goget*

Secrets On *How To* Become A MLM Master
- Act like a Master long before you are one.
- Attend monthly meetings in your area.
- Attend seminars on self-improvement.
- Begin searching out information that will help you improve where you are weakest. Keep building on your strengths.
- Being on top and staying on top takes commitment and constant self-improvement.
- Bolster yourself by attending product meetings and rallies.
- Collect information.
- Cultivate knowledge.
- Consider all of the facts.
- Concentrate positively on learning something and you will.

- Do the job, do whatever it takes and make it look easy.

- Each step on the staircase to stardom begins with being willing to take risks and improve yourself.

- Encourage your team members to improve, so that the entire team will be stronger and better.

- Every MLM Master, the great ones, began their business by sponsoring their first recruit just like you.

- Feed your mind. What you put in your mind can never be taken away from you.

- Find Masters who want to talk about great ideas, not gossip about people.

- Figure out how you can constantly improve.

- For financial freedom, read *The Richest Man in Babylon*.

- Gather ideas that will have an impact on your life.

- Get on with your personal growth.

- Hang out with those who have succeeded.

- How can you learn to earn $200,000 annually from someone earning $40,000?

- How much is it costing you to be weak in your business growth and development? Find those weak holes and plug them up.

- If you do what Masters say to do, you will increase your income. If you have become passive, unable to speak up for yourself, unable to get what you want, you have been held back by the inerts in life.

- Information that's free doesn't stick with you as long as information you pay for.

- Know-how is vital in your MLM business.

- Knowledge is not a gift. It's an accomplishment.

- Listen to motivational tapes.

- Listen to great music.

- Make a decision today not to be average.

- Make the positive way of life your only way of life.

- Memorize noble thoughts, which you then frequently say to yourself.

- Memorize success poems.

And More Secrets On *How To* Be A MLM Master

- Memorize great quotes.

- Mind your own business.

- Obtain resource catalogs that are full of MLM books and tapes to help you in your quest for ultimate success.

- One great way of learning to do something right is to do it wrong first, then make the correction.
- One simple idea might open up a whole new world of thinking and action for you.
- One thought or idea captured can be turned into gold.
- Only listen to those who have succeeded, never to those who are just talking about it.
- Pass on everything good that you learn to your successline.
- Pick up a new thought or new idea.
- Read.
- Repetition is the mother of learning.
- Review information.
- Study Masters.
- Study millionaires, those people with a net worth in excess of a million dollars.
- Study those who have what you want.
- Seek the counsel of wise people.
- Seek out a role model—learn from setbacks of others. Really find out how they do it right.
- Seek out others in MLM companies, and ask them to share their success tips.
- Some of your friends may not like the new, educated you. It's okay.
- Stay ahead of your group if you want to keep leading them.
- Stay current on what's happening in the world.
- Study charismatic people. Learn from them.
- Plan the growth of your business by setting recruiting goals.
- Realize you cannot buy the top positions in your organization.
- Say what you are going to do and do it.
- Stop hanging out with average people who try to convince you that being average is okay. It might be okay for them, but their attitude stinks.
- Take a Master to lunch and let her select the place. Have a list of questions ready and make your time count.
- The biggest room in the world is the room for self-improvement.
- The more knowledge you have, the less you will procrastinate.
- Turn your car into a classroom.

- Take great notes.
- Take notes, write down what the speaker says, and *I mean everything.*
- Teach product knowledge, but focus on the benefits.
- The customer is always right.
- The only way to the top is by high levels of product sales and development of your own sales organization.

And More Secrets On *How To* Become A Master In MLM

- The Master Life Balance is: physical, mental, social, spiritual, financial, home and family. These are not in order of importance. Remember, it is a balance.
- There is constant pressure today to push people downward toward being average. Masters push back.
- Think about a happy future and you will look happy.
- Think the opposite of average, so you can become the very best.
- Time is precious. Don't waste your time. Don't let others waste your time.
- What will you have if you let this opportunity slip away?
- When you are a Master in MLM, the benefits are terrific. You set your own office hours. You will have unlimited earnings, expense-paid vacations, free products, tax deductions, retirement funds, personal growth and financial independence. With proper guidance and coaching, you can be in that one percent who does earn *that phenomenal* income in America.
- When you book a presentation or appointment, keep it.
- When you make the decision to be a Master, it takes practice, drills and rehearsing.
- When you attend a meeting, read a book or listen to tapes, have the attitude that you will learn at least one important tip.
- Work on your business every day.
- Work with those in your organization who are willing to cooperate with your methods. Those who don't want to cooperate normally fall way behind and never catch up.
- Write a recognition-filled newsletter.
- *You can depend on me,* is a great attitude.

Find out:

- What it takes to get to the top of your company and work toward it every day.
- What the average person's sales are in your company.
- What the no-results or small-results people in your organization do and don't do.
- What poor people talk about and don't talk about it. Most likely you will find that they take no self- improvement courses and do not read positive mental attitude books or helpful MLM books or watch videos, nor do they listen to tapes or take action that the Masters are doing.
- What the top people in your company do, how they got there. Ask them what mistakes they made, so that you can gain an edge over the time it took them to make it to the top.
- Where you are weak and seek out someone stronger in that area.

Keep:

- Improving and learning.
- Thinking about being better.
- Thinking about self-improvement.
- Yourself motivated by feeding your mind and by getting positive results.

Know:

- That Masters are their own breed.
- Where you are going. Don't hesitate to invest in your future.
- That being a Master in MLM takes time, patience, training, desire and ambition.
- Unteaching wrong ideas is too difficult.

Learn:

- About yourself.
- At least one idea from a successful person, even if you can't be like them or don't want to be like them.
- From others' mistakes.
- How to make your work pay off.
- How to present a brief company background.
- To make a decision.
- To do more than one thing at a time.

Tell:

- Everyone you talk to that you are in the *greatest business in the world.*

- Others that you will continue to work with them until they reach their goals.
- People about your regular meeting schedule, your travel plans and your newsletter.
- People you are in your company for a lifetime.

And More Secrets About How To Be A MLM Master

You:

- Are the only one who's responsible for your future.
- Have to want to be a Master, more than anything else, to get to the winner's cup and be a Champion.
- Only have to hit the *hot button* of a handful of people to have a fabulous successline and business.

Your:

- Actions speak louder than your words.
- Life can be exciting, dull, frazzling or fulfilling.
- Presentation is a gift, give yourself away.
- Reputation depends on how you conduct yourself.

Vow to:

- Let no one control your future.
- Make a quantum leap in your life.
- Read 30 or more self-improvement books.
- Never return to being average. Not one day, not one minute.

How To Advance Up The Compensation Plan To The Top

If you really, really want to be a MLM Master—a Champion—remember this. No one advances up the comp plan until product is moved. If you contribute by doing more than is expected of you, you create a void which the universe is compelled to fill. You can only advance in MLM because you are advancing others. The quickest way to become a Champion is through Championship performance.

Here's To Your Personal Growth And Development... Happy Holidays!

Invest money on your self-improvement...the best gift anyone can give you is money to pay your way to a great, life-changing seminar, or a fabulous book or tape series that will feed your mind. **From today forward, for holiday and birthday gifts, ask for books, tapes and tickets to seminars.**

MLM
Masters

Are Champions.
Champions are givers.
Champions are flexible.
Champions take chances.
Champions don't give up.
Champions listen and learn.
Champions are eager to win.
Champions are self-motivated.
Champions make commitments.
Champions are positive thinkers.
Champions see good in all things.
Champions do without being told.
Champions know they are not perfect.
Champions fall, but they don't stay down.
Champions refuse to let fear control them.
Champions hang in until the going gets better,
when life gets rough, tough and unreasonable.
Champions get started every day on their own.
Champions realize there is more than one way
and they are willing to try many other ways.
Champions' behavior is not always on the outside.
Champions are like everyone else, they fear failing.
Champions make the extraordinary from the ordinary.
Champions get people involved who want to be involved.
Champions believe the path they have chosen even when it's hard,
even when others can't see where they are going, they can.
Champions don't wait for the world to push them in the right direction.
Champions stubbornly refuse to let a fall keep them from getting back up.
Champions refuse to let others' words and actions affect their attitude.
Champions don't always win, but they always keep a winning attitude.
Champions respect their weaknesses while making the absolute most of
all their strengths.
Champions are people
like you. They make
this world a much
better place to be.

Are You . . .

- ☐ A friend
- ☐ A giver
- ☐ A great listener
- ☐ A positive thinker
- ☐ A risk-taker
- ☐ A self-starter
- ☐ Committed
- ☐ Duplicatable
- ☐ Eager
- ☐ Feeding your mind
- ☐ Fired up
- ☐ Flexible
- ☐ Industrious
- ☐ Ready to learn
- ☐ Recruiting 5 or more people a month
- ☐ Resourceful
- ☐ Self-motivated
- ☐ Selling at least $500 in product every month
- ☐ Training your own recruits

Chapter 15

How To Be A
Master Seller In MLM

Selling is Fun, Selling is Easy, Selling is Important!

MLM is selling! MLM has proven and continues to prove that it's not what you know, but it's what you show!

Poor old selling has really taken a beating over the years. In life, whatever it is you do, you have to sell yourself, your ideas, your product, your service or your talent.

Here's What Selling Really Is...

Selling is sharing, but it is more.

You have to be so convinced about your product that you're able to help your customer find the benefit for them in what you're offering. I believe we do not have to convince—in that pushy meaning of convincing—someone to get something that really does benefit them. But I do believe being a Master in selling requires being a somewhat convincing business person.

Selling is simply helping. Selling is finding out what somebody needs and providing it. If you begin to look at it that way (which is the correct way to view it) you'll find out that Selling is really very easy.

Whether we acknowledge it or not, we are all born sellers. We all innately possess the same selling and negotiating skills. We sell and negotiate all day long, with spouses, children, parents, finding their need and providing assistance.

You Have To Believe In Your Product and Sell It, Because If You Don't No One Else Is Going To Want To Join You and Sell It, Too.

If your doctor is unable to convince you of his/her expertise, you're not going to follow his/her advice. You are not going to believe in or trust him/her. He/she has got to sell you, convince you that he/she knows what he/she's talking about, or you'll find a new doctor and he/she will ultimately lose her practice.

You know the difference between the minister with the full church and the minister with the empty church? The minister in the empty church is just a minister, and the minister in the full church is a minister and a salesperson. He knows how to get his message across in a manner his congregation likes to listen to. They believe what he says, because they like him and trust him. He knows how to sell himself and when he sells himself, he sells his ideas.

So you see, whether you are in MLM, a minister, doctor or teacher, you have to learn to sell yourself, your ideas, your product, your service, your talent, your contribution. Somebody has to buy what it is you do, or your idea or product, or it may as well not exist.

You Have To Be Able To Sell Others On Your Idea

People have wonderful, unique ideas all the time. When you are sold on your product and opportunity, you can catch the enthusiasm, the belief in your company and turn it into recruits, sales, customers, etc.

Selling is business. Selling is what work is all about. Selling is tremendously exciting. It's what makes the wheels turn in all businesses. In MLM, you start a small business and it only grows if you believe in what you are doing. To be successful in MLM , you need to know how to sell.

Selling used to be a man's domain and it required traits women didn't want to acquire, such as pushiness and aggressiveness, or at least that's how the world viewed it. Selling seemed to be somewhat shady. Certainly not genteel. Nothing a "lady" would want to be associated with, so women left selling to the men.

What some people don't completely realize is that selling **is** business. You can't be successful unless you know how to sell. To get ahead in anything requires selling. Many people in MLM don't realize they have to sell themselves and their ideas to get ahead. Many prospects and new recruits believe they can't sell. Well, I know they can, and believe me, in the last 10 years, times have really changed about the concept that everyone can be a salesperson.

How To Get Over Feeling Pushy

Why is it that what we do at home to shape behavior is benign and desirable, but the minute we make the same effort away from the home, we worry that people will think we are aggressive and pushy, rather than seeing it for what it is—assertive and helpful? It's time to reorganize your thinking and realize that selling is very important and fun, because it's a perfect way of helping people. Once you're at ease with the feeling that selling is okay, fun and good to do, and accept it, you'll find all sorts of doors opening for you, because your attitude will change. You'll find selling is both productive and fun.

Here's *How To* Develop an Attitude of High Expectancy of Happiness, Enthusiasm and Success

It's necessary for you to be positive in all your expectations. Expect to be happy. Expect to be enthusiastic for what you are and are doing. Transfer that enthusiasm to others and expect to be successful at it.

Here's an example: A product workshop. You should go with an expectancy of having a good time, helping people, sharing with people. Go with a positive attitude, a smile on your face. You're going to enjoy it. You are going to have fun. You have a right to expect happiness.

Also, go expecting to be enthusiastic and "up" for the presentation. Know that you are going to be able to transmit your enthusiasm for your product to the buyer. Go expecting that you will be successful and that it will be your be best product presentation ever. You have a right to expect success. If you expect happiness, enthusiasm and success as your right, you'll realize it more often.

Selling is not a contest between you and the buyer.

Many salespeople get all mixed up and think that selling is the Customer vs. the Salesperson (sales rep). The true concept of selling (helping) is the salesperson and the customer vs. the want and need. You want to work with the customer. Ask questions and listen and help give your customer what she wants.

Sell the benefits of the product.

The buyer wants to know how your product will fit his needs. Once the buyer understands how the product will benefit him, let him buy. People hate to be sold anything, to be pressured, but they just love to buy. And keep in mind, most of the time people buy what they want, not what they need.

So if you've explained how your product can benefit the customer and she knows you have her desires in mind and you want to help, *bingo*…she moves from prospect to customer and buys.

Customer service is really important.

People gladly buy expensive items. Don't be too concerned about prices. Talk to your customers about the value and benefits of the product.

You are providing them a unique service. Don't make decisions for your customers as to whether the price is too high, let them decide. That's their business. You're not forcing them to do anything. Don't limit your customers' possibilities.

Know your product inside out. The more you know about your product the more you can help others by directing them to the products that will benefit them.

Happy Selling

Here is a letter I send to all my customers. It is in the mail every December 26th. I begin to follow up on the letters every January 2nd. I am booked for the entire year by January 12, year after year. I have more business than I can possibly handle by myself.

This letter only works if you follow up on every single letter you send out. For those of you building a huge MLM business, make sure your successlines use this letter, too.

Dear (put your company name) Customer:

Happy holidays! Thank you for an incredible year. I am a (put your title) with (your company). Because of people like you, my group sales were over (put amount, for example $10,000) in product this year.

I'm part of an organization that really cares about customer service. Satisfying your needs and wants is our top priority. So when you think of (your product name) think of me, not of running to a local store. I am only a phone call away. My number is (your number). You are important and valuable to me. Serving you is my business.

I love what I do. Being a sales representative for (your company) has been such a huge benefit to my family and me this year. It's been a perfect part-time job for me. I absolutely love what I do. This is my career.

After the first of the year, I'll be calling you to see if you would like to schedule a workshop with me. Here's how that would benefit you (and list all the benefits).

We will be partners for your workshop. You get the people there, and I will do the rest.

If you would rather, just mail the enclosed form back to me, that will be fine, too. If I don't hear right back from you, I'll just give you a quick call in the next two weeks to schedule your workshop.

Here are my available dates for workshops this year: Please circle your first and second choices.

January: 8,9,10,11,16,17,18,22,23,24,25,29,30,31
February: 5,6,7,8,11,12,13,15,19,20,21,22,27,28
March: 4,5,6,7,11,12,13,14,26,27,28
April: 2,3,4,8,9,10,11,15,16,17,18,22,232,24,25,29,30
May: 1,2,3,6,7,8,9,13,14,15,16,17,20,23,24,27,28,29,30
June: 2,3,4,5,9,10,11,12,16,17,18,19,20,23,24,28,29,30
July: 1,5,6,7,8,12,13,14,18,19,20
August: 4,5,6,7,8,9,10,11,12,13,14,15,16,17,18,19,20,21,22,23,24,25,26,27
September: 1,2,3,4,5,6,7,8,9,10,11,12,13,14,15,16,17,18,19,20,21,22,23,24,25, 26,27
October: 1,2,3,4,5,6,7,8,9,10,11,12,13,14,15,16,17,18,19,20,21,22,23,24,25,26,27,28
November: 1,2,3,4,5,6,7,8,9,10,11,12,13,14,15,16,17,18,19,20,21,22,23,24,25,26,27
December: 1,2,3,4,5,6,7,8,9,10,11,12,13,14,15,16,17,18,19,20

As always, when you are one of my customers, you benefit even more, because you can always buy my product at 10 percent discount all year long.

This is going to be a great year. I appreciate your business so much and look forward to being your (company or product name) sales rep.

Thanks in advance. I'm looking forward to having a conversation with you in the next couple of weeks. Have your first and second choices marked and have your calendar ready. I'll be calling you soon.

Happy holidays,
(Your name)

Chapter 16

Now Is The Time
For You To
Take Action

From this ultimate Network Marketing/MLM handbook, hopefully you've gotten at least one great idea. Never let it be said that you didn't try in MLM. If you try, and you represent a product you believe in that's backed by a compensation plan you can make money with, and you work daily to achieve your goals, success is yours. . .count on it.

I'm depending on you to be the next success story in MLM. It's wide open. There's more room at the top, it's not at all crowded up here. If I had unlimited personal power, I would grant each one of you the income you deserve, the lifestyle you deserve, all the recognition that you deserve and the total support for you to get to the top of your MLM company. My passion is for you to succeed beyond your wildest expectations. You see, I know you can. It's simply up to you.

How Will You Survive In The 21st Century
If You Don't Get Really Involved In MLM?

Someday I hope to meet you. Please come up to me and tell me that this one *"How-to"* book helped you along your path to MLM success. I hope I shone a light on that path. If you see any breadcrumbs on your path, know that you are on the right path...perhaps they're mine. Maybe I'm right in front of you.

> "Motivation and hard work are not enough;
> concentration and commitment are imperative.
> Concentration is the supreme art,
> because no art can be achieved without it.
> While with it, anything can be achieved.
> The Masters all have the ability to discipline themselves
> to eliminate everything except what they are trying to accomplish."
> — *Dale Brown*

My sincere thanks to my precious children, Sarah, Clayton and Ashley White, my husband Bill Ruhe, Tom Hopkins, Jim Rohn, Randy Gage, John Milton Fogg, Susan Fogg, Lane Nemeth, the Upline® Masters, my family, my friends, my National Sales Directors, my entire Diamond sales organization—which in 1996 numbered more than 7,000—for your gift of friendship, kindness, leadership, training, direction, encouragement, contribution, love, thoughtfulness, joy and self-worth that you have contributed to my life.

Don't Be Average, Be A Champion.
Strive for greatness.
Have fun out there and remember I believe in you.
Enjoy every precious moment, go for being the best.
Shower the people you love with love.
Forgive those who have hurt you.
Be free to be who you are.

I believe in you.
Now is the time to take action.
Ignite your passion.
No Matter What

May you be blessed with health, wealth and happiness

I hope you will remember me for my light, not my lessons.

I love you, I need you and you are beautiful.

With love from the mountaintop,

There's more from Jan Ruhe!

Published by Upline® Press

Motivate Your Organization

Fire Up!
Jan Ruhe

Few people in the world of Network Marketing have discovered and promoted leadership as effectively and in as many people as Jan Ruhe. *Fire Up!* tells you exactly how she did it, and how you can, too. Jan's enthusiastic style weaves personal development and a thorough "how-to" manual into a seamless whole that is now in its third printing.

Jan's insightful words on developing leaders will show you what it means to be a leader, and how to nurture these qualities in yourself and others. Jan offers encouragement, advice, and reassurance on every page as she addresses communication issues, the challenge of keeping your group focused and motivated, and how to maintain commitment.

Fire Up! is a goldmine of business-building ideas and actions (you'll learn 65 crucial points to hosting dynamic meetings!) that belongs on every Networker's book shelf. Call for your copy today, and discover how to "ignite your Network Marketing Business into a roaring blaze of success!" *82 page paperback.*

GB007 $10.95
Quantity Discounts: 2 or more $8.97

To order, call
1-888-UPLINE-1 or
804-979-4427!